Power
OF THE

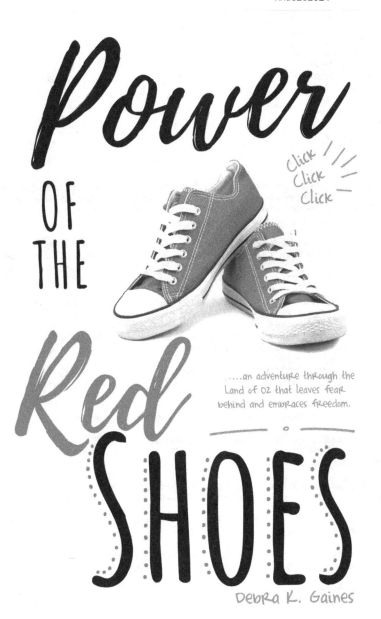

Click Click Click

.....an adventure through the Land of OZ that leaves fear behind and embraces freedom.

Red SHOES

Debra K. Gaines

XULON PRESS ELITE

Xulon Press Elite
2301 Lucien Way #415
Maitland, FL 32751
407.339.4217
www.xulonpress.com

Throughout our friendship, now spanning more than twenty years since 1997 when I first met Debra and her family, I have watched the beautiful creativity God placed within her grow and develop. He knew she would be faithful with His gifts and Debbie is one of the most creative people I know. My life has been enriched by her beautiful paintings, inspired Bible study teaching, deep and loving counsel – she has even expertly helped me choose wall colors for my home!

Here in *Power of the Red Shoes* Debra's creativity has come forth again, speaking to the "Dorothy" in all of us. She has masterfully drawn from that long ago fantastic tale, real life, nitty-gritty lessons that we all come to face at some time or other, seamlessly knitting them together with stories from the Bible of the heroes of our faith.

As you read this unique and thought-provoking book, allow yourself time to meditate and pray and make declarations over your own life as Debra leads you. Journey down your own path as you boldly wear your Powerful Red Shoes and rise up and become an amazing Son or Daughter of the King!

Jervae Brooks

Wife, mother, grand and great-grandmother – and lover of red shoes
Executive Director- International Field, Aglow International

DEDICATION

This book is dedicated to my wonderful husband Mark that has loved me and supported me through every challenge and calling in my life from God. You have honored and loved me dearly through more than 45 years of marriage. Thank you for believing in me, standing beside me, speaking words of continued encouragement and inspiration over me to step out of my comfort zone and reach for the stars. I thank God for you every day.

What an adventure life has been together these many years, I look forward to many more adventures ahead, and I love you dearly!

TABLE OF CONTENTS

INTRODUCTION

CLICK, CLICK, CLICK!

DOROTHY'S RED SHOES from The Wizard of Oz clicked together one, two, three. The image was bright, and the shoes sparkled in my mind. I had not seen the movie in years, but there they were; the memory was vivid, but the timing was odd.

Wow! What was that all about? I was in the middle of praying when that very graphic memory appeared in my mind. *Yes!* I said praying. I was talking with the Heavenly Father. *See, I told you it was interesting.* Now many of you may be thinking that my imagination had taken a left turn off a cliff or that my mind was wandering and that I was not really focused on God. But, I am here to tell you—that was simply not the case. While I can't remember exactly what my conversation at that particular moment with God was; it was definitely not about Red Shoes! My thoughts were totally on point and because I was focused, I knew that God had dropped this memory in my mind's eye for a reason. I just thought the timing of it all was a little peculiar.

My eyes were closed (sometimes my eyes are open and sometimes they are closed in prayer) but this time they were closed because I was being very serious (Smile), that's why it was such a surprise.

I literally stopped, looked up and said, w*hat was that all about God?* I definitely had a puzzled look on my face since I was very confused, but it was then that I could feel Him smile. I love it when God smiles. He smiles more then we realize. His smiles are hugs straight from His throne. So, when God threw the RED SHOES right in the middle of my conversation with Him, I knew He loved my reaction because He loves to show off His sense of humor.

Actually, He was probably laughing but I wasn't paying much attention because in that particular moment I was truly bewildered. I didn't stop to contemplate anything else but the picture in my mind and the reasoning behind it so I could stay sharp with my inquisitive wonder to the Father. I have now come to learn that this experience had a great purpose, but again, in that moment, to my way of thinking it seemed a bit off track.

Adventure

With God, all things are an adventure and since I was up for an adventure, I decided to follow His lead. Now I laughed because sometimes you just have to laugh with Him. After all, His heart's desire is to have relationship with us and that's why when we get stuck in religion and don't even realize it, He is setting us up for a good chuckle.

I personally think that when we focus only on a problem, the Father has to jolt us a bit every once in a while to bring us up to the surface for a breath of fresh air. He knows that if we concentrate too hard on difficult situations and do not keep our eyes on Him, it can be detrimental. There have been times in my life that I literally have felt Him slap me on the back and say, "Deb, breathe!" It's going to be all right! Occasionally, we have unhealthy patterns that need to shift, so I know He purposely creates great moments with Him that will bring a laugh or a smile. He reminds us that our eyes need to be fixed on Him and Him alone!

Hebrews 12:2, (MSG) "Keep your eyes on Jesus, who both began and finished this race we're in. Study how He did it. Because He never lost sight of where He was headed-that exhilarating finish in and with God –He could put up with anything along the way: cross, shame, whatever. And now He's there, in the place of honor, right along side God."

Remember, it is the Joy of the Lord that is our strength. He makes a memory with us, creating joy, just like we do with our own children (maybe He's taking a photograph of us to place in HIS family photo album) for WE ARE HIS CHILDREN. We are made in His likeness, humor and all, and that's what the journey is all about, making memories.

Continuing on, I then asked God a question—Father, what are the Red Shoes all about? He immediately answered me. "Deb, when Dorothy arrived in the Land of Oz, she received the Red Shoes almost immediately, but she did not understand the power and authority that she carried through them until she herself had walked the journey." *WOW! I thought that's really good God.*

I knew immediately He was referring to the blood of Jesus, when we receive Christ as our savior. The authority and power we receive instantly when the blood is applied to our lives through salvation, but it takes the journey and experience of life and making memories with Him to understand what we carry and who we really are. Maybe I should say, who's we are, for we are sons and daughters of the Most High King.

Soon after this encounter, I began to see Wizard of Oz memorabilia everywhere. I walked into a Hallmark store and there, right in front of me, was a plaque with a picture of Dorothy and her companions on the yellow brick road saying: "It's not the destination but the journey that matters most." Off in the distance you could see the Emerald City. I was blown away! I bought the framed picture and the really big, red sparkly ceramic shoe that went with it. They are sitting in my office today as I write this. What a great reminder of the glorious journey we are on.

What a marvelous way of looking at an amazing truth, and this is how it all began. I felt an excitement in the air. I knew God had something special up His sleeve that was totally out of the ordinary. I felt Him say, *Come on Deb, let's go!* Understanding that our ride together would be full of crazy surprises, I immediately accepted the invitation to go with Him down the yellow brick road to a party He had prepared just for us: Dorothy, Scarecrow, Tin Man, Cowardly Lion and of course, the Heavenly Father Himself. What a gift this journey would be!

If you don't mind, let's take a moment and talk about joy and laughter because joy and laughter are one of the reasons that the Lord wanted to share the application of this story with me through a spiritual perspective. The Bible tells us that laughter is good for our bones. (Proverbs 17:22) There are also several scientific studies that show how good laughter and positive emotion is good for your body.

First of all, the Bible tells us that God laughs so we were created to laugh also. Laughter is one of the greatest gifts that we have received from God. Have you ever been with someone that cannot stop laughing and pretty soon, you are laughing too? You don't even know why you are laughing, but you're laughing just the same. Ask yourself, have you ever been really angry and laughing at the same time? Which, is why I believe laughter is one of the most beautiful outward expressions of positive emotion.

When babies giggle their laughter can bring us straight into the throne room of God, at least that's my opinion (Smile). I have such a great memory of my first child laughing for the first time when she giggled at a funny sound that my husband made. It brought such an experience of joy to us that we wanted her to do it again, so my husband created the sound over and over until his throat was sore and he started to lose his voice. She would giggle and then we would begin to giggle with her. And, as the old saying goes, it tickled us pink; in other words, laughter produces life and color, making everything seem so much brighter. What a precious memory I have of this, and I am sure that those of you who are parents or grandparents can relate and also recall times of joy that flooded your heart from your own experiences. I know that Our Heavenly Father experiences the same delight with us when we laugh and have fun because He is our Father. Charlie Chaplin once said, "A day without laughter is a day wasted."

Psalm 126:2-3, (NIV) *"Our mouths were filled with laughter, our tongues with songs of joy....*

I would like to share one more memory with you concerning laughter. I have one grandson that is a little redhead and he loved to laugh and be tickled by his papa when he crawled on his lap. Papa would slowly bring his tickling fingers towards my grandson's bare tummy because my grandson had already raised his shirt up with expectancy. The closer Papa brought his hand; my grandson would just start giggling. Just the anticipation of the tickle monster would bring my grandson into such delight that he would laugh so intensely that he could hardly catch his breath, and his papa had not even touched him yet. We all would be laughing by that time because of this little redhead and his contagious fountain of rolling laughter. The joy spread throughout the room and created an atmosphere of amazing delight and happiness. I still think of this memory today and smile; sometimes it even brings a giggle from me, it definitely brings a smile. What a great memory!

Isn't this how it should be with the Heavenly Father—anticipation of an adventure or moment with Him should always bring us joy. I sincerely hope there are moments as you read this book that will bring a smile to your face, or maybe an outlandish over the top giggle will break forth into the atmosphere to cut through the spirit of heaviness that can so easily slip in and grab hold of our days. So onward we go, as we look at the scripture through a different lens, and in a little different way.

Now I think we all understand that laughter is a major key to health and happiness, so wouldn't you agree that is why the enemy of our soul works so hard to steal it from us? The Bible tells us in Nehemiah 8:10 that it is the joy of the Lord that is our strength;

could it be that joy and laughter is one of the greatest keys to the kingdom? Hmm ... that is an interesting thought isn't it?

I do know through my own experience that if I murmur and complain, I am creating an atmosphere where the enemy of my soul can set up camp. The environment around us that is then full of the sound of discouragement, anger, bitterness and darkness can and will breed additional darkness. But if I choose to speak and live by the living word of God, my atmosphere is charged with the electricity of hope, joy and life, which is His supreme presence. And that is where the Almighty God lives! It is a choice. His presence will bring change for the better and strength for the day. It has been with this key, the key of joy that many doors of hearing and experiencing God in a greater and deeper way have opened to me the realm of grace and hope, where then I am transported into the treasure room of faith! It is there that nothing is impossible with God. So laugh, laugh, laugh! Do not allow Satan to steal your joy!

Scriptures on joy and laughter

Proverbs 31:25-26; 17:22; 15:13, 15:15 Psalm 126:2-3

I began to research and learned that it was the 75th anniversary of when the movie of The Wizard of Oz was released. Here again was another confirmation that God was taking me down a new road with Dorothy and the Word of God! *What a funny combination, I thought.* I was never going to be the same again; I was going to see and think differently about this story that was written over 100 years ago by L. Frank Baum. It was at this time that I decided to buy the movie and Jesus and I began to sit down and watch it together. He began to share many wonderful truths and insights with me throughout this remarkable and very visual tale that was truly extraordinary, that I would never ever forget. Yep, Jesus goes to the movies! I will say this, He did the sharing and I took the notes.

At first, when I sat and enjoyed this feature with the Father, I thought it was just for me. Then I had a suspicion that maybe I would share this experience with others some day in the future. When that became a possibility, I had to remind God that this was The Wizard of Oz, and for this to have a Christian aspect maybe the expression wizard would not be such a good idea. It might be okay to share with me but to share with others, well that would probably not go over so well. After all, the word wizard is not necessarily within our comfort zone, as Christians we just don't do things like that if you know what I mean, right?

I felt like someone needed to speak up and let God know that this is not how things are done down here. Ha, Ha, like He needs me to straighten things out for Him. Now *that* statement brings a big belly laugh, doesn't it? Not really, but for some reason I did mention it to Him, and I think the real reason for that had more to do with what people would think of me.

I have been on escapades too numerous to write about that were a confirmation for this book, and these experiences have led me to this day. It's been kind of like a Hansel and Gretel walk, following one breadcrumb at a time down the road until here we are. Did I always know it would be a book? No, but the adventure in Jesus sure has been a great one!

Come let us go

The scriptures below talk of going up to the mountain of the Lord, and that He will teach us of His ways. Maybe one of those ways will be through a story over 100 years old. Written to entertain but featuring great truths that will visually bring God's word alive, perhaps in another relatable fun way. When Jesus walked the earth, He taught the people through story form several times so that they could understand and remember His words easier. It is not about just hearing; it is also about encountering and believing. Jesus knew how He had created us and that an experience through words with pictures would not be easily forgotten. So ... Come let us go, for the path up this mountain is laid with yellow bricks. (Isaiah 2:3, Micah 4:2)

Get ready, get set! ....Grab the popcorn, sit back, relax, and kick up your feet, it's time to take a trip down a brand new yellow brick street! This road is filled with God's Glory; we're getting ready for an amazing story!

With flashbacks from a childhood movie, let's enter and experience a fun new realm as we seek and undergo God's truth through this magnificent old fable. I am not sure this is exactly what Frank Baum had in mind all those many years ago, but new and exciting revelations through good stories are always a wonderful thrill. Come with me as we step out of our box, stretch our imaginations and catch a glimpse of what is possible in a brand new way, this is what I pray!

Click, Click, Click

Power of the Red Shoes!
This invitation is just for you, to come with me,
On an adventure with Jesus, and Dorothy Gale,
Let's see what we can see.

Skip, laugh, dance and sing,
As we learn who we are in Christ our King!
We have authority because of His Blood,
It will create a joyous beat to your heart,
Let the Red Shoes fill your steps full of zing!

THE YELLOW BRICK ROAD OF LIFE

On this road there are winters
With Jesus it feels like spring
I dance, sing and celebrate
For HE is the mighty king!

Inspired by the Spirit of Adventure
I head for the Emerald City
But I am frightened by the evil one
Oh, what a great pity.

Life more abundant
Life extraordinaire
Life full of promise
Life with Jesus is beyond compare

So down the road I go
I go here, I go there
I follow the yellow brick road
Always starting with a morning prayer

My companions one, two, and three
The great mind of Christ
The beautiful heart of Father God
And Holy Spirit, full of power and might

Life, such an adventure
One could never imagine
But with Jesus
We can live with passion!

So with my beautiful RED SHOES
A gift from Jesus above
I walk in great authority
Because of HIS labor of love

Jesus paid it all
That I might be totally free
So I thank Him, and I praise Him
And raise my hands in worship
So that He might see!

The enemy is so sly
And shrieks with words to scare
I have overcome his power
Soon, I will meet Jesus in the Air!

THE CAST

DOROTHY

Represents us, God's children. The name Dorothy means God's Gift.

SCARECROW

Represents the mind of Christ. *1 Corinthians 2:16*

TIN MAN

Represents the heart of God. *John 14:27, Philippians 4:7*

LION

Represents the Holy Spirit. *Acts 4:3*

GLINDA

Represents an angel, a messenger. The meaning of the name Glinda is Holy and Good. *Daniel 6:20, Matthew 1:20-21, Acts 12: 7-11*

WICKED WITCH

Represents Satan, the enemy of our soul. *1 Peter 5:8*

TOTO

The meaning of the word Toto is priest. Jesus, our High Priest, Jesus the Word of God *Hebrews 4:14-16, John 1:1, Revelation 19:13*

HOME

Represents Jesus

CLICK, CLICK, CLICK

Represents the Father, Son and Holy Spirit

OZ

Is a Hebrew word for Strength, Power, Courage and Might

WIZARD

The original meaning of this word is Wiz, Wise, Sage, a Philosopher, Learned and Intelligent

THE YELLOW BRICK ROAD

Represents the Journey of Life, the Glory of God

SILVER SHOES

Represents Redemption

RED SHOES

Represents the Blood of Jesus, Authority Given, and Protection

RUBY

A stone of Nobility

RAINBOW- GLASSES

Seeing the journey through God's Promises or Perspective

KANSAS

A word meaning the people of the south wind and is also the direction of comfort, refreshment, quietness and peace. *Psalms 78:26, Philippians 4:7, Job 37:17, Song of Solomon 4:16*

CITY OF EMERALDS

Emerald is described as being around the throne of God. Emerald is the background color of the flag of Judah who was one of the four main flag bearers for the tribes of Israel. Dark green includes the attributes of green and black. A fruitful intimacy (*in-to-me-see*) that tramples our enemies under our feet like ashes. Green also stands for intimacy with Jesus. The pastures are green where the shepherd leads his sheep.

SNOW

Sins are like scarlet; they shall be white as snow. Repent ye therefore and be converted that your sins may be blotted out when the times of refreshing shall come from the presence of the Lord.

Snow also represents divine mercy and a good harvest. Light snow means blessing. *Isaiah 1:18 and Acts 3:19*

MUNCHKINS

Small beginnings *Zechariah 4:10*

Once Upon A Time...

1

RUNNING HOME

Wait, Dorothy wait! What's wrong? You seem so frightened and you're running away from someone or something. There is such an expression of terror on your face. How can I help you? Hurry, Dorothy! Run, Run!

Have you ever watched the movie The Wizard of OZ by MGM Studios produced in the year 1939? If you have, you will probably remember the opening scene in which Dorothy and her precious pet dog, Toto, are running down the road towards home.

When I was a little girl, I didn't know what Dorothy was running from, but I certainly experienced the fear she was exhibiting. Let me describe what I saw and felt.

Fear gripped my little heart as I watched the opening scene of the movie; it was dark and felt very gloomy which definitely describes the atmosphere around us when fear is present. At the beginning of the movie the first scenes were filmed in sepia tones, which meant there was an absence of any vibrant beautiful color.

All of us have experienced fear, somewhere, someplace or sometime in our lives. When fear is in control, it strips the moment you're in of all color and beauty and leaves you shaken, anxious, and without joy or laughter. It can grip your emotions and mind like a heavy, gnarly hand that has so much power and strength that it seems impossible to break its grasp! This is exactly how I felt as a child for Dorothy. There was no one on the road with her, she was alone, and her surroundings dripped with a gloomy brown eerie hue. I felt an ominous presence of an overwhelming panic pushing her forward; she must hurry!

As a child, I could sense a storm brewing in the atmosphere, so emotionally and physically, I was right there with her! Wanting to close my eyes, I was so afraid to watch, being fearful of what might suddenly appear in her path of darkness, but then again, I was too terrified not to look. The question running through my mind was, what could be ahead or what might possibly or suddenly, jump from behind that would startle her or me even more?

The look on Dorothy's face was one of anguish. Her eyes were alert and looking for something or someone and you could tell that she was expecting the worst. Dorothy was very aware that there was perilous danger in her surroundings. She was definitely in protection mode with her arms wrapped tightly around Toto, as he was her most precious possession.

I knew someone or something was coming as she heads straight to the farm where she is confident that there will be a sanctuary awaiting her. Dorothy is comforted with the thought that her Aunt Em and Uncle Henry will do whatever is within their power to provide support and a place of refuge; she just knew that her and Toto would be safe with them.

Oh, No! Suddenly, a picture of her nemesis, Miss Gulch, flashes on the screen, the intensity of the music helped me to understand how dire the situation was. Every note created a feeling of anxiety and panic within me as it proclaimed loudly that the enemy was on her way and arriving soon! She rode her bike furiously to catch Dorothy and Toto. With great determination, she was on a mission and rode with great authority, for in her possession were papers from the sheriff giving her the ability to take Toto and have him destroyed! As she rides, the look on Miss Gulch's face is very serious; there is no turning back, she is full of purpose, and anger is the motivating companion that propels her forward with great speed.

I could hear the voice of fear rising up within me shouting tormenting words of intimidation, "Soon there will be trouble!" I felt a confrontation brewing. I couldn't comprehend how I knew, or when it would appear, or how things would turn out, but I did know that a category five storm was on its way!

I was terror-stricken for Dorothy and her little Toto. I asked myself, why did she go by her territory? If you recall, Dorothy walked home from school passing by Miss Gulch's house and we obviously understand now that this was not a very wise decision. My question to Dorothy was *why did you take the chance knowing who she was? Why? Why? Why?*

My heart raced as I continued to watch the wheels of that bike go round and round speeding faster and faster towards the farm, Dorothy's home. To this day I can close my eyes and visualize those wheels spinning and spinning, bringing the enemy closer and closer, hearing the music go faster and faster, causing my heart to race greater and greater!

Dorothy stayed focused on moving towards home. She continued to believe that if she could just get there then everything would be all right. If she could only step foot on her own land, she would finally be safe.

Can you feel the emotional tempest that is beginning to blow as I describe my experience? This storm will soon invade her place of refuge; it will ride in like a runaway train, ready to plunge off a cliff. A whirlwind that, in a moment's time, will shift, shake, rattle and roll then turn everything upside down. Storms tend to do that you know, they blow in, wreak havoc and blow back out, leaving a mess behind. This particular storm will shake the very core of Dorothy's emotions, it will cause her head and heart to spin, it will rumble and rattle her very structure of peace and trust. This storm will cause her to make a decision that will change her life forever. This storm will be like no other she has ever encountered, imagined or faced before.

Reflecting

I think we can all relate because we all have things that are precious to us in our lives which we want to protect, so we find ourselves worrying, which, we need to understand is fear. Then, because of fear we become wrapped or trapped in the effects of the distress and feel out of control just like Dorothy. When fear rules our heart and emotions, we end up running and trying to find a safe place for the things that we love and hold dear. Actually these situations are shouting out for us to STOP and CONFESS; they are

4

revealing that we need someone much greater and higher in our lives that can step in with a helping hand.

Hebrews 4:16, (KJV) "Therefore, let us draw near with confidence to the throne of grace, so that we may receive mercy and find grace to help in time of need."

It has been my experience that in similar situations, I am usually trying to protect my heart from pain and hurt. My coping pattern in the past has been to run to things that will numb my feelings thinking it will help. Whatever it is that causes us to run or hide, please understand that fear is the motivator and the instigator. Fear will stand up, volunteer and take charge! He will be the ringleader of spirits that bring us torment and pain. I am grateful that I have reached a place in my life where I totally understand if I want freedom—true freedom—I will have to stop, identify the fear that is pushing and shoving me around, look it straight in the face, and strip that fear of its power through Jesus Christ and His blood! There is no more running as I capture my thoughts, then renounce and come out of any agreements with the fear. I then break the lies of the enemy that I have believed; at that point I declare the truth of the word of God over myself, and only the truth, filling every cell with life! From that day forward, once the fear has been identified, I covenant with God that I will not entertain that spirit again by giving it power through my attention or my words. I will only fellowship with Him and then, and only then, will the chains of the lying, thieving perpetrators be broken! Let it go, let Jesus and the love of God be your strong tower, run into Him. Take out the fear by the Power of His blood. Too many times we just speak to fear in general and we continue to be tormented. We need to ask the Father to help us identify and call out the name of the *specific* fear and *where*, *when* and *why* it entered our lives. Knowing your enemy is half the battle to freedom just like in the old Westerns. The sheriff use to call out the name of the bad guy in order to meet him in the street for the mighty showdown. Name the fear, call it out, and then take it out! I then suggest you destroy all of his lurking relatives, birds of a feather stick together!

In Psalm 18:2, (KJV) "The Lord is my rock, my fortress, my deliverer; my God, my strength, in whom I will trust; my buckler, and the horn of my salvation, and my high tower."

You can see that Dorothy is most definitely in a circumstance that we can understand. If she would only stand still, look at the fear pushing her around, stare it down and put it on notice. If not, once you start running, it is hard to stop, and turning tail then can become a way of life and soon you even forget why you are fleeing, it just becomes a pattern or a response, never leaving you to be at peace or rest. The culprits, named Running and Hiding have now persuaded you that they are your friends; so you will now overreact every time you feel any kind of fear. You feel safe for a short time until it shows its ugly head again; sadly, these friends only desire your demise.

A moment to pause

The scripture tells us in 2 Timothy 1:7 that fear is a spirit. (KJV) "For God hath not given us the spirit of fear; but of power, and love, and of a sound mind." In John 4:18 (KJV) it says, "There is no fear in love; but perfect love *casts out* fear because fear hath torment. *He that fears is not made perfect in love."* (My emphasis)

Yep, there it is, fear is a tormentor. Let's allow Jesus to fill us with His love. When we are full of His love, fear has no place to live or remain. We can then evict fear by allowing Jesus to heal the places of hurt and pain, which gives the spirit a right to torment! Please take a moment and pause here. Take the time to ask the Heavenly Father what you are afraid of? We must totally comprehend that Jesus died so that we do not have to be afflicted by fear no matter its name.

Have you ever felt like someone or something was right on your heels just like Dorothy? Following and hiding behind every circumstance, waiting for just the right moment to pounce?

Have you ever been so gripped by fear in a certain situation that all you were able to do is run (or feel like running) or maybe you just freeze or hide emotionally and cannot go forward in life?

Well, most of us have, so welcome to the schemes and the ploys of the enemy. Through these experiences, God is reaching out, He is stretching forth His hand and saying here I am. Don't be afraid; with me you can stand.

Now of course we have natural fears that protect us from harm such as fear of a hot stove. That would be something to be afraid of, or fear of a bear that is chasing us in the woods. Yes, in times like that you must run! In fact, in that particular situation, I would probably run faster than I have ever run in my life, even though they say that you should never run from a bear. The only thing that would shift the situation would be a really big gun. With a gun, you could take control of the situation very quickly, either by scaring the bear away or, if absolutely necessary, I would stop this aggressive force of danger coming for me by taking him out!

As we walk through life, we do experience fears that control us and bring devastation in our lives. These emotional fears can run deep; they plague us and keep us from healthy relationships and boundaries. Fear can also keep us bound from doing and being all God has created us to be. In this example of the bear, if we do not take it out when we are threatened, it will over take us and maul us to death. I declare to you that we can take control through the Blood of Jesus, by the Power of His Name and with the Word of God, we can live free of fear. Don't allow it to maul you to a place of emotional collapse. Jesus *is* the big gun; take home the trophy and the prize! Hang the head on the wall like the big hunters and when the enemy comes around again to mock or ridicule to take you down the path of emotional misery, point to the trophy on the wall and say, *IT IS FINISHED!*

Philippians 4:6-7, (NIV) "Be anxious for nothing, but in everything by prayer and supplication, with Thanksgiving, let your requests be made known to God; and the peace of God, which surpasses all understanding, will guard your hearts and minds through Christ Jesus."

Verse 8 then continues to say, "Finally, brethren, whatever things are true, whatever things are noble, whatever things are just, whatever things are pure, whatever things are lovely, whatever things that are of good report, if there be any virtue and if there is anything praiseworthy—meditate on these things."

Jesus is showing us how to escape the cage of torment, being trapped by fear. Wow! What a great solution. I think the greatest thing that God is saying to us is to keep your mind on Him. He is saying, encounter my goodness, my love and stay in me for I am peace. The word of God tells us that Jesus paid the ultimate price on the cross so that He can carry all of your fears. Give them all to Him; He desires to guard our hearts and our minds. Over and over again, the scripture reminds us to fear not!

I do say, "RUN!"
"RUN INTO THE ARMS OF JESUS"
"RUN INTO THE SPIRIT OF PEACE"
"RUN, RUN, RUN!"
"DO NOT STOP AND DO NOT SLOW DOWN"
"ENCOUNTER HIM"
JESUS SAYS, "RUN HOME TO ME!"

Fear and anxiety are so prevalent in the day that we live that if we are not feeling or thinking something negative, the world around us is, and the world is more than willing to share it with us. We cannot be free from it unless we step into Jesus. We must step into Him, the Prince of Peace.

The world today even considers it odd if we are not in fear.

Dr. Caroline Leaf has published many books on the subject of controlling our thoughts because of the harm that it does to our bodies and our minds. She teaches that we only have thoughts of fear or faith. It is how our body receives the things that we think about. All negative emotions and thoughts evolve out of fear. Faith and fear are not just emotions, but spiritual forces with chemical representation in the body. In her book, Who Switched Off My Brain, Caroline states that we were created for love and have learned fear. The way I see it, if we have learned fear, then that means that we can unlearn it and break its hold over us, but we have to want to be free. We are a wonderful creation we have choice!

We must change our thoughts

2 Corinthians 10:5, (KJV) "Casting down imaginations, and every high thing that exalted itself against the knowledge of God and bringing into captivity every thought to the obedience of Christ" Romans 12:2, (KJV) "And be not conformed to this world but be ye transformed by the renewing of your mind.

Scriptures to meditate

1 Peter 5:7

Matthew 7:7 and 6:6-8

Psalm 139:1-14; 46:10-11; 94:18-19; 116:5-7; 107:28-30; 121:2

Pray with me

Heavenly Father, you are good, and I thank you for your love towards me. Help me, Heavenly Father, to look to you and only to you! I want to trust you. Thank you for reaching out to me and sending your son to die for me, which gives me the right to come boldly to the throne of grace and give to you my fear. I do not have to walk in fear. I do not have to live in fear. Fear does not own me. I repent for allowing fear in my life. Father God, I choose to only speak the truth of the Word of God. I choose to meditate on the living word and the truth of the scripture and not the lies of the enemy. I forgive those that have cursed me with and through fear. I forgive those that have abused me or hurt me in any way, physically or emotionally that have created a spirit of trauma in my life and an open door for fear to live. I do not bow to fear but thru You, Heavenly Father, and your love and the authority of Jesus Christ Your Son and the Power of His blood, FEAR MUST NOW BOW TO ME! Amen.

Declaration

I declare today that I am a child of the Most-High God, and He has not given me a spirit of fear, but He has given me the spirit of Love and a sound Mind and the Power to live free of Fear! I declare that fear will not rule me but through the blood of Jesus Christ, the Son of God, I will rule fear!

2

THE FARM

I'm home!

HELP! HELP ME! SOMEONE, PLEASE HELP!

Have you ever felt like no one was listening when you were desperate? That is exactly the situation that we find Dorothy in. Someone needs to stop and listen, but when she arrives home Aunt Em and Uncle Henry were in the middle of saving the little chicks on their farm, shifting them to safety. If they were not moved quickly, they would most likely die. But, because of her own urgent dilemma, Dorothy was actually not paying any attention to the importance of what was going on around her; all she could focus on was her own needs, so she immediately and earnestly launched into a desperate description of how Miss Gulch had attacked Toto.

Dorothy was distraught that Miss Gulch hit Toto's back with a rake! Can you believe it? I mean, really! I know he was in her yard and chasing her old cat, but does that mean that she really has a right to go after Toto? I can't believe she would really do that! Dorothy explains further, "She threatened us!" *How dare she! Who does she think she is?* So, what is the big deal anyway, isn't that what Dorothy's attitude was?

As a little girl, I really did think that Miss Gulch was a very bad lady in this situation and that she was extremely mean. I felt that she should have never done anything like that. Now that I am an adult, I can see more clearly, and I can see the truth of the circumstance from a whole different perspective.

Now don't forget that while all of this was going on, Dorothy continues to look behind herself, watching her back for Miss Gulch. She knew she was coming. She knew deep down that she had definitely crossed the line this time, and there was no going back. You can realize why Dorothy was in a panic, maybe she had cried wolf once to often because no one seemed to be listening. I could feel her desperation, her emotions were driving her and telling her, "If I can just get someone on my side, someone that will listen, when the enemy arrives things won't be so bad. Maybe someone can help me out of this mess that I have gotten myself into."

Dorothy continued to whine and complain, yes out of fear, but also out of frustration because she had hoped that once she was home she would receive help or sympathy and that someone would surely come to her rescue, or at the very least, comfort her. But Aunt Em and Uncle Henrys words were "Don't bother us." Wow! I don't think Dorothy was expecting that. When I saw and heard their response, I know I was certainly not expecting it. My heart was troubled. How could they not listen? Couldn't they see how frantic she was?

Reflection

So let me ask you again, "Have you ever felt or experienced that no one is listening to you, or even has time for you, not even those close to you? Inside you are screaming STOP, I need you to listen! But, no sound is coming out, as you wander helplessly.

The enemy of our soul then takes this perfect opportunity to toss in a few lies such as, "No one really cares" or "No one really loves me." I will say this that the enemy knows the hook to throw our way, *his timing is always perfect*, to see if we will take the bait, and run with it. The enemy is very good at what he does; remember he is the father of lies and his agenda is no different since the Garden of Eden. He desires for us to believe an untruth that will break our relationship and separate us from the Father and others. I personally believe that this is the number one falsehood that he uses, that Father God does not love us. It's not that the Father leaves us; it's that we believe a lie and walk away from a relationship with Him.

John 8:44b, (NIV) "When he speaks a lie, he speaks from his own native language, for he is a liar and the father of it."

When this occurs we must stop and capture the lie of the enemy the very moment it comes charging thru! Bring it into alignment with the word of God, and speak the truth, shouting it right in the enemy's face! Tell him where he can go because if you do not, he will be telling you!

What a blessing and a privilege to live on this side of the cross. Yes it is true that people and loved ones around us can legitimately be too busy and unable to stop for us, but the Father in Heaven is never ever too busy. He will never leave us or forsake us. We are never alone even though the great liar wants us to think and feel that we are. The comforter (Holy Spirit) is a gift from above knowing that we would need comforted.

Deuteronomy 31:6, (NIV) "Be strong and courageous. Do not be afraid or terrified because of them for the Lord your God goes with you; he will never leave you nor forsake you."

John 16:7, (KJV) "Nevertheless I tell you the truth; it is expedient for you that I go away: for if I go not away, the Comforter will not come unto you; but if I depart, I will send him unto you."

Yes it does happen in life when those around us are too busy to stop just like with Dorothy. Goodness how she must have felt! Imagine what she might be saying and or feeling, "Where is the help that I need?" or "Can't you just stop for one moment and listen to me?" Desperate words said in a desperate time!

With no response from Aunt Em or Uncle Henry, she then turned to her friends, the hired hands on the farm. They also loved Dorothy so she didn't miss a beat; she continued to try and relay her story, thinking surely someone would listen. But, the first worker was too busy; the second worker stopped for a moment and then actually gave her excellent advice. But, unfortunately, it was not the words that Dorothy wanted to hear.

Isn't that the way it is occasionally when we look for help and ask a friend for counsel? If those around us are able to help, they can usually see things from a healthier perspective and can share great words of wisdom. Honestly, though, it often ends up not being what we want to hear, so it falls on deaf ears. Dorothy wants someone to take her side, someone to murmur and complain to, isn't there any one that will coddle and comfort her right in the middle of her mess? Unfortunately, when our mess is caused by our own choices, we struggle to hear the truth. For a time we just want to be the victim, even if it is just for a moment. We want people to show empathy towards us, even though it is not what we really need. This is exactly where we find Dorothy.

She immediately spoke up and defended her self, "Well, you just don't understand me!" His advice was not hard; it was actually simple and right to the point. "Do not go by her house and then you will not get into trouble!" (1) Wow! Yep that was it. That was all that he said; it was the truth, it was straight, and it was good, but that is just not what she wanted to hear! Those simple words would have and could have changed Dorothy's life, but Dorothy chose not to listen because it placed her in a situation where she would have had to take responsibility. Her words were, "You're just not listening to me." (1) Simply put she preferred to stay on track with the thought that he just did not understand her, and besides, why couldn't he see that her problem was different! *Can you remember going down that path before?*

Dorothy continues to look to others for the answer instead of looking within.

Here she goes again!

Dorothy straight away walks over to the pigpen and gets herself into more trouble; once again she walks where she should not be walking. Today I am going to call it *riding the fence*, every time we ride a fence on something, and we are somewhere we should not be, we usually fall into a situation that we need help getting out of immediately!

She hops up on the fence and begins to walk it like a tightrope at the circus. My heart leaped out of my chest with an earnest cry No! What are you doing? Stop Dorothy! Oh, no, there she goes! My emotions again sunk in despair as I saw her tipping, tipping and then over she went, down and out of control. Yuk! Sinking into the disgusting mud that is mixed with the slop for the pigs, and the pigs were there too, and guess what else was in that pen? Ha! What a place to take a tailspin!

I could feel my heart pound. Hurry, hurry, help her please! Oh great, now her foot is caught and tangled, and she can't get loose. Goodness gracious, what else could happen? Dorothy, why were you walking on the fence in the first place? What were you thinking? I believe I know the answer to that question, Dorothy wasn't thinking! If only she would have just stopped and thought and made a better choice things would have been totally different. Actually, the whole day would have been different.

Don't we also get ourselves tangled up at times in things we should never have been involved in? All because of an entice-ment or a whim of being somewhere or doing something, or saying something we should not have been around?

STOP! *Let's capture our thoughts and make better choices next time.*

Everyone that is close to Dorothy comes running over very quickly. They love Dorothy, so of course they came to help. Her friends are afraid for her and one was sweating up a storm from worry and fright. This tickled Dorothy, she started laughing as she enjoyed the attention.

Should she have been on the fence? Should she have been walking by Miss Gulch's yard? Should she have made these choices? Those are the real questions.

Remember towards the last chapter, I mentioned second Corinthians 10:5 from the scripture? It taught us to capture our thoughts and to bring them into the obedience of Christ. Let's keep this simple; one of the greatest gifts that God has given us is our free will, the ability and the right to choose. We have the right to make our own choices no matter what that choice may be, but this scripture helps us to understand that we need to bring every thought into alignment with the word of God, and by doing that our preferences will be wise. Here we are once again learning about our thought life and how important it is, by looking at Dorothy and the mess she is in.

Poor Dorothy, she was really on a roll.

1) First, she gets into real trouble by getting too close to a hostile environment. If she would have just walked a different direction when she came home from school, she could have avoided so many problems.

2) Now, she chooses to walk on the fence and ends up in the pigpen. Unfortunately, she keeps going from one thing to another. We learn in life that choices can have a domino effect, and once you're on a roll, you can be in for quite a ride. Now you have to admit that Dorothy is on quite a roll.

My question is, why do we allow ourselves to get so close to certain situations knowing that we need to turn and go another direction and make a better choice, even when we are able to see potential danger? Hmmm … *"That's a good question, Deb,"* I'm so glad you *asked.* I believe the Bible tells us the answer to why we are so enticed.

James 1:14 shares with us that we are tempted by our own evil desires.

To be enticed or tempted means to be attracted by something. You have to admit that when something looks really good or appears really sweet; we take a second look and are tempted whether it is good *or* bad. Our choices then have the potential to place us in situations that put us on the edge or position us where we have to be on guard, always needing to look over our shoulder in fear, just like Dorothy. This is called torment, and yes, our choices will catch up to us. Maybe, from this one simple lesson with Dorothy, we can perceive and learn a lot.

Personally, I think Dorothy really wanted to see Toto chase that ole cat. I don't think she liked Miss Gulch and so she enjoyed watching her dog taunt her. It was bringing her some satisfaction and some laughs, but now the tables have turned, and Dorothy is the one being tormented. There is an old saying that says: Don't play with fire or you'll get burned. Welcome to Dorothy's world right now where she's metaphorically getting burned!

Back to the farm

As Dorothy goes from one person to another, the truth is revealed that this situation has been going on for a while, maybe that is why she was struggling to have someone listen to her. Dorothy knew however, that this time it was different. This walk around Miss Gulch's yard was one too many and that serious consequences were coming down the road (literally) and unfortunately, this time, no one was paying her any attention.

How many times have we continued to make choices even though we were advised by others and directed from God, that still small voice of warning to turn? Yes, sometimes we have made the same choice without a consequence, and because of that, we become quite brave. The Evil One then smiles with confidence as he sets a trap. We become relaxed and continue down a road that leads to destruction or at the very least a very bumpy, quite unpleasant and very emotional painful experience.

John 10:10, (NKJV) "The thief does not come except to steal, and to kill, and to destroy. I have come that they may have life, and that they may have it more abundantly."

Remember, the enemy's agenda is always to kill, steal and to destroy. This is where Dorothy is now, for the road she has chosen is becoming quite unpleasant. Her thought process needs to change, or she is in for quite a bumpy ride, and because we know the end of the story, we know that is exactly what lies ahead. I do love it that the Heavenly Father never gives up, and just like Dorothy, He uses our ventures in life to enlighten us and turn us around.

After Dorothy fell into the pigpen, Aunt Em comes over to where she and her friends are at, scolding everyone for not focusing on their work and wasting time. Once again, Dorothy tries to share with her aunt her concerns, but to no avail, she sloughs Dorothy off and tells her to find some place to stay out of the way and out of trouble. Her choices have created a ripple effect.

The ripple effect

Jeremiah 17:10, (NIV) "I the Lord search the heart and examine the mind, to reward each person according to their conduct, according to what their deeds deserve."

I feel this scripture speaks to us about how the Lord searches the heart and mind, and that we are rewarded according to our conduct.

There is a law of reaping and sowing. If we plant good seeds, we will receive a good harvest. Does that mean that God sits in heaven and looks for us to make a mistake so that He can give us an unpleasant gift? Absolutely not! It means that there is a ripple effect to our choices. When we throw a stone in the water, the ripples continue to build and move and make changes in how the water moves, just as our choices do. We struggle to look at this aspect of having free choice, but it is truth, so let's keep our eyes on Jesus and be wise as serpents (Matthew 10:16). But the amazing God we serve is always there; He will help us turn things around from the ripple effect of our actions if we will just come to Him.

King David and the ripple effect

How can we relate to this situation that Dorothy has gotten herself into?

Let's take a look at someone else's decisions in the scripture and look at a hero of the faith that did not always make the best choices; his name is King David. The Bible says that David was the apple of God's eye. Did that mean that David was perfect? Absolutely not! (*We can all relate to someone that is not perfect, right?*) David unfortunately elected to go down some roads that were not what God had desired or hoped for him. Sadly enough this particular chapter in David's life that we are going to revisit opened him up for great pain and sorrow. What ultimately saved David was that his heart always desired to please God and the Heavenly Father loved that about him; David ultimately always knew where his help came from. If there was anything good that came from the regretful decisions David did make, God used them to bring him back to his heart and then David fell to his knees in honor before his creator. God was always there to help pick up the pieces and put his son (David) back together again, kind of like Humpty Dumpty. Now let's move on and see what we can learn from a great hero of the faith.

In eleventh chapter of 2 Samuel, it is here that we begin to read that it is spring, a time when kings go off to war. But wait, where was David?

Choice number one: Disobedience

In this set of circumstances David made a choice that started him down a very dark path that would almost take him out! It was in this situation that he would become blinded to what he was doing and was unable to see himself.

And this was just the beginning. David was supposed to be at war with the armies of Israel, but he was not; he was in Jerusalem. He was supposed to be with his men, but David was king, and he had a choice. Always remember that we were created with a free will, as we might say today when we joke around, "*It is good to be king!*"

We are kings today. We rule over our decisions. The question is whom do we serve? Do we serve ourselves? (I call this the Kingdom of Self) or do we serve the King of Kings and the Lord of Lords, Jesus Christ our savior? Or another thought, do we serve anger, bitterness, fear, rejection, or even self-hatred? The answer is revealed by our reactions in situations.

The choice that David made at this time in his life was to serve the Kingdom of Self and because of his selection, it placed him in the wrong place at the wrong time. It is a good thing that our Almighty God is a redeemer when we turn to Him. .

As the story continues, he got up one evening and walked around the roof of the palace. Maybe he was restless and thinking about his

23

men? We will never know, but most of us understand that it is hard to sleep when we know we are somewhere that we should not be. We usually find ourselves with a lot of time on our hands. The Bible tells us in Ecclesiastes that there is a time for war and a time for peace, and this time, David chose comfort over obedience. He was supposed to be out fighting the enemy because this was the season for war, but instead he was on the roof of the palace and it is there that he looked out and saw a beautiful woman bathing. So, begins the trail of wrong choices.

Choice number two: Temptation

He sent someone to inquire about her. He had been enticed and his eyes saw something that, if he had been at war, he would have never seen. The enemy of his soul knew David well; he knew how to bait and set the trap. Can you see the pattern already building? The domino effect is already starting to be set up.

David's heart was set on things below,
Not on the things above,
His eyes turned upon himself,
And away from his first love.

Can you relate?
We wander far from God,
Thinking that we know best,
Our choices are so odd.

The many times we choose,
Not to love but to hate.
The dark and not the light,
These choices seal our fate.

But God is always faithful
To help and to redeem
If we will but just look UP
Believe and only dream!

He will take us by the hand
He will always walk us through
He sticks closer than a brother
He will make all things new!

I want you to understand that at any time, David could have chosen to look up. He could have stopped, captured his thoughts and fallen to his knees. But, he did not.

Choice number three: Bring her to me

David had her brought to him even though he knew her husband was at war. She was the wife of Uriah. With full knowledge, he chose to sleep with Bathsheba. I wonder what those around David in the palace thought? Was this really the actions of a king? Their king? Yes, even the meaning of Bathsheba's name means voluptuous. The enemy really knew what he was doing, just like in the garden when the snake enticed Eve with the forbidden fruit. The enemy always makes it look so good and pleasing to the eye. Bathsheba then went back home and both of them (I am sure) were hoping that this sin would stay hidden. But the scripture says that the woman conceived and sent word to David, saying, "I am with child."

Choice number four: The great cover-up

David's thinking was "I must cover my tracks. I have to figure a way out of this situation and what my choices have brought down on me." Oh, if he would have just gone to God then, but we understand shame, and I think probably that was the greatest motivator that joined hands with guilt and fear, for the enemy then whispered in David's ear: "Just bring her husband here! Have him lay with her and then everything will be cleared. Nobody will have to know, or even be the wiser, he didn't even shed a tear."

So, David sent for Uriah, and when Uriah arrived, David masked his intensions by asking how the war was going and how were the soldiers? Is it not interesting that men were dying for his kingdom, but all he could think about was himself? This shows you just how our thinking can so quickly shift from right to wrong depending on the path we choose to walk down. Our eyes are veiled from what is right, we have invited the deceiver in, and at that point, we have given him authority. In Ephesians 4:27 NIV, God instructs us not to give the devil a foothold, meaning a place or a room.

David then told Uriah to go home and wash his feet. Uriah left, but he chose to remain. David was then informed that Uriah slept at the entrance to the palace with his master's servants instead of choosing the comfort of his bed. David then asked Uriah, "Have you not just come from a military campaign? Why did you not go home?" and Uriah answers David in verse 11 in 2 Samuel. "The Ark (which was the tangible visible presence of God) and Israel and Judah are staying in tents and my commander, Joab, and my lord's men, are camped in the open country. How could I go to my residence to eat and drink and make love to my wife? As surely as you live, I will not do such a thing!" So, David then created plan number two when he told Uriah to stay one more day and David ate and drank with him to get Uriah drunk, but Uriah fell asleep and still did not go home to his wife. Isn't it amazing the great lengths that we will go to cover up our sin and our wrong choices! Sadly, if you remember, the story takes even a much darker turn.

Choice number five: The murder plot

David then sent a letter with Uriah to be delivered to Joab; Uriah was literally carrying his death sentence in his hands. What a scheme the enemy had cooked up within David's heart! It is very hard to imagine how far David had gone now. Like I said, choices bring on a domino effect. Or, if you want to imagine a choice as a door, one door will lead to another door and the question that God always puts before us is, which will you choose to open? When we hand ourselves over to the enemy of our soul, the mighty deceiver and destroyer, we have all been surprised where we have found ourselves at times. You see this was not just about David; it is never just about us, but it is about our heritage and our legacy. In this case, the ultimate goal of the enemy was to destroy David's kingdom and his credibility and bring shame that would continue down his family line. The enemy knows the potential in our lives and our descendants, he understands better than we do the power of our choices.

Uriah heads back to the battlefield, ready to fight and defend what is right, all for his king. He unknowingly has been set up by

David to fall in battle so that the King of Self can remain on the throne. How strong it can be within us to protect ourselves from being openly exposed, revealing the darkness within.

The command went forth, put Uriah in the front, in the fiercest part of the battle and then step back and leave him open to the enemy so that he will die. These were David's orders to Joab; this was murder any way you describe it! David had sunk to what I believe was his very lowest. Did David even see what he was doing? I think David knew right from wrong but maybe he was in survival mode thinking he must survive at all costs, and decisions were definitely clouded.

The scripture says in Proverbs 21:2, (NIV), that every way of a man is right in his own eyes; but the Lord knows the heart.

This is the David that loved God, the David that had made so many right choices giving way to now committing such an atrocity. Have you ever thought how could this possibly be? How could this happen to me? I am sure that something like this was running through David's mind as well and that he was wondering how he would ever get out of this mess and how it ever came to this. If he did not have these thoughts, I would be shocked! The sad thing is that it looks like David continued down the road of leaning upon his own understanding and listening to the whispers of the deceiver.

Yes, Uriah did die. Joab sent word to inform David and unfortunately the sadness continues. Others died with Uriah and David was not moved, his heart had become hardened. Satan's plan had gone well, and David was now his accomplice. My what a ripple effect!

Choice number six: No remorse

Now we start a whole new journey of woven lies that will eventually catch up to David. He then sent word to Joab. Don't let this upset you; the sword devours one as well as the other. Wow, had David really become this cold hearted? That is exactly what happens to us when we follow the father of liars, when we seek only what pleases us, our heart begins to shift from the heart of God, which is love, joy, peace, patience, kindness, goodness and faithfulness, gentleness and self-control, to a heart of stone. (Ephesians 5:22-23)

When we shift into selfishness, bitterness, anger and hate, this is who the enemy is. It's always wrapped in a pretty package but it is *always* lethal. I wonder if David even considered Bathsheba's feelings concerning her husband, because the Bible says she mourned. It was all about him! And then, after a period of time, David brought her to the palace and married her. David probably thought all is well; I have been able to fix everything, now things will all work out, and I will not look bad or be caught. Maybe he even had a thought like, I am the King, and I can do what I want. Sadly, He still did not turn to God, as of yet, he still did not repent! This is where we find David now.

But, isn't that where we also find Dorothy in her story? Not willing to admit that she was really in the wrong. She was somewhere where she should not have been. Dorothy's actions were going to catch up with her just like they did with David.

At this time in his life, much pain came from the choices made by David and the Bible says that God was not pleased.

God comes calling

God sent a man named Nathan to speak with David concerning a man that was very rich, and, who had stolen from a man that was very poor. David was incensed. He was very angry and declared he would make the wrong right. However, at this point, David still did not even recognize himself. This is whom Nathan was describing; God had said ENOUGH!

Because David's decisions were made in secret, much would be required of his household, and they would experience a lot of pain. David realized his sin and he repented and because of that God spared his life. And, even though David lost the son that was born from Bathsheba, she bore another son that became a great king and his name was Solomon. *Wow! When God redeems, God redeems!*

Isaiah 47:4, (KJV) "Our Redeemer, the Lord of Hosts is His name, the Holy One of Israel."

Psalm 19:14 (KJV) "Let the words of my mouth and the meditation of my heart be acceptable in Your sight, O Lord, My Rock and My Redeemer."

Psalm 78:35, (KJV) "And they remembered that God was their Rock, and the Most-High God their Redeemer."

Psalm 111:9, (KJV) "He has sent redemption to his people; He has ordained His covenant forever; Holy and awesome is His name."

Psalm 48:17, (KJV) "But now, thus says the Lord, Your Creator, O Jacob, and He that formed you, O Israel, 'Do not fear, for I have redeemed you; I have called you by name; You are mine!"

According to the Merriam-Webster Dictionary, the word redeem means to buy back or repurchase and/or to free from distress or harm, such as to free from captivity by payment or ransom, to release from blame or debt.

Scriptures to meditate

1 Corinthians 10:31

2 Corinthians 6:14

Philippians 4:8

Proverbs 3:5-6; 10:19; 19:2; 22:1 and 16:2

Pray with me

Father God, I thank you for your mercy and your grace. I thank you for the great blessing and privilege of free choice. I thank you for the power of grace that gives us the ability to make good choices. Father God, help me to always make good choices. Help me to keep my love for you kindled at all times. Create in me a desire for you and only you above all other things. Create in me a clean heart and always renew a right spirit with in me. Let my choice always be to choose you and your ways, for your heart and your love towards me is to protect and to bring life and not death. Your ways are boundaries that will lead me in the paths of righteousness. Thank you, Father, for giving me free choice and the right to choose. You always gently lead me you never push! Give me strength and wisdom and discernment in the choices that I do make.

I choose to follow You!
I choose your way,
I choose You,
I choose a better day!
In the mighty name of Jesus!
Amen.

Declaration

I declare that I am a child of God. I declare that I will trust you with all of my heart. I declare that I will not lean to my own understanding, and in all my ways I will acknowledge you.

Bibliography

1. *The Wizard of OZ*. 1939.

ABIDE IN THE RAINBOW

(THE DREAM)

Is there such a place?
That truly does abide,
Is there such a land?
Is there a place that I can be satisfied?

Is there a place with colors so true?
Where all the skies are a beautiful Blue,
Where I can hope for peace and joy,
Where every child can laugh and sing,
Every girl and every boy!

This is the day I start to believe,
This is the day I will start to see,
The colors of God through you and me,
In His presence this place provides,
Rainbows of beauty that is always alive!

As we play in the amazing hues,
Shades and tints will color our day,
The beautiful rainbow shows the way!

In these amazing skies of blue,
Yes happy little birds will live in the new.
They will dance across the colored sky,
All with the rainbow by their side!

So let's get ready to choose,
The life of a rainbow in dancing shoes,
Let us slip and slide with a happy grin,
Knowing that Jesus' blood paid the price,
And with His colors we Win Win Win!

It's a place where every girl and every boy,
Will live in peace and perfect joy,
Where the love of God is all around,
Where each and everyone wears' a crown!

3

THE DREAM

Aunt Em's heart- penetrating attitude and words towards Dorothy was, please go somewhere and stay out of trouble. Dorothy is all alone. No one has stopped even long enough to really hear what she has to say.

My heart ached as I watch her loneliness become apparent. I could see and feel the sadness and the pain piercing her emotionally very deep as she is continually rejected and brushed aside. She finally shrivels within from the disappointment of not being heard. The expression on Dorothy's face reflects the endurance of her suffering and she now resigns herself to the fact that her aunt is not going to be attentive to her crisis or her cries for help.

Aunt Em walks away.

Dorothy sighs, looks down at Toto and asks a question, "Do you suppose there is such a place (2) where there isn't any trouble?

She makes a statement that if there is such a place you would not be able to travel there by a boat or a train, and if this place does exist that it must be far, far away. She turns her face towards the sky with an expression of desire and a look of longing in her eye.

Have you ever dreamed and felt like your dream was impossible? I have and I am sure you have too. Possibly this is what Dorothy is feeling right now; even if this place were real, we would never be able to get there.

Dreaming of a better world, a place that is beautiful, sweet and pure. She begins to sing the most moving song, with the most moving lyrics.

Even today, I can still hear this amazingly simple melody in my head. It is probably one of the most recognized songs in the world. To this day I can still see Dorothy as she gazes up to the sky where there is a sudden sunbreak and you know, you just know that this perfect place has to be beyond that cloud, just beyond that ray of sunlight that you can perceive with your natural eye. (It made a little girls heart so glad). You can almost reach it; it's with in your touch, if you just close your eyes and let your imagination fly!

I continue to feel and experience the melody as the notes flow through my thoughts. I see the longing in her heart and the desire and emotion in her voice; they sweep us up to this place where there is only splendor, peace, joy and happiness, all things that are good. Something inside Dorothy understands and she speaks; this dream of mine must be over the rainbow.

This desire—is it real? Surely there is such a place and it is but a heartbeat away. I could sense it then and I can sense it now when I think of or just hear the sound of this music. To this day I can be transported back immediately in time and find myself reliving each overwhelming sentimental moment of emotion from so long ago as a child.

Dorothy continues to dream through this song and the inspiring words, as she continues to dance with the rainbow right by her side, she felt as if she could fly!

If you have heard the tune, I would be surprised if you are not reflecting on this precious and very simple melody in your head and experiencing the memory of that famous scene in your mind, inducing great hope and peace as it flows over Dorothy. These words, this music and this scene birthed a desire within me to find and experience, a rainbow encounter. It calls to your spirit, being created to desire and to seek out wherever loveliness reigns, and where our troubles melt away. I will now state, "There is such a place."

Dorothy continues to raise her amazing voice, singing about the bluebirds flying over the rainbow and wondering why she can't do the same.

Where is this place? When can we go there? How can we get there? We have not yet experienced this place on earth, but the desire is still deep within us to fly way up high and want to be where the skies are always blue and rainbows live and *Yes, we do too!*

As Dorothy and I dreamed together, I began to wonder what heaven must be like. This place of paradise where there are no more tears and there is no more agony, this place that is somewhere over the rainbow. I have many loved ones that are in heaven and are waiting for when I will join them, Yes, there is a place where I believe the skies are always blue and bluebirds sing, and yes, if I want to fly, I believe I will fly, and there will be no more asking, why not I?

It is at this instant that the Father reminds me that we sit with him in heavenly places, and this is our rainbow experience here on earth; our place is *IN HIM*. Oh, what a price that was paid that reconciled us for today.

Ephesians 2:6, (NIV) "God raised us up with Christ and seated us with Him in the heavenly realms in Christ Jesus."

This is now. He extends His hand that we might follow Him, the place where the skies are always a vibrant blue, and the birds are always singing. We fly high in Him for there is peace and joy and all things good. He desires for us to live there with Him, not only at the end of our days but now, today and tomorrow.

He extends His hand,
And says, Follow me.
Up where dreams come true,
Up where you can see.

Each day is like spring,
The skies are blue,
There is peace everywhere,
Let me make all things new!

It is here that the Father took out His sense of humor card and played it again, so I looked up with a great big grin. He spoke to me about rainbow glasses, I said WHAT? Again I must have had a most curious look on my face as I asked him, what are rainbow glasses? The Father answered me by asking a question, "What is a rainbow?" I replied it is a promise. "Yes," the Father responded,

"Wearing rainbow glasses is viewing all things through my promises from the word of God!"

Wow! I had to stop and think for a minute. That would cause everything to shift. If we made sure we viewed everything, every situation, every day sad or glad through the promises of God, in Him and through His Spirit, we would live over the rainbow. Put on your rainbow glasses and view things from His perspective, see what He sees and live life *in* and *thru* Jesus.

I believe that is what Paul (in the New Testament) called living and walking in the Spirit. Not of our own thinking but experiencing life through the promises and living word. There is an old hymn written by The Sensational Nightingales that I sang as a child that stated, "Every promise in the book is mine!" (I still go to the piano every once in a while, pull out the old book and declare these words over myself).

There is another old saying, view the world through rose-colored glasses, meaning that everything you see will be altered by the color of the glass. Everything would be rosy, so that if we looked through rainbow glasses and viewed everything through their colors and promises of heaven that would be a big wow! Our attitudes, feelings and perspectives in life would shift dramatically. My prayer to the Father is to let everything come up in rainbows. Don't you just love a beautiful rainbow? When we see one in our yard or even a far off, it lifts our spirit and we know that God is good, and that He is good all the time. We are reminded that He has never forgotten His covenant and promises to us, that He is a faithful and true God, and that He is a personal God, so let us view and see the world around us through His rainbows.

My challenge to you is to put on the rainbow glasses. Get into the word of God. Live *in* the promises. Live *with* the promises. Live *through* the promises. Jesus is the ultimate promise; *experience* Him, *be with* Him and let Him be in every situation and a part of every challenge or adventure that comes your way. Look at the scripture from the perspective that it is a love letter to you, for *you are* His love child.

The Father sent His son to pay the price that we might have access to the throne 24/7. Use that access, for Jesus is the code for entrance! Put on the rainbow glasses and view the world in a whole new way. Experience new colors and feelings and strengths like you have never encountered before. It is free; the debt has been settled. The promises are yours for the taking. Reach out, pick them up, and put them on! With them you will enjoy the new and go beyond!

Promises from God
Exodus 14:14
Isaiah 40:29; 40:31, 41:10, 41:13, 43:2, 52:10, 54:17
James 1:5
John 1:19

Pray with me
Heavenly Father, I thank you and praise you that you are always with me and that you have prepared a place for me in heaven. I also thank you and praise you that I can experience hope, peace, and love and your goodness here on this earth in the midst of darkness. I thank you that I do not have to wait until I am with you in heaven to know who you are and your amazing goodness, for you are with

me now. I am grateful that I can see those around me and the experiences that I am walking through now through the power of your beautiful promises. Father, help me see what you see and let me see your good in all things. You have great plans for me. You are for me and not against me. I choose to praise you and encounter you in all things.

In Jesus name, Amen.

Declaration

I declare that though the mountains are shaking, and the hills are removed, that your unfailing love for me is not shaken. I am a daughter, I am a son, I am amazingly loved. I will see and I will hear the voice of the Lord. Your covenant of peace towards me will never be removed.

Bibliography

1. *The Wizard of OZ.* 1939.
2. **Fleming, Victor.** *The Wizard of OZ.* MGM, 1939.

4

THE THREAT

Around and around go the wheels, closer and closer she comes, faster and faster she pedals, the enemy is quickly approaching with a fierce determination to take Dorothy's precious companion! What Dorothy fears most is fast approaching!

The farm, a place of safety, will soon be invaded with threatening words that will carry great authority. These words will bring enormous fear and anger. There is a vendetta in the heart and mind of Miss Gulch, to destroy Toto! Her face reveals what is within, as you watch her continue down the road with unrelenting purpose and sternness.

As a child, my heart was beating faster and faster and seemed to be beating to the rhythm of the ever spinning wheels, understanding that Miss Gulch will be a force to be reckoned with. I can see that she is very close and is on a mission that nothing will prevent her from finishing.

She sits straight and sure. The paper that she carries will give her the legal right to come on the property and take Toto. The explosive sound of the music unites with the fear-gripping anxiousness of the moment; it shouts determination and intimidation into the air. She rides high on the saddle, (as the saying goes) advancing with the understanding that she has the power. It is amazing what sound does, you can feel the very atmosphere shift depending on the resonance that you are listening to or speaking. It can shift your day, your heart, your mind and your life. This dynamic frequency that is coming down the road to Dorothy's farm will shift everything! It will even shift Dorothy's sound, her reactions and her choices.

Can't you relate to that? Forceful and unpleasant situations that we find ourselves in can and do squeeze us so tight that at times we feel that we'll explode and sometimes we do! The words or the sounds that come out of our mouths can be very alarming and quite a shock. Alarm is right! Pay attention because there is a reason that it is going off. These moments truly bring great understanding of what really is deep within.

We need to shout Hallelujah for the revelation in these moments! The exciting thing about discerning what resides deep down, is that we are able now to address them with the Lord. My response is usually, *"Wow! What was that?* Or, *"Where did that come from?"* It is then that we need to go immediately to the beautiful throne of grace and the Heavenly Father. He will then place His arm around us and whisper how much He loves us. Let the Father then graciously share the exact memory that holds the pain that needs healed. Jesus is *always* in the healing business. Thank God for revelation, take these opportune moments that God is offering to us through these disclosures and go to Him. We simply must go to Him!

This is exactly where we find Dorothy in this story, right in the middle of angry words, spewing fear and feelings of utter helplessness. Her pain within is definitely erupting. What a mess! The question is—what will Dorothy do now?

The enemy has arrived and the door is open to her and cannot be closed. Miss Gulch enters and she feels quite comfortable and secure, as we find her dressed in a haughty, high and mighty attitude knowing that she has all power as she takes a seat. Sitting straight and tall she begins to present her case, stating why she has arrived. Dorothy, Aunt Em and Uncle Henry know that they have no alternative but to listen to what she has to say.

Dorothy's choices have now caught up with her and have given Miss Gulch the right to come onto their land and release abusive horrifying threats. The sad part is, that the enemy's words are more than threats. Poor choices that were made in the past are now dictating the present and perhaps the future. Yes, Dorothy walked too close to the enemy's yard one too many times. The enemy's net has been cast and now the law is on her side! I am sure that is not what Dorothy had envisioned. If only she had realized the consequences of yielding to the temptation of going down the wrong road and allowing Toto to chase the old woman's cat. What fun it must have been in the moment and how she must have laughed, but now it was bringing serious trouble right to her doorstep, yes, trouble literally entered her house with great command, and sat down in her very own chair. Dorothy is now being forced to deal with her decisions and look them straight in the eye. There is no escape!

The amusing pleasure of letting Toto run after her the old cat was felt only for a moment, but now what was she going to do? Her choices have unlocked and opened wide a door to the tormenting spirits of regret, shame and guilt. These spirits sauntered in with an arrogant demeanor and were provided with a deed of ownership that is now in full operation. We can surely relate to Dorothy with how these spirits have tormented and manipulated us in our own lives many times, can't we? Just because of the life experiences and the responses we have made, they slip in unbeknownst to us like secret agents on a mission to seek and destroy. Well, it takes one secret agent to take out another, don't you agree? The most exciting part of this scenario is that we have the most exceptional unparalleled undercover operative working for *us*; Holy Spirit is the greatest sleuth of them all! He can see and expose where these spirits are lurking and hiding in the dark and through His great power, we can take them out. Yield to His lead and don't get caught in a ball of tangled, frustrating turmoil like Dorothy.

Regret and fear are in control; desperate words are quickly coming out of Dorothy's mouth as she tries to defend herself. She holds on to Toto with a fierce and frantic grip! Take me, it's not his fault, I am the one that is guilty, as she pleads with Miss Gulch. Please! Fear and anger are striking out like a hot iron; the insults are bursting forth, but to no avail Miss Gulch will not budge. Sadly enough Dorothy's words and actions were all noise with no authority. Unfortunately it created a heightened determination with a greater resolve to rise up within the old woman. Miss Gulch now begins to raise the stakes as she states that she will take everything away from them, even their farm, which of course is their very livelihood, if they did not comply with the law and comply now! She takes out the paper that declares

HER authority and thrusts it towards them. Waving it in their faces she is relentless, and will not back down! No matter the words, no matter the pleading, no mercy is found!

She now sternly presents to Dorothy the basket that will imprison Toto and the words are released that he will probably be destroyed! Put him in! (2) Dorothy fights back, she pushes and shoves and again in anger she explodes as her insults saturate Miss Gulch, but to no avail, nothing can be done. The law has to be obeyed. Dorothy looks to Aunt Em and Uncle Henry in desperation, hoping for some kind of help, but of course, there is nothing they can do. Their hands have been tied. The written law makes the final decision. It is done.

Dorothy began to cry, her heart was literally breaking, and the anguish was too much. One of the dearest things to her is now being ripped right out of her hands, and she literally has no power to change the direction of these circumstances. Feeling utterly defenseless and reacting in hopeless despair, she runs to her bedroom, throws herself on the bed, crying uncontrollably. Her face buried deep in her pillow as the loss is grieved. There seems to be absolutely no solutions on the horizon that could possibly arrive in time or is readily available to change the situation. Dorothy needs a major miracle!

Just a little girl, but I felt her pain. This is unimaginable, she loves Toto so much. He means everything to her. He went everywhere with her, he was her constant companion, and she loves him dearly. As I watched the screen, tears ran down my face, I cried out, no, no, don't take him, please, don't take him! Can't you see that she is so sorry for what she did? Please, have mercy! This was so hard for me to even conceive, I totally could not comprehend how anyone could be so cruel. I wept with Dorothy for her loss, her suffering and discouragement overwhelmed me.

Stop let's reflect

Let's take a couple of moments to reflect. I am hoping you can recall from the last couple of chapters that the voice we listen to and the choices we make do matter. Dorothy and the anguish that she is walking through at that very moment are definitely connected to her choices. We can all identify to that somewhere or sometime in our lives. All to often we have run to our own bedrooms (so to speak) and sometimes literally, we have buried our head in a pillow and cried out for answers. The agony of the trauma can be so deep, that as the tears fall, feeling your heart bleed emotionally is a reality. When we experience this depth of a wound, you are usually unable to put it into words or communicate it to anyone, not even to God. It is then that our wonderful Heavenly Father sees the very depth of our soul and is there for us. He is there to heal the suffering as we give it to Him. It may not happen overnight, but as we continue to bring our sorrows to Him, it will happen, one layer at a time as they come to the surface. Lay them at His feet, forgive and let go. He will continue to lift us up, replace the tears and sadness with joy that is so sweet.

Joy will come in the morning,
His Love will heal the wound,
Come give Him your pain,
He will keep your heart in tune.

Seek the one that seeks to save,
He is the one that will rescue in every way!

Psalms 30:5b, "Weeping may endure for a night, but joy comes in the morning!"

Sometimes life will hand us a situation that has nothing to do with choice and we find ourselves in the same exact desperate place where we too need a miracle like Dorothy. The scripture shares with us that we have a good, Heavenly Father that cares way beyond anything that we can ever imagine. He will never, let me repeat that again, He will never leave us or forsake us.

Psalms 139:1-18 (NIV)

1You have searched me, Lord,

And you know me.

2 You know when I sit and when I rise;

You perceive my thoughts from afar.

3 You discern my going out and my lying down;

You are familiar with all my ways.

4 Before a word is on my tongue

You, Lord, know it completely.

5 You hem me in behind and before,

And you lay your hand upon me.

6 Such knowledge is too wonderful for me,

Too lofty for me to attain.

7 Where can I go from your Spirit?

Where can I flee from your presence?

8 If I go up to the heavens, you are there;

If I make my bed in the depths, you are there.

9 If I rise on the wings of the dawn,

If I settle on the far side of the sea,

10 Even there your hand will guide me,

Your right hand will hold me fast.

11 If I say, "Surely the darkness will hide me
   And the light become night around me,"

12 Even the darkness will not be dark to you;
   The night will shine like the day,
   For darkness is as light is to you.

13 For you created my inner most being;
   you knit me together in my mother's womb.

14 I praise you because I am fearfully and wonderfully made;
   Your works are wonderful, I know that full well.

15 My frame was not hidden from you
   When I was made in the secret place,
   When I was woven together in the depths of the earth.

16 Your eyes saw my unformed body;
   All the days ordained for me were written in your book,
   Before one of them came to be.

17 How precious to me are your thoughts God!
   How vast is the sum of them!

18 Were I to count them,
   They would outnumber the grains of sand,
   When I awake, I am still with you.

These verses tell me that the Father cares about every detail of our lives. Do we make mistakes at times? Yes. But as I have continued to experience life, I have come to realize that with God, that there are no mistakes, there are only challenges and these challenges are the steppingstones to power, authority and freedom. When I am at a place in my heart where I am unable to make the better choice, my God works with me to turn it around. Do we need Jesus? Yes. Do we need the Holy Spirit to guide and direct us? Yes.

Do we need the Father to heal us from the past so that we are able to make better choices? Absolutely." *He is our Absolute!*

The word of God says in John 16:13 that the Holy Spirit has come to lead and guide us in all truth. Jesus paved the way. He ascended back to heaven that He might send the Comforter. If He sent the Holy Spirit (the Comforter) then I do believe that it is a sure bet that we will need comforting in this life. Do we need guidance? Yes! His promises are "Yes" and "Amen."

2 Corinthians 1:20, (NIV) "For no matter how many promises God has made, they are "Yes" in Christ. And so through Him the "Amen" is spoken by us to the Glory of God.

The Father already knew that as we walked this yellow brick road experiencing life that we would need freedom, comfort and guidance, which needed to be paid for through the cross of Calvary by His son, Jesus Christ. This was the highest price that ever could be paid, so take ahold of this receipt and when life gives us an unexpected turn, pull it out and show the enemy that it's already been paid in full! "Yes" and "Amen." Our Father *will* come through.

In Revelation 13:8, (NIV) states that the Lamb was slain before the foundation of the world. Our Father God has set the stage for amazing miracles in our lives; some are small, and some are large, but all are mighty and amazing. Look for and expect Miracles!

Dorothy in a place of desperation with no place to turn needs a miracle!

Important points

Now, while most of us comprehend that there are things that come our way in life that we do not choose, but I want us to understand and reflect that, in this particular story, that is not the case, Dorothy is definitely facing circumstances that were created because of her choices. Now the important truth to recognize and receive in this lesson is that we must take responsibility when it is needed. The scripture teaches (and is clear) that we have the authority over the enemy of our soul to take away any rights of torment to us. It was a real eye opener to me when I came to an understanding in my life that sometimes the enemy has rights even after I had given my life to Jesus. This is where we find Dorothy in the story; she had given the enemy the right to come on her family's land, she pushed back and shoved and spewed words, but it did no good. It frankly was of no effect against the legal authority that had been given, Miss Gulch simply pulled out the paper and demanded Toto!

As mentioned before, the scripture tells us in Ephesians 4:27 that we should not give the devil a place in our lives. Now that is an eye opener, let us remember that we can actually give the enemy power. In other words, don't give the enemy of your soul any kind of opportunity. Don't let him live in any area of our heart and minds. Do not give him a room and don't let him be a guest in your house.

Matthew 18:22-34 shares the story that Jesus told about forgiveness. In this particular account, he tells how a man was forgiven a great debt that he was unable to pay. The master was merciful, but unfortunately, the man that was forgiven went out and found a man that owed him very little money and did not forgive him. The master then took the man that was forgiven of great things and because he did not forgive the other man, the master cast him into prison, and he was given over to the tormentors. The tormentors were given the authority, yes, to torment. I am sure that at this moment in her bedroom, Dorothy felt quite trapped. She had given away her right to be free by her own choices. She was definitely in torment. Dorothy needed to repent and acknowledge the truth of her participation and her wrongdoing. She needed to go to the authorities, confess, and then everything would change and begin to shift.

My encouragement is to be vigilant. Be alert to any lie that is not in alignment to the word of God. Don't allow the enemy of your soul any place. Confess, repent and then you can live free and in peace.

Psalms 119:11, speaks of hiding the word in our hearts that we might not sin against the Father. Let the word of God become like a precious treasure to us, more valuable than anything we own. Indeed, it is a treasure. It is a gift. It is life. It is everything. Eventually all things temporal will fall away, but the word of God will stand forever.

As Dorothy desperately hung onto Toto with everything she had, I believe this gives us a great picture that describes how precious and how desperate we need to be holding onto the living word of God. Jesus is the Word. Let there be a resolve within us that no matter what the enemy is throwing at us, that we will hold on tight and fight with everything that is within us to not lose the most precious gift we could ever be given. Remember that Toto actually means priest, and Jesus is our High Priest. Hang on and squeeze tight!

Sadly enough, we leave Dorothy in a place of shame and pain, in need of a great miracle, buried deep in her pillow without a hope or a prayer.

Don't let any temptation come between you and the word of God. Let go of anything that could steal this treasure. It is life. It is power. It is relationship. *It is the case that holds and protects the rainbow glasses.* Without them, we cannot see properly, and our visions perspective is distorted. We need our glasses to see, believe and to experience miracles! Miracles come in many shapes and forms. Yellow represents the glory of God, so enjoy his presence on this yellow brick road of life, pick up the Word, put on your glasses and see what you have never seen or encountered before. See what God has for you through a kaleidoscope of living color. Let your life erupt with joy and laughter infused with His beautiful rainbow promises. Untie the bow and open the gift!

Hebrews 4:12, (NIV) "For the word of God is alive and active. Sharper than any double-edged sword. It penetrates even to the dividing soul and spirit, joints and marrow; it judges the thoughts and attitudes of the heart."

Scriptures to meditate
Isaiah 40:8
James 1:22
Luke 11:28
Matthew 7:28; 24:35; 4:4
Psalm 119:105; 119:9; 18:30; 119:130
2 Timothy 3:16

Pray with me

Dear Heavenly Father,

Draw me close to your heart. Bring me to this place where I can see and hear only your words and your ways and see life through your rainbow of promises. Let me hang on tight to the word of God and never let it go. Let me understand how precious the word is and that I must hide it in my heart. Let me abide in you and you abide in me. Let me experience and encounter your power through the power of your word! Let me understand that your word gives life, and I must do everything I can to protect the words of life that will lead and guide my steps. Help me, Heavenly Father, to recognize anything or anyone that the enemy is putting in my path to take the place of a face-to-face encounter and relationship with you through your word.

Thank you, Father, for the living word! Amen.

Declaration

I declare that the word of God is life unto me, and I will walk in its wisdom. I will choose to protect and hide the word in my heart. I declare that I will follow His word, and I will put it into practice by the power and the might of Holy Spirit that dwells within me. I will allow the word to judge my heart. I choose life! I choose Jesus! My choices do matter. I choose to look at life through the promises of God.

Bibliography

1. *The Wizard of OZ*. 1939.

2. **Fleming, Victor.** *The Wizard of OZ*. MGM, 1939.

3. *https://nameberry.com/search?q=meaning+of+Oz*. [Online]

4. **Nemitz/Facebook, Colors by Carol.** [Online]

5. www.sheknows.com. [Online]

6. http://www.netstate.com/states/intro/ks_intro.htm. [Online]

5
MY BAGS ARE PACKED

Into the basket he is pushed!
Toto is trapped!
It looks hopeless!
But this mission is about to collapse!

Toto is in the place prepared by the enemy, locked up and held captive. It looks like there is no way out. Dorothy is dealing with this situation the best she can, but emotionally she is a wreck. Tears are flowing like rain as her heart breaks from the pain. Sadly, her head is positioned down; she can see nothing but darkness, which in the moment is her chosen companion for comfort. The uplifting light that shines through the window is shut out since her eyes are cast down and buried. Could this possibly be a time where hope could appear?

Looking down and shutting everything out around us is not an uncommon coping mechanism, and we undoubtedly can identify. I'm sure you can also recall memories of hopelessness that have walked through your door with their buddies named sorrow and despair? This is where we find Dorothy as she weeps in her desperate hour of need.

In just a few moments, Dorothy's home life went from a place of safety and comfort to a location of pain and destruction. A whirlwind came rushing in and shifted everything. My head was spinning from the momentum of what just happened. Think back in your life when literally things came to a screeching halt because of the turbulent chaos of circumstances that blew in like a roaring lion and disrupted absolutely everything in your path! Those times are real.

There are pages written in our life that have literally taken our breath away; because of this we can totally relate to Dorothy's emotional reaction. As a little girl myself, I was right there with her as she ran to a place of comfort, the place she could allow her emotions to pour out freely and no one else could hear or see. The wrenching of my feelings for her situation tapped deep into my empathy gift. But as I write, my memories now flash back to the times in my own room, with my own pillow, and my own uninterrupted flowing tears as I shared my troubles and heartbreak with Jesus, so, I do understand her passionate wholehearted cry of desperation.

The scripture tells us in Psalms 147:3 that "He heals the brokenhearted and binds up their wounds." Matthew 5:4 tells us that "Blessed are those who mourn, for they shall be comforted." And 2 Corinthians 1:3 talks about "the Father of mercies and the God of all comfort."

Our heavenly Father has provided a way of escape through His grace during life circumstances that take our breath away. He offers comfort that surpasses all other sources; comfort that goes so deep within that it *can* heal the emotional bleeding and torn heart. People have said to me that time heals all wounds, but I am here to declare that Jesus is the only one that can heal the pain of a trauma completely. Time may pass and we may learn to deal or survive, but total healing comes from heaven above. The Father doesn't want us to just survive; He wants us to thrive!

It's a miracle

Dorothy's head is buried, everything seems dark, she cannot see what is happening, but there is a miracle in the making! Yes, Miss Gulch thought all would go in her favor as she once again pedaled with great confidence, this time heading away from Dorothy's farm. She moved forward in confidence, thinking all was under control. In fact, she was quite pleased with herself. Her eyes were solely focused on the road ahead. Little did she know that an amazing miracle was taking place right behind her back! That's exactly what God does for us so He can play His hand. He allows the enemy to be distracted with confidence so that the impossible can take place. Toto popped his head out, sees his chance, seizes the moment and jumps! He is clear. He is free, yes free indeed. He is on his way home as fast as his little legs will carry him. How wonderful the air of freedom must feel to his lungs as he races back towards Dorothy. Freedom is good. He is close. He begins to signal that he is coming home. His barking tries to bring an alert, but despair, disbelief and the agony of defeat muffle the sound. She was not expecting any kind of sign or wonder.

I laugh here because I am thinking of a story in the Bible when the church was praying for Peter to be released from jail and God sent an angel. In Acts 12:1-16, Peter came to the door of the house where they were praying, and a young girl named Rhonda heard his voice and was so excited that she forgot to open the door. She ran and told those praying that it was Peter at the door, and they told her that it must be an angel simply because they were not expecting. Even though they were praying, they had no expectation. Peter was in what seemed like an impossible situation because Herod the King ordered that four soldiers guard him. They knew that every precaution had been taken to keep Peter from escaping. The great part of what happened in this story is that Peter was actually sleeping in between two soldiers when the angel appeared. This amazing miracle arrived, and Peter was set free. The Heavenly Father kept the enemy asleep. God comes into our situations when it looks and feels infeasible, just like Peter, so when it looks like the enemy has the upper hand God breaks through with freedom, hope and the impossible.

In this story with Dorothy, I think that is exactly what was going on. She found it hard to believe that the sound she was hearing was actually the bark of her precious Toto; after all, she understood the reality, wasn't he locked up and being taken away? I believe her cries were exposing the feelings of "if only I had not made those choices!" Or maybe she was thinking, "It's all my fault!" She was overwhelmed and lost in grief, pain, shame and guilt so how could she ever expect a miracle?

The blame game had begun, and it was bringing good results, at least for the enemy. Blame, blame, blame, that is all the enemy of our soul does. He whispers constantly in our ear everything that is a lie, hoping we will listen and agree that it is entirely our fault and that no one will ever help us, especially not God. If we come into agreement with self-blame, our anger then turns inward and not towards the real culprit. The enemy knows that if he can convince us to live in sorrow, disbelief and self-hatred, that we are not going to look out the window of expectation towards the light and see the miracle and the promise that God is bringing. The wonderful part about who our Heavenly Father is, is that He doesn't bring us gifts because of who we are but because of *whose* we are. We are His children; we belong to Him and He loves to shower us with goodness. No matter the choices we have made, He will walk us through the consequences if we will just look up and call upon his name.

James 1:17, (NIV) "Every good and perfect gift is from above, coming down from the Father of the heavenly lights who does not change like shifting shadows."

1 Corinthians 10:13, reminds us that God has always given us a way of escape from the temptation of the enemy. Proverbs 3:5, tells us to trust in the Lord with all of our heart and not to lean to our own understanding. Philippians 4:19 promises us that God the Father will meet all of our needs according to riches of His glory in Christ Jesus.

Look up!

Look up, Dorothy! Look up! Look out the window, put on your rainbow glasses and believe that something amazing is on its way, look, listen and pray!

Yes, it is dark, but she knows that she hears a bark! She turns her head and in springs her little marvelous wonder, alive and well.

Dorothy is elated and the excitement of the moment overwhelms her. She hugs Toto and is thrilled!

Suddenly, her thoughts, and emotions are gripped with an unnerving fear once again. It is like a chokehold to the death, death to any reasonable thinking process. She pulls Toto close, so tight I felt he probably could barely breathe.

Instantly and abruptly, Dorothy realizes that Miss Gulch will come back, and she will still have the legal right to take Toto once again. Quickly the thought leaps into her brain to run! She feels this will be the answer to all of her problems: run, run, run.

Oh noooo, Dorothy, don't run away; that won't be any fun! I had an immediate thought that was driven by panic when I was little—where will you go and what will you do? Even when I was young, I knew this was not a good decision!

As quickly as the thought came into her mind, she unfortunately allowed no time or space for reason to set in. She sprang into action, grabbed her suitcase and began to pack. You can see that she will do anything to ensure the safety of Toto, and I guess to her, running away was the only option. So, just as suddenly as Toto leaped through the window and arrived home safely, the two of them were out the door and down an uncertain pathway. Tears welling up in my eyes, I looked on in despair, hoping she would turn, hoping that she would arise with courage and face what needed to be faced. With my heart in anguish from the uncertainty that lied ahead, I watched her slow, dejected walk take her further and further away from home.

A different thought

I think the real question is, "What if Dorothy would have faced the situation straight forward and went to the sheriff herself? What if she had faced up to what she had done and took responsibility? She could have pleaded her case and made arrangements to keep Toto away from Miss Gulch's yard and her cat. She could have repented, turned from her immature ways and promised to walk a different route. Do you think that would have made a difference? I bet it would have, but sadly enough, fear was in complete control of her reasoning and actions, this put her in a downward spiral. Fear was calling the shots. Fear was making all of Dorothy's decisions. Fear was like a cue ball, wrecking havoc, bouncing here and there, ricocheting wildly and allowing no peace.

When fear is in the driver's seat gripping the steering wheel of life, it generally causes us to go down a road that we regret, and we usually end up in a bigger mess then we were in originally. This is where we find Dorothy right now, not knowing where she is going, leaving her place of safety and the protection of Aunt Em and Uncle Henry. This really is not looking good and as a child, I wanted to shout out so loudly for her to stop! Dorothy, this is crazy! Don't do this!

All packed and nowhere to go. The road ahead looked gloomy. "Dorothy, Dorothy," I pleaded, "You must not leave!" She stepped out, the door slammed from behind, walking slowly away, she had no purpose and definitely no direction. I found myself raising my own hands in a stop sign of objection!

Fear is the puppeteer as he pulls the strings,
Dorothy is the puppet dancing to everything,
Letting him dictate her destiny,
How much sadness it brings,
Down the road she goes,
On a path that she has chose.

Let's reflect

2 Timothy 1:7 shares with us that God has not meant for us to have a spirit of fear. His heart desires for us to walk this yellow brick road with power, love and a sound mind.

"This is just the way it is" or "I have no other choice." These thoughts must be swirling around in her mind. I can't help but think that if Dorothy would have put on her rainbow glasses, looked at this situation through the promises of God, not allowing intimidation or fear to rule, she would be walking down a whole different path. A road filled with power, love, and a stable mind, full of light, beauty and wondrous adventure. It didn't look to me like the choice to run was really a very good one. We usually understand that running away rarely is. Have you ever noticed that when we decide to run and not face the problem or truth at hand, that no matter where we go, the trouble always reappears again and again? It may look a little different and wear a different colored dress, but yep, underneath it all, it's still the same old issue and the same old mess. It continues to chase us down, spit straight in our eye and challenge us over and over, oh my oh my!

I love God because He has a promise in the first chapter and fifth verse of the book of James stating that if we ask for wisdom that He will give it to us freely and generously. Wow, the wisdom of God is *free,* and we all have access to it because of the cross. There it is again, the same simple rule; we just need to stop, ask and look to the Father. I exhort you again to learn from this simple illustration of how Dorothy continually reacts and responds out of anxiety, stop, ask for wisdom and let God bring His peace! The Father desires (and asks) for you to stop and spend time with Him. In the Song of Solomon 4:9, the scripture shares with us that we have captured His heart and just one look from us captivates Him. Look up! Don't bury yourself in darkness as Dorothy did. Look up! Father God is waiting with open arms.

As I stated before, the name Toto means priest. I love that! Let us cling to Jesus (our High Priest) just as Dorothy wrapped her arms around Toto and was not going to let anything or anyone get between them. Nothing was going to steal or capture her love away from her again.

Hebrews 4:14, (NIV) states that since we have a great high priest who has ascended into heaven, Jesus the Son of God, let's us hold firmly to the faith we profess.

Scriptures to meditate
Psalm 119:89-91; 112:6
1 Corinthians 15:58
1 Timothy 6:12
Galatians 5:1
James 5:18
Matthew 24:13
Philippians 4:13

Pray with me

Dear Father,

Thank you for the precious price you paid of giving your Son on the cross that I might freely access your throne of grace. I thank you and praise you that I can freely come to you for wisdom to make sound choices when I am feeling completely overwhelmed by life's circumstances. I thank you that I do not have to live under the influence of fear, shame, guilt or self-bitterness because Jesus paid the price for us. I thank you that miracles are made for me, that you love me unconditionally, and that you are there for me no matter what the circumstances that I find myself in. I ask that you help me believe that you have great plans for my life and that I do not need to pack my bags and run away from facing things I need to take responsibility for. Father, forgive me for running away from you in the past, forgive me for the times I have not listened to you and have not taken responsibility for my actions. Father, I now choose to take your hand, allow you to walk me through the tough times and allow you to heal my heart from the brokenness of life. I will use the word of God to be my guide.

In the name of Jesus. Amen.

Declaration

I declare that I am a child of God and that I have the mind of Christ. I will follow his voice and not the voice of fear. I am an amazing creation, created to do great things. I will stand firm, and I will not run!

6

A VOICE IN THE WILDERNESS

Bag in hand,
Toto beside her,
Now leaving the land,
Her home is a blur.

Dorothy has decided that the best course of action is to shut the door to her past. Yep, leave it closed behind her and start walking down an old, dusty road on her way to nowhere. She has no purpose or direction; she is just leaving. Her emotions have hijacked her common sense and are totally and completely in charge, which is not always a bad thing depending on what is driving your feelings. But unfortunately in this case, distress caused by fear is the nasty culprit!

Now because her emotions are shoving her around, Dorothy is beating tracks out of town. The scene is fresh in my memory even to this day of Dorothy walking slowly down the road with an unhappy and resigned countenance on her face. Just the look of it told everyone she felt there was no other choice. I could really feel her despair; she felt she had no voice!

Talk about something that should bring up a hair curling emotion of fear—I think walking this road would be it! No plans in place, just wandering aimlessly without any direction, going wherever the road led with no thought whatsoever to what might lie ahead. I wondered who might be around the next bend. The road literally reeks with the stench of despondency, and hopelessness, which, as the Bible explains, will actually make our hearts sick. I could feel her overwhelming desire for a safe and secure location to take Toto and as the old expression says, to live happily ever after. She has given up everything to protect Toto as she keeps her gaze straight ahead, locked on the horizon with just one thought: "Toto and I have to get out of Dodge." In her mind, there was absolutely no other option; it doesn't matter where she runs to, just wherever the wind may blow, as the saying goes.

Fear can be like a wave from the ocean, depending on how it comes in and how it hits us, it then dictates where we land. Unfortunately, we usually end up landing somewhere we should not (or do not want) to be, and we end up feeling totally helpless and downhearted just like Dorothy. The scripture in James 1:8 speaks about what it is like for a wave of the sea to be tossed about by the wind. James refers this to someone that is double minded because, just like the wave, it is unstable and so is a double-minded man who is being tossed here and there by everything in life. When our trust is not in the unmovable stability of God, we are depending on man's ways, which shift and change continuously by different whims. We are then tossed here and there, and every which way but loose!

Fear drives us here and there,
It pushes and it shoves,
It is trying to control,
What we hear from God above.

We must come into peace,
And hear what God has to say,
Follow His word in life,
Then we are safe every day!

Come into the Father's safe hands,
Look to Him on high,
He will lead and He will guide,
In His sheltering wing we can hide.

The voice
Oh, what do Dorothy's wandering eyes see?
What, oh what could it be?
There is something off on the side of the road,
It's something exciting to check out I do believe!

Hmmm … It does look very interesting. In fact, it is quite a bit out of the ordinary and it's definitely not your average everyday Joe. I do surmise that it is a voice in the wilderness.

Dorothy does not realize it, but this is a "suddenly." something that will stop her immediately in her tracks and cause her to take a second look at what she is doing and rethink her choice to run. God is so gracious that he puts stumbling blocks in our path to cause us to stop, look and listen. That is such a good lesson that we were taught as children—before crossing a road, stop, look and listen. Wait and see what may be coming that could be harmful before we decide. I thank God every day for the many interruptions that He allows in our lives that usually change everything. I love the goodness of God.

Oh yummy, Dorothy and Toto can smell the fire and the wonderful aroma of cooking food. *Can you tell I love hot dogs!*

Now, it's true, Dorothy probably did not stop just because of the smell of food. What really caught her eye was the probability (and great possibility) of transportation that would further her travels down the road.

There it is, *the suddenly!* Dorothy stops, she looks, and the next thing coming will be to listen. She reads the sign.

This is definitely intriguing. Wow! Mr. Marvel, just his name alone is inspiring and invokes wonder. This man must have an exciting life, full of amazing opportunities and adventure, a life that is much more exciting than the one on the farm. If Dorothy didn't think this, I sure was. Mr. Marvel sounded like he lived an unusually thrilling existence, and here he is, right in Dorothy's path. She found him right in the middle of an old dusty, boring road that needed a shot in the arm with some laughter, joy and wonder. This was definitely a great start to her journey; it must be fate, it's never to late!

Dorothy is ecstatic; this could be her ticket out of town! A wonderful prospect is being presented right before her very eyes. She is just certain that this is someone that she and Toto could hook up with, travel and see the amazing world.

Personally, I thought it was a little strange that she was willing to head down the road with a complete stranger, don't you? She really must be desperate. Have you found this pattern in your own life that when you are in a place of complete and utter agonizing moments that some of the strangest opportunities come your way and that some of the funniest doors open and the most fascinating characters appear out of nowhere to help us through? I believe these are angels in disguise. Let's just look at Dorothy in this case — even though it's just a man at a campfire cooking a hot dog, we need to be aware, very aware.

Oh yes, there is a definite purpose for this little interruption along the road, but little does she know it's definitely going to change her path.

This voice in the wilderness will point her back home to safety. This voice will completely shift her direction. This voice will cause her to refocus, recalibrate, put on her rainbow glasses and view her circumstances from a whole different color scheme. She will then stop, look and listen and then realize what is truly important in her life. This voice in the wilderness will help her to see and hear her situation from a much different perspective.

When we soar like an eagle,
Our problems appear so small,
So take a look around and be aware,
With wisdom we can overcome it all.

Dorothy had been very distracted because the focus of her attention was always on the enemy and the power that Miss Gulch carried. This distraction opened the door; fear then moved in and took control. Fear then became the overlord. I also like to describe it in this way: fear became the puppet master and when he pulled the strings, Dorothy danced. As we described before, Miss Gulch was running her life at that point. The enemy said jump, and Dorothy asked how high?

Dorothy stops, sits for a moment and listens, which positions her to hear the voice of wisdom.

Father God, help us to stop in this busy and overwhelming world of chaos that we live in and listen to your voice of wisdom (James 1:5). Ask for wisdom and God will give it liberally.

The scripture also tells us in Romans 8:28 that God works all things for good for those that love Him. If we look to Him, He will use all of our circumstances for good, even if we have made the choice to run away. He will send "a suddenly" to turn us around and use it for His Glory—that is how much he loves us. Let us stop, look and listen.

Scriptures on guidance

Psalm 5:8, 27:11, 31:3, and 61:1-2

Now in the movie, the traveler beside the road took out his crystal ball, but I declare to you that we do not look to magic or sorcery for our guidance. We look to the word of God and only the word of God! It is the truth, the whole truth and nothing but the truth. We look to the only source of power that gives all power. We look to the true power source. Many people in this day and time have become lax in this area and have allowed the enemy of their soul to veil their eyes concerning witchcraft. Our culture has opened itself up to believing that the power of darkness is no big deal. Even in the Body of Christ I have seen and heard those that have been enticed by the power of darkness. Father God is very up front and very straight that there is no way we can serve two masters! (Matthew 6:24) Choose this day to serve the Living God! I Samuel 28, shares the story of Saul turning to witchcraft and then because of that choice God turned Israel over to the Philistines (enemy). The bible says that he is a jealous God. (Exodus 34:14)

Dorothy stops to talk to Mr. Marvel. He invites her to sit and have a chat. Seeing the circumstances and realizes that a shift from the road that she is now traveling is a must, he hopes that he can help.

Now in the story the traveler asks Dorothy to close her eyes so that he could deceive her. He tricked her into thinking that he had great power, which was not the truth. This is exactly how the enemy will fool us; he is never up front with where his power comes from, but I will say this, God gave it and God will use it all. We repeat this again in Romans 8:28. All things work for good. In other words, whatever the enemy brings our way, God turns it around if we look to Him. In Psalms 2:4 it states that God laughs at the plans of the enemy. He sits, watches and then turns the situations in our favor and for His Glory!

A turn around moment

Dorothy jumps up—she has seen and heard the truth! She must change the course of her life; she must head back home. Her thinking has been adjusted; she realizes that she is heading in the wrong direction. It took a voice in the wilderness to bring her to that understanding. Wow! One thing I love about Dorothy is that when she heard and understood, she moved instantly to turn things around. She didn't waste any time deciding. She knew it was the truth; it resonated deep within her. She felt remorse and plunged into action! She grabbed Toto, her bag and off she went in a hurry back down the road to home sweet home. It was a turn around moment; it was a turn around day! She was back down the path in a hurried way.

What a different and interesting journey it would be this time though. The wind began to kick up its heels and let out a ferocious howl. A gust came to torment and pitch a fit, it was like a mighty attack! It pushed her around as if to say, "It is okay to leave, but don't come back!" If only she had put on her rainbow glasses first thing in the morning and seen her situation through the promises of God that infuse hope and direction, she would not be in this position of trying to frantically return to her safe shelter. She would have realized that safety was already in her possession. Dorothy is now bulldozing her way through. She grips tightly and hangs onto everything dear to her with all of her might. She is determined to win this fight!

Let's put on our rainbow glasses

I love God and how He is relentless in bringing us into His fullness, which is the fullness of His love, our destiny and purpose. Fears push us to the right and anger pushes us to the left. We are out of control with our decisions, oh but for the love of God. He moves to correct our direction, He moves to cover us, and He moves to surround us with His goodness.

Micah 2:13, (AMP) "The breaker [the Messiah, who opens the way] shall go up before them [liberating them]. They will break out, pass through the gate and go out; so their king goes on before them, The Lord at their head."

Several years ago I asked God the question, "What is destiny?" I had heard it so much that I actually told God that I wanted to gag on the word! I was feeling so pressured by it constantly being used by others, that it made me afraid that I was going to miss whatever God had for me, so I asked Him the question. He answered me immediately and so simply. He said, "Deb, I am your destiny and absolutely nothing else." He told me, *"Remain in me and everything else will flow out of that relationship."* Now, I want you to understand, I knew that in my head, and I knew the scripture in Matthew 6:33 that says, seek me first and my kingdom and all other things will follow, but I had never thought of Him and my relationship with Him as a destiny.

The Father continued to speak, "If you are not careful, you will seek destiny (your promise) like a carrot on a string and just when you think you have it within your grasp, the enemy will jerk the carrot out of your reach." I felt such relief that I immediately replied, "Oh Father, I can do that!" I will just stay in relationship with you. That moment changed my life because I now had a whole different perspective and the pressure was off. I now totally understood that it was all about my relationship with Him, and there is nothing more. From that day to this the Father has continually shown me that walking the yellow brick road of life with Jesus is the true gift, the most beautiful gift of all. When I am distracted and my focus is on problems the Father has gently placed His hand on my chin and brought my attention back to Him. He somehow brings a Mr. Marvel experience into my life and it turns me around to the right path, which is actually very simple— just be in Him. It really is not about the promise at the end of the road, but it is totally about the adventure along the way. We often forget that Jesus is the adventure!

This is why we want to look at this story of Dorothy from a whole new light. This is why we want to put on our rainbow glasses the first thing every morning, the start of every day, and let God reveal to us His viewpoint in all things along the way.

1) Let us recall the picture of Dorothy heading down a dark, desolate, lonely and wrong direction, and making incorrect decisions all because of fear. Remember her eyes were on the power of the enemy, her vision was distorted by terror, which then had the right to pressure and torment her until she felt she had no other choice but to run.

2) Let us understand that when we find ourselves in a situation of life that is unbearable and squeezing us, God has given us the ability to stop, look and listen. It is then through Him and His wisdom that we are able to keep our eyes on the things above, and our vision and hearing will be clear and peace like a river will then flow deep in our soul.

3) Let us always remember Romans 8:31 which says that if God is for us, then who can be against us? He is working for our good and that even though at times when we have made a choice to walk down the wrong road or go in the wrong direction, God is ready to place powerful voices in our path to turn us around. Be aware and be very sensitive to the Holy Spirit because His voice can come in the most uncommon ways and at the most unusual times. It can also through the most strange people and places. Just like with Dorothy, the voice came from a man sitting by the side

of the road named Mr. Marvel that was cooking a hot dog. Who could have ever imagined that?

4) When God speaks, stop, look and listen. Turn! Don't wait, don't waste time, respond quickly and choose Him.

5) The Voice in the Wilderness is mentioned in Isaiah 40:3 and John 1:23. Can you remember when Isaiah prophesied about John the Baptist? He was to be the voice in the wilderness, which would prepare the way for Christ. It said, "Prepare ye the way of the Lord, and make straight in the dessert a highway for our God."

Now I understand that John the Baptist was preparing the way for Jesus to arise, take His place and step into His destiny on this earth to be the savior of the world, but I would like for us to put on our rainbow glasses and look at this for a moment with a little different overview.

We know that it is true that still to this day, the Holy Spirit prepares the way for Jesus to bring salvation. He goes before Him to prepare our hearts and is the highway for God. The Holy Spirit speaks to us so that there can be a breakthrough in our lives and in the lives of others. I encourage you to listen for the voice of the Lord when you are in a wilderness; He will speak, He will lead, He will give direction with wisdom and discernment when we need to find our way back home just like Dorothy. Be aware that He is preparing the way for you. Your glasses will allow the beauty of His promises to erupt into your circumstances as the highway of God is opened up in and through you. Expect a suddenly! Expect His beauty to burst forth! Expect His voice!

Scriptures to meditate
Ezekiel 1:28 and 43:2

1 Kings 19:12
1 Peter 5:6-7
Jeremiah 33:3
Numbers 7:89
Psalms 29:3-9
Zephaniah 3:17

Pray with me

Dear Father, I thank you that when I make a wrong turn or a wrong choice that you never ever give up on me. You continually send a voice to speak to me in many different ways to turn me around and to get me back on the right path. Father, I repent for the times that I have reacted in fear and obeyed the voice of fear and made choices that harmed others or myself emotionally or physically. I repent for making fear my God and letting it rule my life at times and not listening and obeying your voice or your word that says to remain in peace and to trust you in all things. I thank you for turning me around and sending me home to you where there is peace and safety. I thank you that you are my high tower and I run into you and not away! Father, I expect your beauty to come alive in my life. In Jesus name, Amen.

Declaration

I declare that I am a child of God. I declare that I hear the voice of God and I will listen and respond to the Holy Spirit. I declare that when you call me, I will answer! I also declare that I will hear great and unsearchable things through you. I receive this promise, and decree that it is mine!

7

THE MIGHTY STORM

Dorothy is up and out a new door, running down the road heading back home! I can't wait to see what is in-store!

Realizing her mistake, she listens to the voice and receives the word. Once again, with her bag in hand and Toto by her side, she is off. She is pressing forward with complete determination, leaning into the wind with all of her strength. Wow, what a storm! Yes, the adventure of trying to get back home will be quite different then her quiet, uneventful experience when she left. No one seemed to even notice when she walked out the door. It was sad and a bit boring until she came into contact with the voice in the wilderness. That's when things shifted, and Dorothy's life was altered immediately.

Have you ever noticed that when we turn and choose the right direction, there always seems to be a tremendous opposition, just like Dorothy is confronting. But, no matter the sudden fierce winds that have risen up and are wreaking havoc, Dorothy unwaveringly continues to push back and press forward.

This huge resistance that is coming against her continues to bully, hassle and shove her around, it seems like an invisible force, an enemy that does not want her to return, but Dorothy is determined. Her sight is restricted from the flying dust that is swirling around her. She raises her arm as a shield for protection, moving forward only by instinct. Objects are now being tossed through the air from the power and strength of the wind. The winds could have been a great distraction, but Dorothy did not look to the right or to the left; she knew that safety was just ahead, she was almost there, and there was no Dread!

For me, memories of feeling great terror and anxiousness flood to the surface when I recall watching the effects of this cyclone as a child. I knew she must get home and she must get there immediately! Again, I could feel the urgency that was churning in the atmosphere. It seemed that Dorothy was always placing herself in desperate situations that created in me a state of fretfulness for her welfare.

Meanwhile, Dorothy's friends and family have headed for a place of security, down, down, down, deep underground, to a cellar built specifically for ultimate protection. Her aunt and uncle and the farm hands are calling Dorothy's name, but she is nowhere to be found! Where could she be? Oh how this scene raised my heartbeat just from the sight of her being stuck in the horrific atmospheric chaos.

Yes she has turned and is on her way back, but the timing of her arrival home is not quite perfect, or is it? When we are caught in the uproars of life that God never intended for us to have to go through, relax for He is always there with us. Storms are like rollercoaster rides; they are up, down and all around, and sometimes even upside down. Dorothy was not in the place that she was supposed to be, or was she? At this point, her family and friends have no choice; they must enter the place of refuge without her. They must go down into the cellar with the absence of Dorothy and pray that she will be safe. They enter the underground sanctuary and lock the door, they are sheltered, waiting to be restored, but as a child watching this movie, I was in a place of torment, I was definitely not bored!

This is a twister! A tornado! It's ugly and scary and brings agonizing trauma if you continue to look at it. They can come suddenly and twist with such a violent force that everything in their path is brought to rubble. We then look at the path of destruction and think, "What do we do now? The answer is for us always to keep our eyes on Jesus and never the storm. He is there riding it out with us, our eyes must be kept on Him.

You have to understand that I grew up in the Northwest, so I had never seen anything like this violent twisting monster that I was experiencing vicariously through this movie. I very quickly and clearly perceived that if you were not in a place of protection, you were at its mercy, and I certainly did not believe or see that it had any mercy!

Just like Miss Gulch and how the intense music announced her arrival to the farm, the sound of this storm did the same, announcing its arrival with threats and intimidation. To say the least, I did not enjoy this sound. Like a frightening growl, the roar of the winds pierced my senses and touched off every emotion of fright imaginable. It awakened within me such agitation from its loud threatening voice that seemed to be shouting, "I am after you, I will stop you, and you will not get away from me!"

Watching the TV screen, I could see that the threat of this sound only placed more of a resolve upon Dorothy's steps; they were more and more consumed with a sense of purpose, "*I WILL* make it home!" Yes the ferocious rumble actually did activate an amazing perseverance within Dorothy, but for my kind and gentle spirit, the cruelty of the sound and significant danger created a fierce concern because of her vulnerability. In my thoughts I was crying out, please hurry Dorothy, take cover, hurry! Get back to your house where you will be safe and secure. The sound of the storm was like the rumbling of the tormenting Egyptian chariots that chased the Israelites through the Red Sea; she must get across!

Dorothy finally arrives, thank God she is inside, she calls out, but it is pointless she cannot be heard; they have already gone to the place prepared for such a time as this. The location is deep beneath the ground where there is peace and calm as the storm passes by overhead. Dorothy realizes where they are and races to the cellar door and knocks and stomps relentlessly to no avail! Frantically, she tries to open the door with her own strength but it is hopeless, it's too late, the moment is lost! She turns towards the house, desperately hanging onto Toto with everything she has, battling and maneuvering the furious out of control tempest.

There seems to be a common scene throughout the story so far, *HANG ONTO TOTO!* Making sure not to let go, she finally reaches the bedroom, and once again, there is another suddenly. The same window that brought the miracle of Toto back into her life in the past is about to bring another! It blows off its hinges and hits Dorothy smack on her head, she stumbles and staggers to her bed, and it almost looks like she is dead! Wow, she is out! I do believe another amazing miracle is on its way; in fact, I think it has already arrived. I have to laugh because I think there are so many times that God has had to literally and intentionally hit me on the head with a window of revelation to bring me to my bed of rest, which is In Him. HE is our place of peace, and has always been.

It is interesting and quite fascinating to me that Dorothy has arrived right back at the exact same room and bed that she was in before she made the frantic decision to run away. The same window that brought the last revelation and miracle is now about to bring another. Dorothy's bedroom should have been a place of rest. I sure do wish she would have stopped and thought things through before that lying, ugly, threatening fear started crashing in on her so hard with the situation of Miss Gulch. If she had come into rest, she could have clearly heard a better direction to go. *If only!* The past few hours of her life would have been so much simpler, and at this very moment, she would have been in the shelter, far away from the storm. My encouragement at this moment is to say, "Stay in the peace of God! Stay in His rest, stay in the secret place!" Unhealthy reactions to the threats and sounds around us can take us down roads of torment and fear just like it took Dorothy. So, always be very aware. Listen for the still small voice! (1 Kings 9:11-13)

But, the awesome thing about God is that He sends miracles in many different shapes, sizes and at the most odd and peculiar times. In fact, real life supernatural interventions usually come right in the middle of our storms, right in the middle of our messes when we need them the most, just like Dorothy!

What an experience for Dorothy. Something just shifted. Here she was, frightened and not knowing what to do, and there it is, another suddenly. Remember when I made the statement a few lines back, "She is not in the place she was supposed to be, or was she? From a different perspective, I think she was right where she was supposed to be. Well, here we go, the ride is about to change, the switch has been pulled, the track has been adjusted and her direction totally rearranged. The next stop? Welcome to The Land of Oz.

Rainbow glasses on

We see that Dorothy has just walked through a very dangerous place because she allowed fear to rule her in this situation. She ran away from home thinking that would be the answer to all of her problems and the threats from the enemy would be left far behind. She was sure that running would keep Toto safe. A voice in the wilderness turned her around which headed her back to safety, but on the way, a huge storm of opposition surfaced, and she was caught right in the middle. But, the beautiful thing about storms is that they relocate things and they uncover and bring revelation. This is exactly what is coming for Dorothy, a new revelation and a huge discovery and understanding of the choices she just made and the new ones that are ahead. She has arrived back home by the power of the storm, and has been placed on her bed of rest with an open vision to come, I love it, this is the very best!

Yes, many times we are caught in the middle of a nasty tempest because of our choices. It seems frightening, as we are being tossed about like a rag doll with no ability to stop the wind that is propelling and manhandling us. I have memories in my life when I have felt exactly like that rag doll, how about you? I can relate that just the sound of a storm can be so incredibly terrifying that I feel overwhelmed and at a loss for how to even prepare for it. It is in that situation that the voice of my enemy doesn't dare miss a beat; he steps up his game and will continually accuse me of failure and weakness to try and serve me a platter of yet more panic!

So, let us put on our rainbow glasses and see what God has to say!

Where oh where are my rainbow glasses?
I need them now as I live my life,
I place them on and then see beauty,
With them on there is no strife.

Let me walk in the power of your promise,
With rainbow glasses I am no doubting Thomas,
I must view life and be able to see,
That life is an amazing, colorful giving tree!

Full of fruit that feeds the world,
Full of life from God above,
Full of promises to be fulfilled,
If we can only see everything through His love!

It is good when things shift! We need change because change brings challenges and challenges create growth. On this exciting train of change, we adapt, experience adventure and learn to trust God. It would be terrible to just think and not to believe or encounter that God has our back. We must have hope in all of these places in our life; we must be kept on track!

In the books of Matthew and John, the disciples were in a great storm, but God had their back. The scripture tells us that they literally feared for their lives even though Jesus was on board the boat. We need to understand that this was a very fierce storm and being on a boat was not uncommon for them, so they definitely understood what they were up against. I picture them probably bailing water as fast as they could, who knows, but I can say this, they were disturbed that Jesus was sleeping. They felt that He was not concerned for their lives after all. He wasn't even helping! They were offended. They woke Him up and made this statement right to His face, "Do you not care that we perish?" They must have thought that there was something He could do about the prevailing wind, or they would not have awakened Him. We can relate to this, I know we have felt the same thing. *God, where are you in the middle of my storm?* Help God! Isn't even any of the loud noise disturbing you? How can you sleep? And there He is, right in the middle of the boat at rest, and we are in shear panic! I wonder if the disciples thought that He did not totally understand the situation and really how serious it was, because after all He was a carpenter and not a fisherman!

I've experienced that very thought process before, haven't you? We have all had questions at times. We see in the scripture that they felt He didn't really care, or He wouldn't be sleeping. They were not yet in a place where they could take this storm on by themselves; through that statement they were professing that they actually didn't even realize who Jesus was, at least not yet. Isn't that what the journey is all about? As they continued to walk with Him, they began to comprehend. In the future they would encounter Him greater and become known as those that turned the world upside down! (Acts 17:6)

I'm grateful that the disciples stopped and woke him up because I can associate with that better, that heart felt cry. The more time that I have walked with the Lord my relationship has shifted from fear to trust. I think that is where His companions were at in this moment. I know the scripture states that Jesus asked them where their faith was, but I believe Jesus knew exactly where their faith was, but he needed them to know. Wow! What a revelation just because they asked a question. In order for their spiritual eyes to be opened, they had to go to Jesus, ask for help, speak up, and express their hearts.

So, I declare to you that the Father wants us to stop and pursue Him when life is crashing all around. He never meant for us to shoulder life alone. His desire is for us to come to Him and share every feeling. He has the power to change the atmosphere and everything around us, what ever is rocking our boat, but we need to reach out and receive His peace. In this case, the disciples had not really come to perceive who Jesus was yet, because we see they were astonished and afraid when He silenced the storm, and they spoke among themselves saying, who is this that even the winds obey Him? (Luke 8:25) Continued relationship with the Master would bring great understanding, but, by stepping up and asking on this day, it set them free to see, an amazing miracle.

Jesus is the silencer of the wind! When the storm is howling, spitting and growling, and your boat in life is being violently rocked to the point you think you are going overboard and will drown, either physically, emotionally, or spiritually, please step up and call out His name and let Him calm the upheaval! Be at rest and be at peace because that is who He is, He is the Prince of Peace (Isaiah 9:6). Our faith is built in Him through life. The scripture says that the disciples were astonished and afraid; they had never seen any man like Jesus before.

They encountered Jesus through a new facet, never seen before, and it all started with frustration and alarm that thrust them to the edge, pushing and encouraging them to express their hearts. They were living real life with Him.

Praise is another weapon that will destroy the spirit of chaos around us and in us. Paul and Silas praised God and worshipped in the prison cell in Acts 16:16-40. It was in this place of thanksgiving that ushered in the angels from above, the chains broke off and the cell doors swung open wide. It was worship during adversity (the storm) where freedom was born. I recently heard a statement, "God doesn't want worship; He wants worshippers!" Let us be a worshipper!

1) Will we be in storms? Yes, some from our choices and some from just living life. Is God with us? Yes, all of the way and all of the time. God has a plan for us and is always working on our side to set us free and complete the plan. Just like Dorothy, a storm presents the opportunity for an adventure of a lifetime where we can live, learn and experience who we are and who He is. Experience the supernatural! Allow your wings to sail on the wind of adversity, be lifted up, and be free to see.

2) Let's talk about the safety of the innermost place in Jesus. He is our strong tower and we run into Him for protection. Dorothy should have been home but because she was not, it set up a whole different scenario. Always remember that the Father desires for us to be in Him and that He is prepared for any storm and that He is

our protection in all situations. Just like in the story of Dorothy and the cellar, there is a secret place in Jesus at the throne of God. Let us choose the secret place that is prepared just for us. As it says in Psalm 91:1, (KJV) He that dwelleth in the secret place of the Most High shall abide under the shadow of the Almighty.

I am reminded of a song from many years ago that I heard as a child called, "Till The Storm Passes By" that was written by Mosie Lister. The words are awesome, and I hear it in my spirit still to this day, as they share about being held in the hand of God until the storm passes by.

Scriptures to meditate
Jeremiah 29:11
Luke 8:23
Mark 4:38
Matthew 14:22-27 and 8:24
Psalm 91

Pray with me
Father God, I thank you that you are with me in every storm of life when the wind blows and the rain falls. Father God, help me to believe and see that you are always there and to know that I am always safe if I stay in you. You ride the storms with me, and you also silence them. When I am with you, all is good. During those times when the storm is severe, let me always know and remember that you will never ever forsake me and that I am your child! Thank you Father that your peace is not as the world gives but it is supernatural from heaven and of the spirit. It is a peace that no one can take away! Father, keep me in the palm of your hand, protected

and always safe. Thank you, Father, for the revelation of who you are that is revealed through the storms of life. You are constantly overwhelming me with your amazing love and that you are faithful to the end. Amen.

Declaration

I declare that I will believe and know that in the middle of the storm I am protected and safe in the arms of God. I declare that I will look to Him, even though my boat may be rocking and shifting violently. I declare that my peace is supernatural and is not of this world but from heaven above. No one can steal my peace. I declare I will not trade my peace for fear. I declare that I am safe and secure in Jesus and can do all things through Him.

8

THE WINDOW OF REVELATION

OOM! Dorothy is down for the count!

She walks into her bedroom looking for a place to hunker down and ride out this violent cyclone. The next thing that happens is a total and complete surprise. The wind ramps up so violently and blows so hard that the window lets loose from its hinges, flies across the room straight at Dorothy, and hits her directly on the head. Oh my goodness, now wouldn't you say that that was a definite suddenly?

Dorothy is down for the count as she falls helplessly on the bed and passes out. I wanted someone to help her, someone to rescue her. As I watched, this was almost too much for a little girl's heart to bear. Dorothy had already been through so much, what else could happen, doesn't anyone care?

Our next thought should be to call the paramedics, rush her to the hospital, and pray. If there had been a referee, I believe the count would have been 1-2-3-4-5- ... but things are not exactly what they seem. As we wait for just a moment, it's becoming extremely clear that she is entering the greatest ride of her life. Now ... 6-7-8, Whoo hoo – she's up! Dorothy is awake! Her vision and all of her senses have been restored.

Can't you just hear those words from the song composed by Johnny Nash that say, "I can see clearly now ..."? Well, it's exactly what has happened to Dorothy. She rises up, places her feet on the ground, moves to the window and looks out. She is horrified comprehending that they are right in the center of the cyclone, the eye of the storm. (I think it is very interesting that cyclones are also called dust devils.). Dorothy is being transported up, up, up, higher and higher. There is no other choice now and no way out. Our vision and observation of things in life always change dramatically when we go up higher and view things from God's arena, truly a heavenly perspective. Dorothy is about to experience a heavenly view; she is headed to a place where she is about to see things clearly where everything is true and brand new.

Never forget that it was the power of wind that shifted the window. Wind is mentioned throughout the scripture on many occasions, but let's recall when the Holy Spirit first invaded man on the earth in a new and mighty way and it was described as a wind!

Acts 2:2, (KJV) "And suddenly there came a sound from heaven as of a rushing mighty wind, and it filled the entire house where they were sitting."

Once the Holy Spirit came to the earth and lived within man, it was a game changer. The window of heaven was opened for new understanding, direction, revelation and power. It was the prophesied promise of God fulfilled. Man and the earth would never be the same!

Let there be wind!
Exodus 14:21-22: God opens the sea with the wind for the children of Israel to walk on dry land!
Amos 4:13: God dispenses the wind!
2 Samuel 22:11, God is in the wind!
Ezekiel 37:9: Wind is the breath of God!

As Dorothy was viewing the outside like a movie reel through the open window, she was also becoming much wiser with the understanding of who people really were. The wind was doing a great job of blowing away the façade, which was meant to mask and cloak the deep reality. We need to be praying in our lives, let the windows of heaven open, and blow wind, blow, let us see!

Let's talk about windows for just a moment. Windows allow light to come in; they allow the sun (the Son) to shine on us. The sun (the Son) "brings warmth, revelation, knowledge and understanding. Windows are an eye to the outside and the inside depending on where you are positioned. Windows are positioned so we can see clearly.

We need revelation concerning the condition of our own hearts so that we can allow the Holy Spirit to do His work of healing and set us free. We must see what is on the inside.

We need to see outside ourselves (and beyond) for an open revelation on situations around us to receive wisdom on where and how to walk the yellow brick road but above anything else, we need the true unveiling of who God is! Jesus died so that there would be no separation, that we might truly experience and see our Father. What a privilege it is to now be able to enter boldly into the Throne of Grace because of the cross.

At this moment in the story, Dorothy is on the inside looking out. In the middle of the whirlwind outside her open window, she sees her family and her loved ones smiling and happy, but then suddenly Miss Gulch appears and there is total understanding that she is still on a mission. Dorothy's eyes are now opened to a revelation of great evil and she is quite alarmed! Cringing as the scene changes, she watches Miss Gulch turn into the very picture of wickedness. What's really amazing is that we now have a great epiphany; the wind that seemed to be destructive is actually a blessing, for it is through the raging storm that the underlying truth has been unlocked.

Just then, a sudden evil sinister cry causes Dorothy to tremble, turn away and bury her head. The evil one continues to cackle with a menacing and threatening sound. The book has been opened and the page has been flipped to reveal who Miss Gulch really is. Terror strikes Dorothy! Remember, revelation is always good. Since we must have the ability to recognize and see the enemy and see where he is hiding.

2 Corinthians 2:22, teaches us that we must know our adversary. 1 Peter 5:8 shares with us to be alert and sober minded. Let the Father reveal to you through the Holy Spirit the enemy of your soul; be wise to his tactics and maneuvers. Let the Heavenly Father strip him of the camouflage clothing that hides the truth behind his schemes.

In wartime, each adversary studies the tanks, battleships and weaponry of their opponent. They must recognize whom they are and what they are up against to discern and destroy the enemy. The same is true with *our* adversary, Satan. We must recognize his strategies with great revelation from a heavenly perspective. We need to go up higher just like Dorothy, through the power of the wind (Holy Spirit). Discerning that it was at this elevated place she suddenly could see very distinctly and properly without any hindrances in the way.

In an instant, the house shifts into reverse, and is falling, falling, falling! Down, down, down, Dorothy's bed of rest is twisting, turning, sliding and bouncing around! Things everywhere seem totally out of control, so Dorothy is hanging on for dear life! She lets loose a massive scream as the downward spiral continues at an intense speed. Not knowing what will happen next or where the next stop will be, Toto is tight in her arms. The house comes to an absolutely screeching sudden, complete and totally abrupt stop. *BAM! BOOM!*

There is an overwhelming piercing silence. Dorothy's eyes open wide. She's alarmed as she comes to realize that the sound of the storm is gone and that her house is no longer spinning or shaking. Her bed has traveled around and around, side-to-side, a little up and a little down. It was quite the adventure, but she is completely and totally safe. Dorothy rises slowly and cautiously as she looks around to investigate, what has just happened? What's going on? Where is she and what's behind her bedroom door?

Wow, what a whirlwind of events,
Wow, what a wild ride,
Wow, where am I at now?
Wow, I'm a little afraid to look outside!

What do I do now?
I know some things have shifted,
What is behind the door?
Help my fear to be lifted!

Pulling out the rainbow glasses

How many times in the middle of riding out a storm have we been hanging on for dear life, with everything shifting and moving around and beneath us, where nothing seems to stay in one place, and all we desire is just one stable moment. I am here to share with you that Jesus and the word of God is the only stability in this world. When we are caught in the eye of the storm and we are riding it out, it is Jesus. There is no other. He is the same yesterday, today and forever. He is the beginning and the end. When we are hanging onto everything precious to us the best we can, hoping all will be calm soon, hoping for a place where we can just walk without wobbly legs, the scripture tells us in Psalm 46:10 that in those times to be still and know that He is God. In Ephesians 6:13, it also says, when you have done everything you know to do, put on the whole armor of God so that when the day of evil comes, you may be steadfast and unmovable. Trust that He will bring an abrupt safe suddenly.

Put on your rainbow glasses, look at these scriptures through the love and promises of the Father and who He is. He will give us the supernatural strength to stand in faith.

Hebrews 13:8, (NIV) "Jesus Christ is the same yesterday today and forever."

Revelation 22:13, (NIV) "I am the Alpha and Omega, the First and the Last, the Beginning and the End"

Come to rest in that the Father knows the beginning, but He also knows the end. His omnipotence is our security!

With our rainbow glasses we can see that the Father is with us no matter the situation and He is willing and able to be with us until the very end. He doesn't get tired, grow impatient or weary of us, He will stay. He will hold fast and we can stand in the time of need.

Psalm 6:1-3, (NIV) "God is our refuge and strength, an ever-present help in trouble. Therefore, we will not fear, though the earth gives way and the mountains fall into the sea, though its waters roar and foam and the mountains quake with surging."

I don't know about you, but I am in constant need of the Heavenly Father. My physical body would grow weak without daily nourishment, just as my spiritual man becomes weak without daily communing with Him. I put my rainbow glasses on each day and look ahead through the word of God and the heart He has for me. These words penned by Robert Lowry many years ago in 1872 speak loudly: "I need Thee, oh, I need Thee. Every hour I need thee; oh, bless me now, my Savior! I come to Thee." Relevant then and relevant now.

A shift

A suddenly, the storm has ceased; it is quiet and very still, it is almost eerie, and it actually feels a little awkward. Sometimes we are so used to so much going on around us that we don't even know how to relate with peace. When it is quiet, it can be almost deafening. The calm after a storm is very surreal and can even feel strange. That is why I encourage people to stay in Jesus and let the peace of God be our normal, not the abnormal. Let His peace reign at all times. Nothing shifts the Father, nothing takes Him back, nothing surprises Him, so let us be in Him and let who He is rule our body, mind, emotions and spirit. So whether we are in mayhem or not, we will not alter, we will not move either way. There is another old hymn from my childhood composed by Paul Heaton and Stan Cullimore, an African American spiritual used during the Civil rights movement, "I shall not be moved just like a tree that is planted by the water, I shall not be moved."

Psalm 1:3, (NIV) "That person is like a tree planted by streams of water, which yield its fruit in season and whose leaf does not wither. Whatever they do prospers"

Jeremiah 17:8, (NIV) "They will be a tree that is planted by the water that sends out its roots by the stream. It does not fear when heat comes; its leaves are always green. It has no worries in a year of drought and never fails to bear fruit."

The greatest radar that I depend on for myself is the peace of God. When I realize that I am not in peace I immediately ask God the four W's: what, where, when and why. The Father is faithful in setting us free from the turmoil within, fear of the times that we live in and the fearful experiences that we have lived through. Be free! Learn from Him. Learn where it's coming from, what is causing it, when did it attach and why did it attach. Take time with the Holy Spirit to look at what the storm has revealed and uncovered; movement always bring revelation. Use the power and authority of Jesus Christ with the weapons you have been equipped with and destroy the tormenter! Be the *Terminator*! Your greatest weapon: the Power of the Red Shoes, The Blood of Jesus!

Scriptures on peace

Colossians 3:15: Peace of God rules your heart.

Galatians 5:22: Fruit of the Spirit.

1 Peter 3:11: Pursue peace.

1 Peter 5:7: Cast your care on Him and remain in peace.

Pray with me

Dear Heavenly Father, I thank you that I have the privilege to come to you personally, that I do not need a priest to give a sacrifice for me, for you gave the ultimate sacrifice, your son Jesus. Father, I thank you that Jesus Christ is the Prince of Peace and He dwells within me, therefore I am at peace and have the ability through you to live a life of peace within and without. I am thankful that no matter what comes or goes, you are with me and your promises are true and faithful. Lord, I am thankful for revelation in the middle of the storms in my life and for the wind of the spirit that opens up my spiritual sight when it takes me higher into your heavenly realm. Help me, Heavenly Father, to always choose to go higher with you, and when the unexpected comes and it feels like the bottom has dropped out from underneath me, I feel unsteady and my legs feels wobbly, I believe and know that You are there to hold me up and give me strength and guide my path. Amen!

Declaration

I declare that I am a child of the Most High God and that I will stand in strength and courage and choose to look at life through your prom-ises. I declare that I have peace within me because the Prince of Peace is my Lord and Savior! I choose to let the Peace of God rule my heart. I declare that the wind of the Holy Spirit has full reign over my mind, soul, body and spirit. I declare that I will see from a higher perspective through the Holy Spirit. I choose to go higher!

Dorothy gathers a few things in her basket that she might need and heads for the door. What is behind door number one?

9

BEHIND DOOR NUMBER ONE

Dorothy has an expression of perplexed wonder on her face. Hmmm … slowly she sits up and then stands up. Her arms are still around Toto holding him close, picking up her basket she now steps forward. What do you think is running through her mind now as she leaves the bedroom and heads towards the front door, looking around very cautiously and not knowing what lies ahead or where she has landed?

Dorothy knew as she looked out of the window into the eye of the storm that she was being carried somewhere new, somewhere different. I held my breath comprehending her apprehension. What is behind the door? She forges straight ahead. It's the same door she has known all of her life and she has walked through many, many times before, but in another place and what seems like another lifetime. Bracing herself for what is ahead knowing on this occasion, things are definitely not as usual.

There is an immense consciousness that this door is going to open up to a new situation that is out of her world, so, what is behind it now, where has she been hurled?

Being little I had an overwhelming feeling and thought that Dorothy should probably not even open the door. I wanted to shout it out loud! Nooo! After all of the calamities and (literally) devastating blows that have just taken place, I was definitely not very excited for her to see what was behind that door.

An enormous amount of curiosity was pulling Dorothy like a massive magnet, closer and closer. She knew there was no other option; she had to open this door. Closer and closer! It was the undeniable power of the unknown that enticed Dorothy nearer and nearer to that door. Then, with her arm outstretched, she reaches for the handle, her hand grips the knob, it begins to turn, and slowly as it opens the door swings inward. Wisely she stays covered from behind to peer outside. We both sucked in air reacting with a loud gasp! The sight is astonishing! It brings an emotion of delight all over her as Dorothy's heart is filled with joy when the colors burst forth in the sunlight—it is a whole new land. This is the beginning of a whole new world for her!

Now, we have to remember that Dorothy has just gone through a very intense time of experiencing heartache, separation, fear, and anger, not to mention a cyclone of a storm that tried to tear everything she knew and loved away from her. Personally, I am not so sure if I would have opened that door. I kind of felt like she was in a Jack-in-the-Box moment, one of not knowing what, when, where or how the next thing was going to pop up! What did you think? I was thinking what a ride! In all probability I would have just stopped and contemplated for a bit the last few hours of my life to see if I had enough courage to move ahead, or at least taken a good nap! You see like I said before, as a child, I wondered if it was really such a good idea to open that door. Don't you feel that Dorothy actually showed quite a bit of courage to move forward and inspect what was beyond that door?

What a reward!

Courage does have its rewards! Dorothy quickly finds this out. Is this the same timid girl that shrank back from facing her fears? Is this the same girl that had just run away from it all? Hmmm ... has something changed? The storm has placed her in a position that requires her to stand up, step forward and step out. The alternative would have been to sit in a dark house, hoping someone would rescue her when all of the time, beauty and adventure would have been just around the corner

Doors

With a feeling of wonder and delight,
We open a new door, to find colors so bright.

We step outside on the fresh new land,
This is the place that I am!

Oh, what an adventure that lays ahead,
I am sure that this is what she said!

Everything around her seemed filled with wonder,
This is a brand new start,
This is surely what she needed for her heart!

Isaiah 43:19: I am doing a new thing!
James 1:17: Every good and perfect gift is from above!

Let us learn from this creative fable not be afraid to open new doors when they are presented to us through the various experiences and encounters we will have in life. The moment Dorothy chose to open and peer around the door, what to her amazement did she see?

The colors are exquisite; the flowers have a new smell,
Things will be different for sure; I can tell.

Dorothy knew and had no doubt that this was a new day. She has realized that she is obviously not in Kansas anymore. The storm has taken her and shifted her to a new place. Maybe this was the place over the rainbow because it was just so over the top beautiful. It looked like the place she had dreamed and sang about right before everything seemed to fall apart. The place she had so desired for her and Toto to be able to go, the place that only her imagination could take her before, she has arrived over the rainbow, through this brand new door!

A time to reflect with rainbow glasses

Ask yourself this question, what if Dorothy had never opened the door? I find that life is about circumstances that present us with an invitation to open different doors, but because of fear, shame, rejection or regrets from the past, our mindset keeps us in bondage from experiencing something fresh from above. Let's be brave. Take hold of courage and trust, fuse them together and expect a miracle that comes from His love.

Isaiah 40:31: If you hope in the Lord, you will renew your strength.

Isaiah 43:2: Be brave because when you pass through the waters, He will be with you.

Joshua 1:9: Be strong and courageous.

Help us Father not become victims of our circumstances. Let us be more then willing, just as Dorothy was to face the unknown, to step forward, and let you be God. Help us to be fearless and open the doors that are set before us from heaven above. Swing them wide and help me to step through and enjoy the new.

I recently had a lovely friend that passed away. She walked through the door of this world into the next, and no doubt, this is the greatest transition of all. She continually spoke of life and love, as she would make these statements: "Don't let the fear of the unknown take away the comfort of that which is sure." She also would say, "Worry empties today of its strength." What truths these are, real truths that will take us far!.

Don't be afraid of transition, for life is full of transitions from one season to another. Life is full of exploits if we will just walk through the enticing portals of festivities. We continue to move and grow in relationships and through adventure. As we begin each day with God, lets ask him, what new experiences do you have for me today? Let us be like little children, always excited for the next learning phase, pushing forward and experiencing the new—rolling, crawling, standing, walking, and finally running. Running with Jesus to the next opening, it all starts by going through door number one.

Door #1

The first door that I want to mention from the scripture is Jesus. He was represented in Exodus 12:22-23 during the first Passover when blood was applied to the doors of the children of Israel. They were told by God to place blood on the doorposts and as they did this in obedience, they all were saved; the blood protected them. The blood represented Jesus and the sacrifice that would come to save the world and all that would apply His blood to their lives through receiving Him would be saved.

The scripture states in John 10:17, that He is the door. There is no other way, He is the way, the Truth and the Life, and no one comes to the Father but through Him. Yes! He is *thee* door!

Revelation 3:20, describes another door, the door of our hearts. Jesus stands at the door and knocks. He is a gentleman; He waits for us to open and request His presence. He doesn't push, shove or bully. He asks to be invited.

And just like Dorothy, she had a choice and so do we. If you have not accepted Him as your personal savior, I would say to you, open the door, repent and receive Him in. You will then experience a brand new day of sunshine and flowers, a brand new land, a place of peace, love, acceptance, authority, and an adventure in Him that is new every morning. Hear the saviors knock; open up your heart to salvation, a life of hope, and grace will be unlocked!

If you are reading this and you know him personally already, follow the Holy Spirit as He leads you to open new doors of experiences in Him and through Him. Don't be afraid. Let the winds of change bring you to transition, from one room to another. Always remember that the greatest adventure of all is Jesus Himself. He is the greatest door, to all things, all adventures, all peace and all life! As we view Jesus through our rainbow glasses, let every new adjustment that is presented by Him bring us to a setting where our senses are set on fire with joy just like Dorothy!

Jesus' blood paid the price,
Let's walk through the door,
To see the other side,
Let's see what He has in store.

Yes, God, let's go through a new door!
Yes, God, I am ready for more!
Yes, God, I am ready to go with you,
Yes, God, I am ready to be renewed!

What is behind door number one?
What have you prepared?
Let me not be afraid to look,
At everything you want to share!

Scriptures to meditate
Psalms. 24:7
Matthew 7:7-8 and 6:6
Acts 5:19 and 14:27
John 10:7
Revelation 3:7-8

Pray with me

Father God, I thank you for the new experiences and challenges that come into my life through new situations, even though I do not always understand them at the time. I thank you, Father, that you desire to walk with me through every new door that is presented that brings transition from one season to the next. Just like you have created the earthly seasons that change and bring a different source of beauty in a new way each year, so it is in my life. I need you, Father, to walk and talk with me through these times, to secure my heart from the fears and sometimes pain that a new door may bring. Thank you, Jesus, that you are the ultimate door and the ultimate joy and peace. You gave your life that I might walk and talk with you in an amazing personal relationship. I can do all things through you Father, so I choose to trust and obey as I hear you say, "Let's go through the doors together and shift the world around us by the power of my blood and Love." Amen!

Declaration

I declare today that I will choose to walk in Your Peace and Joy through every door that presents itself in my life because you are the Prince of Peace! I declare that the Peace of God resides within me and fear has no place. I declare that I will arise above every situation by the power of the Most High God. I declare that I will walk in authority through every door that lies ahead and declare that it is an adventure in Jesus!

10

THE LAND OF OZ

I feel so excited
I feel so alive
Yes, oh yes
We have arrived!

The first thing I would like to share is that the word Oz is a Hebrew word for strength, power and courage. (3) When I learned this, my heart skipped a beat. Wow, that is amazing! Dorothy has just entered the land of strength, power and courage; instantly, in my mind this put a whole different spin on the story, especially with the understanding of what she has just experienced. This is significant since she is coming out of fear, rejection and trauma. We can all relate to needing to live in the land of power, courage and strength. God is so faithful to take us unto Himself and pull us close to His heart during these times in our lives when we are overwhelmed by a storm of troubles. He invites us to lay our head upon His shoulder, rest, and be alive with His amazing power, strength and courage.

The meaning of the Land of Oz and how it applies to our personal story is just ahead. As we look through our rainbow glasses we see a fantastic invitation to skip and dance in this new land of great promise. Dorothy is coming out of a place where she has experienced a lot of pain, hurt and disappointment, but now, great things are ahead for her. Come with us as the new door opens and we view this magnificent country through the eyes of Christ. We have crossed the threshold, and there is no turning back.

What marvelous things we are going to learn and see, hurry, please come with me!

If you will recall, the voice in the wilderness that turned Dorothy around was named Mr. Marvel. The meaning of the verb marvel is to be astonished, to be surprised, to see a miracle, and to be in awe. Let us stand in awe of the Lamb of God. He desires our love and friendship as we walk this glorious road called life. He desires that our days be filled with joy and laughter. He desires for us to marvel at who He is and enjoy this kingdom that is full of expectations, great strength, power and courage, for it is Jesus. Jesus is always waiting our arrival and the Holy Spirit is always pointing the way for an encounter of unbelievable wonderment with our Savior.

2 Corinthians 3:18: He desires for us to go from glory to glory.

Be aware; be very aware of the signs all around you. The land is speaking life and vitality and the skies are always blue!

What beauty

When Dorothy and Toto peer around the door, they are in awe of the beauty that they are now beholding. She continues to hang on ever so tight!

Hebrews 4:14-16, (NIV) "Therefore, since we have a great high priest who has ascended into heaven, Jesus the Son of God, let us hold firmly to the faith we profess. For we do not have a high priest who is unable to empathize with our weaknesses, but we have one who has been tempted in every way, just as we are, yet He did not sin. Let us then approach God's throne of grace with confidence, so that we may receive mercy and find grace to help us in our time of need.

Dorothy steps through the door to the outside, she walks around admiring all of the amazing new scenery. She has arrived where the Munchkins live, in the wonderful Land of Oz. I loved this place of music and laughter then and I still love it today. Dorothy has no idea that these delightful little people are watching her every move behind the scene. Hidden and disguised in the dazzling surroundings, for me they are creating an expectation that something magnificent is about to happen. Even their hats, shoes and dresses are literally springing up flowers. Their very essence speaks of exuberance and life. Everything you see and everything they are, illuminate joy.

When I was a little and watched this part of the movie, it brought me such pleasure because it personified fun. I was unable to watch without smiling and giggling the whole time. It brought a bubbly giddiness to my spirit. Munchkins were spreaders of joy that made you feel as light as a feather.

So, between the colors, Glinda arriving, the singing and the dancing, it is definitely a place that lifts your spirit high. The presence of Glinda brought such peace; even when she was arriving you knew that it had to be something absolutely astounding that was on its way because of the way she made her grand entrance.

Let your mind resurrect the memory of this scene where Dorothy catches a glimpse of this splendid, small, pink bubble coming towards her. She watches as it floats closer and closer and then becomes larger and larger, and then poof! Suddenly Glinda arrives, Wow! What a surprise!

I would often giggle with such anticipation after the first time I saw this scene, when I would watch it again because I knew who was coming – Dorothy's guardian. No matter how many times I watched it, I wanted a dress and a crown just like hers. She arrived like an angel, her voice was sweet but carried authority and her magnificent staff was crowned with a sparkling star.

I look through my rainbow glasses and what do I see? I see Glinda as a guardian angel, bringing a message of peace, hope, protection and direction. I see all of these attributes today when God sends an angel as a messenger through people or heavenly beings from above. They still come today to help us in life as we face new or overwhelming circumstances or when we face new doors that seem like impossible challenges. Glinda brought a voice of direction and clarity when Dorothy was baffled as to where she was, where she was going or what she was to do now that she was in Oz.

The color pink is the combination of red and white. The color stands for holy awakening or new birth, the womb, the breath of mercy, being born, and being awakened into sanctification. (4) The color is also said to represent the Father's care and love. Isn't this exactly what happened to Dorothy? Glinda was coming to care for her and protect her in troubling times. The very name Glinda means holy and good, (5) She had come to bring goodness and guidance.

Glinda invited the little people to come out of hiding, saying, "Come out, come out, wherever you are" out from under the influence of fear and begin to rejoice and celebrate the death of the wicked one. They also began to celebrate Dorothy as the words of their song explained, she fell from a star and Kansas was that star. When she fell out of Kansas, a miracle occurred!

Oh, the music that came from this land,
Oh, the beauty in this place,
How she felt renewed and refreshed,
How we change by the power of His grace!

Rainbow glasses on

Let's take a quick look through them at the name Kansas and its meaning. It is a North American people of Eastern Kansas. It comes from a Sioux Indian word for South Wind people. (6) The Bible talks about the four winds in the scripture, so for the fun of it in the next chapter, we will begin to find out about the South wind in the scripture and what it blows in.

Dorothy knew that it was not within her power to kill the witch; she knew it was the storm that had brought this great victory! The house made of wood had come hurling into the atmosphere at just the right time and landed on the exact right spot to destroy the tormentor. It is the cross (also made of wood) that was the simple instrument that was used to crush the enemy of our soul, the accuser of the brethren. Satan has been defeated and his plans have been foiled, it is finished!

There was a great storm that took place in the atmosphere on that day in the spirit realm when Jesus, the son of the living God bowed His head and said, "It is finished" over 2,000 years ago. The earth shook, it became dark, and the veil in the temple, the Holy of Holies, was torn from the top to the bottom, the graves were opened, and many bodies of the saints, which were sleeping arose! All things on earth shifted that day as the enemy was crushed under the weight of the cross just as the old witch was crushed in this story with Dorothy's house! This is such a wonderful picture of what happened that day at Calvary.

Come to Jesus today,
Enter into His rest,
Be free of the old
Experience the best!

Walk away from the fear,
From the lies and the threats,
Rejoice in the Land of Oz,
Courage, strength, and power
For the cross has paid your debts!

There is no other way,
There is no other choice,
That will give you peace within,
Come please listen to His voice!

John 19 and Matthew 27: *It is finished*

Isn't this just like God? He uses us in the middle of a whirl-wind through the power of the cross to take out the enemy and his plans. I love God.

Luke 10:19, (NIV) "I have given you authority to trample on snakes and scorpions and to overcome all the power of the enemy; nothing will harm you."

Through the power of the Red Shoes, the blood of Jesus that was shed on the cross, we are now able to arise in authority as a royal priest (1 Peter 2:9). Let us stand and be God's children, let us now rule over the tyranny of the enemy and bring forth the Kingdom of God on earth just as Jesus did.

Isaiah 59:21, (NIV) "As for me, this is my covenant with them," says the Lord. "My Spirit, who is on you, will not depart from you, and my words that I have put in your mouth will always be on your lips, on the lips of your children and on the lips of your descendants from this time on and forever."

Isaiah 60:1, (NIV) "Arise, shine, for your light has come, and the glory of the Lord rises in you! "

1 Peter 2:9, (NIV) "But you are a chosen people, a royal priest-hood, a holy nation, God's special possession, you may declare the praises of Him who called you out of the darkness into His mar-velous light."

Scriptures of power, courage and strength

Ephesians 6:10

Isaiah 40:29, 31

Nehemiah 8:10

Philippians 4:13

Psalm 22:19, 119:28, 46:1 and 28:7-8

2 Corinthians 12:9-10

Scriptures on Angels

Acts 12:5-17

Hebrews 1:14 and 13:2

Luke 4:10

Psalms 103:20

Pray with me

Father God, I thank you that when I come to you that I live in the land of strength, power and courage! I thank you that in this new land there is great rejoicing. I thank you that through every storm in life you will be there to give us great strength and courage if we abide in you. I thank you that through the power of the cross, the enemy of my soul has been placed under my feet. I thank you and worship you that I can live with great victory through the cross. I thank you that in this land of new birth there is an amazing experience of your holiness and your goodness. I thank you that you are color and life and that I can encounter this because all things become new through you. I thank you that you are my over-the-rainbow experience and that you are the rainbow. Thank you for the blood that makes all things possible. Amen.

Declaration

I declare that I will walk with courage. I declare that I will walk in great strength. I declare that I will walk in great power through the amazing blood of Jesus. I declare that I am a royal priesthood and that I am chosen to do great things. I declare that I will change the world around me, affect my sphere and I shall praise the Lord all the days of my life and be a rainbow for Jesus.

Bibliography

1. *The Wizard of OZ.* 1939.

2. **Fleming, Victor.** *The Wizard of OZ.* MGM, 1939.

3. *https://nameberry.com/search?q=meaning+of+Oz.* [Online]

4. **Nemitz/Facebook, Colors by Carol.** [Online]

5. www.sheknows.com. [Online]

6. http://www.netstate.com/states/intro/ks_intro.htm. [Online]

11

CELEBRATE! EVIL IS DEAD!

Yes, let us celebrate that the evil one is dead. The power she carried has been broken and the time of rejoicing begins. The age of grace, adventure and power has arrived.

The celebration begins

In Munchkin land there is rejoicing, there is song and there is dance. Songs of jubilation ring out in the air. The young and the old join together with ecstatic delight as the smiles on their faces reveal what is within their hearts, oh what a sight!

Celebrating that evil is dead! Hooray Horray is what they said!

Who knows how long this evil one has afflicted and tormented them, maybe days, maybe weeks, maybe months, and maybe years? The Munchkins had to have felt trapped with no hope of being free from the Evil One's constant torment, never knowing when she might drop in, understanding that they had no great power over this evil. Awe… but then came a wow moment! Then came an instant that not one of the Munchkins could have ever dreamed. It was something they had never seen before or imagined, something that would shift their land forever.

Just when the Evil One had come to afflict and abuse them, up they look and what did they see but a twirling, swirling, whirling, tumbling down house. Watch out! Run for cover!

Ka-Boom! Right in the middle of this beautiful land came the arrival of a massive old farmhouse. And its bold entrance has now changed absolutely everything. Glinda has also arrived, and she is coaxing the little people out from hiding and announces that the Wicked One is dead!

What do we see?
What is the new?
I am bewildered,
Don't you agree?

Wow! What just happened?
What came crashing down?
It is beyond words.
What arrived in our town?

Never forget to look above,
Never forget the answer is on High,
Never forget miracles are real,
Never forget the answer is nigh!

Let's adjust our glasses and look at this part of the story a little closer through a rainbow of color. The enemy has been crushed under the weight of the almighty cross. We are celebrating a victory like no other victory, a victory that has never been seen or experienced before. A victory that will empower all other victories to come, and this victory has paved the way for a brand new day.

Isaiah 52:7: describes the good news of Jesus and all that it brings to this earth. Where the enemy has ruled, Christ has come and the age of Grace now reigns. The angels have appeared and announced the birth of the Prince of Peace. Jesus, the Son of God, has arrived to pay the price for all mankind, to pay the price for peace, joy and love to rule.

Luke 2:14, (KJV) "Glory to God in the highest, peace on earth, good will towards men."

The Munchkins begin to sing and rejoice, they are singing that Dorothy fell from a star and Kansas was that star.

I remember another star, the star that brought the wise men to Jesus from afar and it was the heavens that showed the way. In our story of the powerful Red Shoes, Dorothy did drop from the heavens, and it was a mighty wind that blew her in. Now, if you recall, Dorothy came from Kansas, so let's take a closer look.

As stated earlier, the word Kansas is a Native American Sioux name meaning, "The people of the South wind." I have to smile since it was definitely a wind that blew Dorothy in and because of that storm a major source of evil was destroyed. Now there was celebration over Dorothy, just like there is in heaven when we come to Christ. Our sins are dead. What a time of rejoicing! A celebration begins over the new birth and the new adventure in Christ. There was also great celebration in the heavens the day Jesus was born. The heart of God is to bring celebration to our lives, to bring hope and love. He continually celebrates over all of His sons and daughters.

Zephaniah 3:17, (NLT) "For the Lord your God is living among you. He is a mighty savior. He will take delight in you with gladness. With His love, He will calm your fears. He will rejoice over you with joyful songs."

Rejoice over you literally means, dance, skip, leap, and spin around in joy. Rejoice is translated from a Hebrew word that Strong's Concordance defines as: to spin around (under the influence of any violent emotion), that is usually joy and rejoicing or dancing. That is exactly what was happening around (and for) Dorothy in Oz.

Through the people of the South Wind and through the rainbow glasses, we can see a whole new perspective!

Obadiah 1:19, denotes that the South will possess the land and take out the evil of Esau. They will be people of deliverance. The cities of the South denote the knowledge of truth and good; they are in the light of truth from the word. The interpretation is that the South Wind is a delivering wind, to set captives free from tormentors. Drawing out, setting apart rescue, escape, delivering or birthing Kingdom purpose in the earth. (Luke 4: 4-19)

The South wind is the Spirit of deliverance generated to mark a people prepared to inherit the promises. It is to rescue, recover and cause to escape enemy oppressions by a body of people delegated the freedom to worship God in Spirit and Truth.

(The Winds Of Heaven: Bob Jones and Paul Keith Davis)

Job 37:17, (KJV) He quieted the earth by the South wind.

The South wind brings a time of refreshing in our lives.

Psalm 78:26, (KJV) ... and by His power He brought in the South Wind.

The South Wind brings the peace of God!

Philippians 4:7, (KJV) "And the peace of God, which transcends all understanding, will guard your hearts and your minds in Christ Jesus.

The South wind speaks of comfort, refreshment and quietness. Isn't that who the Father is and who we are through Him? The people of the South wind bring direction, comfort, refreshment and peace through the mighty power of God. Peace brings deliverance from pain and heartache. It also brings refreshment to a tormented soul. Jesus was the ultimate South wind when He walked the earth. When He was born He brought peace and good will to man.

Now in Dorothy's case, she did not plan to destroy the enemy of the land, but the winds set her up to bring the perfect storm, and it brought freedom. Yep, she was more or less along for the ride! That's why when we are in turbulent times of life we can see the importance of staying in peace and rest in God and He will bring the freedom.

Let's recall Mark 5:1-20. When Jesus arrived on the shore of Gadarenes, there was a man that lived in the tombs; he was harassed day and night from evil spirits. No one in the village could control him. He had been chained but he tore the chains, night and day he would cry out and cut himself with stones. When he saw Jesus from afar, he came running and fell at his feet and the spirit cried, "What do you want with me?" The tormenting spirit recognized the Living South Wind, the Wind of deliverance and peace.

When Jesus steps on the land where the enemy rules, the Prince of Peace rises, speaks, and then shifts emotional or physical tortured lives into a beautiful place of rest and tranquility. There is a song that states, "When He steps into the room everything changes." This is Jesus.

Isaiah 9:6, (NIV) "For to us a child is born, to us a son is given, and the government will be on His shoulders. And He will be called wonderful counselor, Mighty God, Everlasting Father, Prince of Peace."

Run and fall at the feet of Jesus

Let Him free you from the past that keeps you bound with chains emotionally and hidden away in the tombs prepared by the enemy, that keep you from community and relationship with others. These tombs or caves are full of accusing and criticizing spirits that lie to keep us imprisoned within. Let the wind of peace blow over and through your heart and mind. As soon as the man was set free, he was released back to the city and he lived vibrant and whole. He immediately began a ministry of worship and praise by lifting the Son of God up as he shared all of what Jesus had done for him.

When we think tomb, we understand it is where the dead are buried but isn't that exactly what happened to this man? But through Jesus he was resurrected spiritually and emotionally, ready and able to live life again. No longer entrapped or tortured within his mind, The Prince of Peace came with power and authority, destroyed the assignment of the evil one on the life of this man, and all things became new.

2 Corinthians 5:17, (KJV) "Therefore, if anyone is in Christ, he is a new creature. Old things are passed away; behold, all things become new."

Again, we speak this scripture out loud as it resonates what is happening in this new land. All things are becoming new.

We are the people of the South wind! Let us bring the peace of God and let us shift the atmosphere just as Dorothy did when she arrived in Oz, the land of power, strength and courage. We bring peace and love by the power of the cross, and we are the presence of Jesus on earth, bringing the good news, which is peace on earth, good will towards man. He dances over us with His love and rejoices as we stand in this new land. Be a daughter or be a son of the Most High King, worship Him and sing!

Come on down this yellow brick road with me and continue to learn who you are, see that you are a person that brings deliverance and peace through the South Wind, the very breath of God. The more we are free, the more we have to give. His life-giving breath resurrects dry bones that looked like they would never live again.

Ezekiel 37:1-14: God was directing Ezekiel to prophesy, to speak to a valley of dry bones, and as Ezekiel obeyed, the bones came together, flesh developed, and breath entered the bodies. They stood as a vast army. God used Ezekiel and breathed life into a situation that seemed impossible.

Breathe Him in,
Breathe Him out!
Rejoice in His love,
Dance and shout!

Stop and celebrate
Colossians 3:16-17
1 Chronicles 16:34

2 Chronicles 5:13

2 Corinthians 4:15

Jeremiah 30:19

Luke 15:22-24

Philippians 4:6-7

Psalm 9:1; 107:8-9; 95:2-3

Colossians 3:16-17

Pray with me

Father God, I worship and praise you and celebrate that you celebrate me. I celebrate that you gave your son that the enemy might be under our feet, that through you we can dance and rejoice each day as we live in you. I thank you that you are the ultimate South Wind and that you breathe through me and bring me to life when I feel alone and afraid. I thank you that I do not have to live in fear no matter the storm that is around me. I thank you that you declare peace and I declare peace and there is peace! Father, I want to breathe your spirit in every moment of every day. Help me to always to look to you no matter where the storms of life take me and where I land. I thank you that the cross has won the ultimate victory, and I can live from victory to victory. In you, I bring the deliverance of the South Wind! Amen.

Declaration

I declare that I am a child of God and I celebrate who I am. I celebrate that through you Jesus, that I carry the very presence of peace because you are peace. I declare that I have unspeakable joy and that your joy will resonate through me to others. I declare that I am victorious through the cross in the mighty name of Jesus.

12

THE ACCUSER

A ll is good! The celebration is alive with joy and ecstatic expressions of rejoicing.

Yes, this is a great Day! The evil one is dead! Suddenly, there is a loud noise and a huge billow of smoke as shrieks of fear arise! Out of the ominous smoldering mist steps the very essence of wickedness! Now, who in the world is this?

Dorothy is startled and quite shaken! Fear grips her heart as she sees this evil presence moving towards her, spewing vile accusations and threats. Closer and closer she comes, with her green boney finger stretched out and pointed straight at her face. As far as I could see pure evil is looking sweet Dorothy straight in the eye, and with a sinister voice continues to harass and terrorize, Dorothy is emotionally paralyzed! Now this ugly spirit of intimidation has materialized! She now challenges Dorothy's arrival to this great Land of Oz and is accusing her of killing someone near and dear.

Dorothy feels the need to try and defend herself. She jumps into an immediate explanation of what just happened. Isn't that how the enemy of our soul comes calling?

Revelation 12:10 and 1 Timothy 4:13 state that Satan is the accuser of the brethren, and that is exactly what he does. He comes to us with accusing words and makes us feel that we need to defend ourselves in situations that we have had nothing to do with. Usually they are circumstances that he has actually created, not us.

With words of accusation or downright lies, he tries to get us to accept responsibility for things we have been forgiven of and that have been placed under the power of Jesus' blood. If he can get us to receive the lies that we are not good enough, or that everything is our fault, he knows that he can assign the spirits of shame and guilt to plague us, and those accusing spirits will never let up or relent!

Dorothy is wide eyed and in total disbelief of what is happening now. Here she is, in this beautiful land, enjoying all of its splendor and wonder, and trying to get a grip on how different everything is when suddenly, out of no where in the middle of this great celebration comes an evil that she has never witnessed or experienced before. Didn't they just say she was dead? Were we not just rejoicing that the tormentor was dead? But, here she is, staring her down right in front of her face! There was no denying that this was not real!

Dorothy was just about ready to step deep into a mucky, miry mess of receiving and agreeing with a lie when Glinda steps into the conversation.

Dorothy makes a statement, "I thought she was dead?" (2) Glinda pulls her close, wraps her arms around her, keeps her safe and calms her spirit with reassuring words. Glinda's staff of authority that she carries shelters Dorothy from it all. The answer is .... this evil one is the sister of the dead witch—and she's known as the Wicked Witch of the West!

Glasses on

With my rainbow glasses, I see Glinda carrying a scepter of authority that is topped with the Star of David. I envision that this is a great picture of how Jesus Christ left His heavenly kingdom and He came to shed His blood that we might be protected, and because He went back to the Father, He sent the Holy Spirit that leads and guides us. The Holy Spirit wraps His arms around us and speaks truth in our ear when we are facing great opposition. He reminds us daily who we are, and that the enemy has no power over us. He sent the comforter to be with us in times like these, and yes, He also sends ministering and guardian angels.

Hebrews 1:14, (NIV) "Are not all angels ministering spirits sent to serve those who will inherit salvation?"

Psalm 91:11, (NIV) "For He will command His angels concerning you to guard you in all your ways."

Psalm 34:6-7, (NIV) "The poor man called, and the Lord heard him; He saved him out of his troubles. The angel of the Lord encamps around those that fear Him, and He delivers them."

The evil that was once in hiding has now been uncovered in this beautiful Land of Oz. Without the revelation of the enemy, what would be the need for power, courage and strength? I am grateful that when the enemy overplays his hand in our lives and reveals himself that we are then able to see where he is, and it is at that point God always gives us a strategy for prayer that we can use through the power of Jesus and His authority to take him out!

When I pray with people, I let them know that instead of shrinking back from intimidation when the enemy shows up and is up front with what his plans towards us are, I let them know that it is a halleluiah moment! When he is out of hiding and in the light, yes this is a halleluiah! This is a great truth that was taught to me through Wellspring Ministries in Alaska. Praise God for exposure!

Let's just imagine if we were in a physical natural war and we were in the middle of a jungle and its nighttime, so it's extra dark. We persistently shoot blindly at an enemy sniper that we cannot see, and the harassment continues since he is well hidden. What would be the answer in this crisis? LIGHT! Then suddenly, a flare goes up and because of the great light the enemy is exposed. Yes, light is the answer!

The Heavenly Father actually answers our prayers by revealing the dark hiding places of our spiritual tormentors. Just like the witch suddenly appeared in the Wizard of Oz! Now Dorothy is capable of doing something about this confronting evil knowing where she is and who she is! It is then by the power and authority of the cross and His blood that we look the enemy straight in the eye as he points his gnarly finger in our face with accusing lies, and back him down! We have the ability to dismantle the enemy's assignment. But first, we must have the revelation of where he is hiding, and then using the word of God, we slice and dice.

Look to the Father and dance a dance of victory. Praise His name and allow His love to flow over your body, mind and spirit. Refuse to accept the enemy's words over you. Just like Glinda, meaning Good and Holy, allow Him to wrap His arms around you, keep you safe, and with His authority, resist the Devil and he will flee.

James 4:7, says to submit yourselves to God. Resist the Devil and he will flee. In this story, Dorothy trusted and allowed Glinda to surround her and protect her. In the same manner let Jesus the living word fight your battles. We are shown through the scripture how the enemy came and accused, brought fear, rejection, shame, guilt, and many other spirits that wanted to destroy God's children. Do you recall that King David felt overwhelmed by the enemy of his soul and his enemies on this earth? But God! The scripture tells us also that when the angel appeared in front of Mary, the mother of Jesus, and shared with her God's heart and plan for her life, even Mary felt overwhelmed. But God! No matter who we are or where we are at, rest in the arms of the Father and trust His wisdom and love. Know and follow His voice, He will protect and place a shield around you!

Psalm 3:3, (ESV) "But you, O Lord are a shield about me, my glory and the lifter of my head."

John 10: 27, (NIV) "My sheep, hear my voice and they follow me. And I give unto them eternal life, and they shall never perish; neither shall any man pluck them out of my hand."

Follow my voice,
Listen as I speak,
Go where I go and rest in me,
It is your heart that I seek!

I am your God,
I see all things,
I know the way,
Fly, I have given you wings.

You are safe within my hands,
I am your shelter and your peace,
Raise your eyes to mine,
My love will never cease!

The accuser will bring fear,
But his power has been stripped,
If you release yourself to me,
By the blood of Jesus, you are equipped!

Just as Dorothy is looking in the face of her accuser, Glinda reminds the evil one of the Red Shoes. Oh, that's right! The enemy turns and goes towards the shoes when suddenly they are gone, and the legs shrivel up and disappear under the weapon that crushed her!

Scriptures to meditate

Deuteronomy 31:6
Isaiah 41:10
Proverbs 2:11 and 4:6
Psalm 5:11; 34:19; 46:1; 57:1; 138:7; 140:4
2 Thessalonians 3:3

Pray with me

Father God, I thank you that when the enemy comes and accuses me and desires for me to receive a lie about who I am, that you have given me the power to take him out by the word of God and I am able to resist him. I thank you, Father, that you send angels to protect me. I thank you that you wrap your arms around me, and you step into situations that want to take me out emotionally and spiritually. Help me, Heavenly Father, to always turn to you and to never receive the lies and accusations that torment me. Help me, Heavenly Father, to believe who I am in you and the power that I carry through the blood. It is not by my strength, but by yours, for when I am weak, You are strong. Amen.

Declaration

I declare that I am a child of God and when I resist the enemy, he has to flee according to the word of God!. I declare that I am a child of God and I hear your voice. I declare that I may be hard pressed on every side, but I will not be crushed, perplexed or in despair! I may be persecuted but I declare that I am not abandoned. I may be struck down, but I declare that I will not be destroyed. I declare that God is my rock, He is my stronghold and He is my refuge! I declare that I will stand strong and in the power of His might.

Bibliography

1. *The Wizard of OZ*. 1939.

2. **Fleming, Victor.** *The Wizard of OZ*. MGM, 1939.

3. *https://nameberry.com/search?q=meaning+of+Oz*. [Online]

4. **Nemitz/Facebook, Colors by Carol.** [Online]

5. www.sheknows.com. [Online]

6. http://www.netstate.com/states/intro/ks_intro.htm. [Online]

13
THE RED SHOES

What just happened?

H er Evilness watches in horror and disbelief at what she just witnessed! The wicked one jumps up and briskly returns to Dorothy and Glinda, asking, what have you done with the shoes? She declares, "They are mine! No one else should have them or can have them!" As a child I trembled at her voice and her threats, but Glinda remains calm and smiles with no sense of any fear, she then points to the beautiful Red Shoes that have been transferred on to Dorothy's feet. Oh, how exciting, oh what a treat. Glenda lets the evil one know that the shoes will stay with Dorothy.

It is time it is now!
Choose Jesus today!
Celebrate it is His blood!
Lift your voice and pray!

His blood applied upon our lives,
Instantly, we receive,
All we need to do,
Is believe!

I declare to you today that through the mighty choice that Jesus made in the garden as He prayed to the Heavenly Father, it was His choice that instantly shifted our lives just as it did when Dorothy received the red shoes.

Okay, it's time to pull out your rainbow glasses again and let's look at this picture through God's beautiful colors. With the power of the Red Shoes, now the real adventure can begin.

Did Dorothy understand this at all? Did she really understand anything that was happening? I would say that the answer to those two questions would be a definite and resounding No!

The immediate threatening response from Her Evilness was for Dorothy to give them back, and to give them back now! Fortunately Dorothy's guardian Glinda, impressed upon her not to give away the shoes, which definitely implied that Dorothy had the power to do so.

We will learn later in this story that the enemy did not have the power or the authority to take the shoes, but she was trying to convince Dorothy through fear and intimidation to give them up. The enemy was informing Dorothy with all of her menacing threats that she would never ever give up trying, and she would get those powerful Red Shoes!

The enemy understood the ultimate power they carried. Her threats became more intense but Glinda kept her arms securely wrapped and tight around Dorothy the whole time, never letting go. And then when Glinda had simply had enough, with ultimate dominion, with her soft beautiful voice she commanded the Wicked Witch to go, informing her that her power was useless here and that she needed to leave before someone else dropped a house on her. The enemy quickly responded by looking up to the sky, with fear in her eye!

Stop, look and listen

Let's stop and think for just a moment and remember where they are. Awe yes, the Land of Oz, the land of strength, power and courage, and it is through the blood of Jesus that we can choose to remain in this land by the great power of the Red Shoes.

I want to mention another old hymn called, "There is power in the blood." Maybe you have heard this song that was written over a hundred years ago; the words are so powerful that I remember them to this day. Let's reminisce a bit with the lyrics, please enjoy them as I share the chorus: "There is Power, Power, wonder working Power in the Blood of the Lamb; there is Power, Power, wonder working Power in the precious Blood of the Lamb!" Lewis Edgar Jones wrote these words in 1865. The same power that he experienced back then has never changed to this day! It is the same God and the same blood and the same savior!

The blood of the Lamb,
That laid down His life,
Because of His yes,
There is no bondage in sight.

What an amazing moment when Jesus said yes. He loves us so much that He was willing to carry the sin of the world to freely give us the authority and power to rise above every situation and assignment from the enemy on this earth by the power of his blood. Herein lies the understanding of the power of the RED SHOES.

Luke 10:19, (NIV) "I have given you authority to trample on snakes and scorpions and to overcome all the power of the enemy; nothing will harm you."

Let us wear them with great honor,
Understanding the price that was paid,
Let us receive them and learn,
Our assignment for this day!

For such a time as this,
We wear the Red Shoes,
Equipped with the power from above,
Arise and shine, for you will be used!

Isaiah 60:1, (KJV) "Arise. Shine, for thy light is come, the glory of the Lord is risen upon you. For behold, darkness shall cover the earth, and gross darkness the people, but the Lord shall arise upon thee, and His glory shall be seen upon thee."

The blood shifts everything. When it is applied to our lives it shifts how we see, who we are, how we hear and who we will be. It shifts the now and it shifts the future. There is new light for our path, the world around us may grow dark and even darker, but our promise, our rainbow, is that His glory will be the light. The Lord has risen upon us. His light will show the way!

These powerful new Red Shoes that Dorothy has just received will now take her on an adventure that could have never been imagined. All she will need to do is follow the yellow brick road. This is where we find ourselves, on the yellow brick road of life, surrounded by His glory full of adventure and the goodness of God.

Many months ago as I was spending time with the Lord I learned a great truth. We were sharing from one heart to another. We were conversing about the things in the earth that are very dark. The enemy was using the darkness of heartache and pain that I see in the world to push his agenda of heaviness upon me, hoping that I would come into agreement with despair. The Father told me not to be afraid, for when he walked the earth in human form, there was heartache, pain, hopelessness and evil all around, but He had come to bring healing and life. He shared with me all that was needed is for His light and love to flow from His children. He said rest in Me and to be My presence. I will never forget the other words that the Father spoke to me. He said, "Deb, never forget that it is the journey that is the true gift." It was really such an eye opener. I knew He was always the gift, but suddenly, because of this one heart revelation, things became so much clearer in such a different light. It is the journey of life with Him, through Him and in Him that is the ultimate gift! Wow! Never be distracted by what the enemy desires for us to focus on, things that are fleeting or you will miss the most precious moments of all.

You see, He was showing me that if we are not careful, we will always be enticed by the enemy to look far ahead, far into the future at the goal or the promise and we will miss encountering Him today, which I suddenly understood is the real gift. Be aware of the trap of distractions that the enemy sets to keep our eyes off of Jesus. If we are caught up in all of the pain, destruction and chaos around us and miss who we really are and what we carry in life, the light will be diminished, and so much will be lost.

Remember the story of Peter and John when they were going into the temple and the crippled man held out his hand for money. They could have been discouraged because of all the sadness and the pain around them and at that time, they had no money to give, but instead they gave him what they did have. Peter and John were focused on the gift of the journey. They spoke to the man, told him we don't have any money but what we have is healing and life, at that moment they took the man by the hand, helped him up and His life was changed forever.

(Acts 3:6-7)

Yes, I realize that our salvation is the ultimate gift, but this gift includes living the adventures of life with our Father so let's choose adventure like Peter and John. What thrilling times these Red Shoes were created for.

It's amazing to me that our Creator would want to spend personal time with us. He craves for us to laugh and cry, sing, love and be with Him. He desires to be our friend and our Father. He wishes to be it all. He desires the gift of relationship that was supplied by His son. And it is the blood of Jesus that opened this door up to all of us. It is the power of the Red Shoes. You talk about a personal custom fit; this is it!

I will reiterate and shout out, walk on the enemy, stomp on the enemy through the power and authority of the blood. Expect encounters that you can't even imagine, let the journey be the gift. Learn how to walk, run, skip and jump in these new powerful Red Shoes.

These shoes will overtake the enemy; they have the ability to take back what the enemy has stolen. Remember that the first thing he stole from us was our personal one-on-one, face-to-face connection that we were created for in the garden. We are His sons, and we are His daughters, again through this sacrifice, there are no more veils and no more walls. Praise God for the power of the Red Shoes!

We have the power
He is the power!
Thank you for the blood,
The enemy cannot devour!

Thank you for the Red Shoes
Thank you for the blood,
Praise your name on high,
It comes in like a flood!

The enemy's power has been stripped,
His days are drawing near,
Thank you for the blood!
We stand up and cheer!

I am a firm believer that the Red Shoes are like transformers! Whatever is needed is supplied. If we need to run, we can run. If we need to dance, we can dance. If we need to go to war, they are combat boots. If we need to climb, we have cleats. The blood supplies whatever is needed. I hear the Lord saying, "Be ready!" Come with me down the yellow brick road and learn the true power of the Red Shoes.

Scripture to meditate

Ephesians 1:1

1 John 1:7 and 5:6

Hebrews 9:12-14 and 13:11-12

Matthew 26:27-28

Romans 3:25

Pray with me

Father God, we thank you for your plan that was before the foundations of the world. Father, you knew there would be a fall of mankind into sin. You knew that your children would struggle. But, Father you still chose to create us and allow us to choose, even knowing the choices we would make. Thank you, Father, for loving me even in my imperfectness. Father, you are so good, you sent your son from heaven to die for us, knowing many would reject the gift. Lord, I choose the gift. I choose to receive your love, and I choose to say yes. Help me to receive the power of the blood. Father put your shoes on my feet and help me to walk in authority and power over the enemy that you fully intended from the very beginning of the ages. Father, I receive the Red Shoes. Let me follow you and your glory that lights the way on this great gift called life and the journey that you have ahead for my legacy, my heritage and me. Let me be your presence in the darkness; through me you will radiate light. Let me make a difference for this day and this hour, for such a time as this, for your glory, in Jesus mighty name! Amen.

Declaration

I declare that I am a blood bought child of God! I declare that through the blood I have a mediator of the new covenant Jesus Christ. I declare that I have a great high priest that I can take all of my shortcomings to, and that I am loved and set free by His forgiveness and grace. His blood is my shield. I declare that by the power of His blood I can and will walk in power and authority for His glory!

Bibliography

1. *The Wizard of OZ.* 1939.

2. **Fleming, Victor.** *The Wizard of OZ.* MGM, 1939.

3. *https://nameberry.com/search?q=meaning+of+Oz.* [Online]

4. **Nemitz/Facebook, Colors by Carol.** [Online]

5. www.sheknows.com. [Online]

6. http://www.netstate.com/states/intro/ks_intro.htm. [Online]

14

THE KISS

The enemy cowers low as she looks around in fear to see if a house might be coming to strike her down. The words that Glinda peacefully spoke, but with such great authority sent the Evil One into a frightened state of shivers running through her spine. She knew her time was up!

The enemy has now been given her marching orders, but before she left she spewed a few last sinister words, one last threat! Her final menacing words that pierced the air like arrows towards Dorothy were to let her know that she would never ever give up, and that no matter the price paid, she eventually would conquer and retrieve those powerful Red Shoes! Dorothy was wide eyed with horror!

Poof! As quickly as the enemy appeared, she vanished in a very explosive and loud billow of fiery smoke!

As the saying goes, I shivered in my boots for I can personally relate this situation to my own story. Boy, could I feel this threat as a child, because I knew she meant business! The enemy of my soul is always pushing and poking me, always trying to stick his finger in my face and cause me to lower my head, cower and curl up with fear. His scheme is to have the last word hoping that I will fall for the trap to believe and receive. His plan is to make me feel that he has the upper hand. There it is again—fear, fear, fear—one of his greatest tools. Imagine if you could see the enemy at a card game holding his cards close, for he knows that if we were able to see his hand that we would immediately understand. His bluff with all of his terrorizing words would disintegrate and disband!

Colors of protection

Putting on the rainbow glasses, I can see clearly why the Father instructs us to be continually in prayer and to always have the words of Jesus in us. When the word is in us it fuses to our very DNA! Our mindset becomes the mind of Christ as the word of God is alive, and it becomes who we are and shifts our belief system! When the enemy shoots his darts of accusation, containing rejection or lies of shame or guilt, it will then bounce off of us, like a ball hitting a cement wall for we are protected by the shield of His righteousness and the belt of His truth. His truth must become who we are. Crash, bang, boom, the arrows are deflected and destroyed. The thought is rejected and not allowed within; stripped of its power, the threat fizzles and dies, melts and dissolves. It lies on the ground like a muddy puddle that we can splash, dance and have fun in; the victory party has begun!

Have you ever noticed that a child loves to wear boots, especially their rain boots? Number one, they are easy to put on. Number two; they are usually decorated with fun colors. It seems to me that they love to be prepared because children are enticed and drawn to a puddle of water like a huge magnet. They love to walk, run and splash in the water, in fact they will go way out of their way on a walk just to splash! And they are never afraid to get wet! Let us be expectant and prepared just like a child to do the same with every evil dart that the enemy throws at us. Let it melt away, drain to the ground and have fun with it. Splash, splash, splash!

Ephesians 6:10-11, (NIV) "Finally, be strong in the Lord and in His mighty power. Put on the whole armor of God, so that you can withstand against the devil's schemes."

It is at this time that Glinda gave very important instructions to Dorothy concerning her Red Shoes. We have to keep in mind that Dorothy, as of yet, does not truly comprehend the power and authority that these shoes carry and the depth of the gift that she has just been given. Glinda specified to her that she was never to let the shoes out of her sight, and she was to never ever to take them off. This is very crucial, for her Guardian understood the extreme danger that was lurking about. Like a spy that lurks in dark shadows, the enemy sits and waits for the perfect time to pounce and destroy! Glinda, with her words of wisdom and warning, knew what lay ahead. Within herself, Dorothy does not have the power to restrain the Evil One. It would take the protection and power of these Red Shoes to keep Dorothy safe and the enemy at bay.

The kiss

Glinda adoringly kisses Dorothy on the forehead as she sends her off down the road and on her way. Keep her safe Heavenly Father is what I prayed.

Psalm 85:10, (KJV) "Mercy and truth are met together when righteousness and peace have kissed each other."

I love Glinda with her spirit of gentleness; remember, her name means holy and good. God is always good! What a beautiful picture of the Father and His goodness and righteousness, kissing us each morning through the Holy Spirit as we start our day. It reminds me of Snow White and Sleeping Beauty as the kiss of true love woke them up to life and a new way. As a child, this kiss represented true love sent from heaven above.

As we start down the glory road,
His presence is so very near,
Let His kiss start each day,
My heart now moves away from fear.

Psalm 34:15, (NIV) "The eyes of the Lord are on the righteous, and His ears are attentive to their cry."

Lamentations 3:22-23 (ESV) *says,* "The steadfast love of the Lord never ceases; His mercies never come to an end. They are new every morning; great is thy Faithfulness."

Think about it, *New Every Morning.* We don't have to worry about His grace and strength running out, losing it, or that there will not be enough to get us through a day, a week, a year or a lifetime.

We literally only need to go to the Father boldly, go to His throne the scripture says, and ask. His grace is sufficient. Praise

God! He always has one more kiss, one more hug, one more miracle set-aside just for you and me; all we need to be is open to His affections. Sometimes we understand that our greatest miracle is to just get through one day at a time. When the pain and tragedy of this world touch us, and it touches us all, Jesus, the great healer, is there to lift us up emotionally, physically, and spiritually. Reach out, look up, He is there. Don't let the moment pass you by, just give it a try.

Mark 10:46-52, (NKJV) V.47, "And when he heard that it was Jesus of Nazareth, he began to cry out and say "Jesus, son of David have mercy on me!" Bartimaeus called out to Jesus and because he did, he received all that he was looking for and all that he needed."

It is in these times that the Father whispers our name and encourages us with an embrace through the Holy Spirit that only He can do. When our spirit is one with His, we can even be at rest in a place that David describes as the valley of the shadow of death. Life does hand us many situations that are dark, but it is in those times we really come to know who He is. It is in this darkness that you can see His light the greatest. The Father spoke to me once specifically about darkness. He said, "Deb, the enemy uses the darkness to bring great fear, but I created the darkness, so don't be afraid for I am in the darkness." It was in that moment I saw the Lion of Judah in the darkness watching over me; I felt His presence so strongly. I knew that I was not alone no matter how dark things looked or felt. I created a painting portraying this experience that I had with the Lion of Judah, and to this day, it is a reminder that He is always there.

I have thought how a physically blind person places their hands on the face of someone so that they can imagine what they look like and connect them with their voice. I have envisioned this in the spirit realm with Jesus. When it is so dark that I can't seem to see Him in the midst of my troubling circumstances, I close off my desire for natural sight and reach out through my spirit to feel and know where He is. It is in this kind of blindness that I experience Him more intimately through the hands of my heart. It is in this posture that I can hear, see, let go, come into rest and trust His presence. Let Him kiss you each morning with His grace and love.

Down the road we go

Glinda and the Munchkins have pointed Dorothy in the right direction. "Go to the Emerald City and seek out the Great Wizard of Oz!" (2) Being in a new land, Dorothy does not know the way so she asks, "How do I get to the Emerald City?" Glinda's replies, "It's always best to start in the beginning!" (2)

Dorothy embarks on the next phase of the journey by putting one foot in front of the other. The yellow brick road originates in the center of the city and around and around it goes. Those around Dorothy give her words of encouragement, they begin to chant nd then to sing, *"Follow the yellow road, and see the amazing wizard of OZ, Because he is wonderful he deserves an applause."* With Toto in her arms, she is off, one step, then two, and then here we go, one, two and three! Her legs shift her body into a joyful skip as she starts to sing along and feels the beat. Here she goes as she is light on her feet! This is exciting, for this journey is going to be sweet.

And my, how the Red Shoes sparkle and glisten on the beautiful, bright yellow brick road. As a little girl, I remember how those Red Shoes fascinated me; they were so engaging, they twinkled and shimmered so vibrantly. The sight of the shoes literally caused my heart to jump with joy. I was captured like a hug from your grandma that snuggles you in so tight. Yep, what can I say? I wanted a pair of those exhilarating shoes for myself! There are just no words to express how I felt. Oh, the power of those Red Shoes!

At this moment, my heart and mind are spinning with glee because of the thought of my spiritual Red Shoes. I can see myself dancing like I know this earthly body cannot dance, but only in the spirit. Such a smile and such joy are being showered from heaven above. In my thoughts, I am able to jump, whirl and twirl; I am airborne in my body soul and spirit.

That is the power of these Red Shoes
With these shoes, my spirit can rise above,
I can ascend to new heights,
Through their power and His love!

Now, as an adult, I realize that in the motion picture they had a special way of making the shoes sparkle with brilliance that is not a reality in real life. But, when you're a child, it's okay not to understand everything. The beautiful canvas of color painted on the screen has stuck in my mind throughout the years and even today with knowledge and understanding of movie making, I still love the beauty of those sparling Red Shoes. These shoes made such an impression in our culture and around the world, that 80 years later these shoes are still recognized and speak loudly of a great adventure.

Rainbow glasses out and clean

Now clearly through them I can see the brilliant contrast of the yellow road and the Red Shoes. I see it as an illustration of God's beauty and magnificence. The Red representing His blood and the Yellow representing His glory! The combination of the two colors is an impressive way to begin this next bold and unusual undertaking. As sons and daughters, His blood and His glory should never lose its attraction or illustrious beauty in our spiritual eyes. May we always be captivated by who He is and His splendor and glory. The scripture tells us that we go from glory to glory; He is that Glory.

2 Corinthians 3:18, (AMP) *"And we all with unveiled face, continually seeing as in a mirror the glory of the Lord, are progressively being transformed into the His image from (one degree of) Glory to (even more) Glory, which comes from the Lord, (who is) the Spirit."*

Our journey in life with Jesus starts with a kiss of mercy, peace and righteousness. He has equipped us with the power and grace to walk this road, with many things ahead, let Him lead you; He will do just what He said.

John 1:3, (NIV) "Grace, mercy, and peace from God the Father and from Christ Jesus, the Father's Son will be with us in truth and love."

Take hold of Jesus our great high priest, turn and receive the challenge of walking in His glory. Just like Dorothy, look to the future and the things to come, get ready to run! Not knowing the journey each day but knowing that He leads the way. So, let us go forward, step one, step two, step three …

Let me again share words to another song that I think of often. *"I don't know about tomorrow, but I know who holds my hand."* One statement in the song also says, *"But His presence goes before me and I am covered with His blood!"* Ira Stanphill penned this hymn during a very difficult time in his life. No matter where the yellow brick road of life takes us, let us always remember He is the one that lights our path, He is the one that shows the way, he is the one that holds our hand, He is *the* way!

2 Corinthians 3:18, (NIV) "And we all, who with unveiled faces contemplate the Lord's Glory, are being transformed into His image with everlasting glory, which comes from the Lord, who is the Spirit."

There is excitement in the air!
She begins to skip, sing and dance for she has no dread,
She leaves her fears behind and leaves them for dead,
Dorothy turns and waves goodbye,
Looking forward to the road ahead.

I open my heart to Him each day,
And start with a kiss from above,
A kiss from the Father, who sent His only son,
Because of His wondrous love.

John 3:16, (NIV) "For God so loved the world that He gave His only Son, that whoever believes in Him shall not perish but have eternal life."

With Toto by her side,
She starts down the yellow brick road
Looking neither to the right or left,
She is in a fast forward mode.

Turn! Open your hands wide and loosen your grip. With a wave goodbye we release the fears that want to keep you from moving forward. The fears that would try to keep us from the greatest adventure of all, our adventure in Jesus! Here we go ...

I love this visual picture with my rainbow glasses. Toto (the high priest and the word) by our side, we cannot fail. The yellow brick road (the glory of God) holding us up, for it is beneath us. *Now the Red Shoes (His blood) give us the power to walk, dance, and sing, as we wonder what else He will bring.*

Psalm 28:7, (NIV) "The Lord is my strength and my shield; my heart trusts in Him, and He helps me. My heart leaps for joy, and with my song, I praise Him!"

Scriptures to meditate
Isaiah 30:18-19 and 40:11
Matthew 11:29-30
Mark 1:40-42
Song of Solomon 4:9

Pray with me
Heavenly Father, I thank you that each day I am awakened by your presence. Father, I thank you that you eagerly wait for me to arise from my sleep so that we may be able to spend time together. Help me not to become so preoccupied that I miss even one moment with

you. Forgive me for being too busy to see that you are always by my side and desiring a greater relationship. You are good and you are faithful, and your mercies are new every morning. You desire for me to receive your expressions of love that are continually being professed towards me through the Holy Spirit and your word. Help me to see and hear these expressions of love that come in unexpected ways and packages. Keep me alert to your mercy and grace even when things seem cloudy and unclear, let me always see the light of your glory leading the way. Thank you, Father, for your patience that you have towards me concerning many of my unwise decisions. You are always there to turn me around. Thank you. In the mighty name of Jesus. Amen.

Declaration

I declare that the Lord is my strength and my shield. I declare that my heart will trust in Him and He is well able to defend me in times of need. I declare that I am being transformed into the image of Christ, and I am going from Glory to Glory.

Bibliography
1. *The Wizard of OZ.* 1939.
2. **Fleming, Victor.** *The Wizard of OZ.* MGM, 1939.
3. *https://nameberry.com/search?q=meaning+of+Oz.* [Online]
4. **Nemitz/Facebook, Colors by Carol.** [Online]
5. www.sheknows.com. [Online]
6. http://www.netstate.com/states/intro/ks_intro.htm. [Online]

15

DOWN THE GLORY ROAD

Okay, here we go! Do you have your shoes? No, I mean your Red Shoes. Make sure you have your Red Shoes on, for it is an absolute necessity on this trip. Today is the day we start down the new yellow brick road. Today is the day the adventure shifts into high gear. A journey that will change our hearts and our thinking, but, isn't that what all adventures do?

Maybe we should start with the words "Once upon a time ..."

Let's begin with singing. *We're on the way to see the Wiseman, hooray for you and me! Exiting things are ahead, our hearts are filled with glee, I love feeling so free.* I can hear the music now and see Dorothy as she is skipping down the road, ready to face this new world, bring on the show! This is the experience that I want to participate in with a live active joyous heart, embracing the road ahead and the unknown with gleeful expectation. I hope you will come with me as we join Dorothy and position ourselves with an open heart and mind. Ready, set, go! When I was little the thought of being in this land was so very exciting; I just knew something amazing was about to happen.

I do want to start off our journey with sharing the original root meaning of the word wizard since that is where we are headed now, to see the wizard that lives in the Emerald City. I don't want anyone to go off the deep end with fear concerning the mention of the word wizard before I clear a few things up. According to Google dictionary, in late Middle English, the original word is Wiz-ard, which means a profoundly wise man, philosopher and sage. The definition of sage is knowledgeable, sensible, intellectual, discerning, judicious, insightful, thoughtful, profound and deep, just to share a few descriptions. Now, isn't that a lot different then what you were expecting me to say? (According to the online etymology dictionary, the word wizard is also connected with Lithuanian magic. The distinction between philosophy and magic began to blur in the middle ages). But in the very beginning the word meant wise man. So let's stop, take a look and listen to what the original definition was really saying, and of course, we must have our wonderful rainbow glasses on.

Don't you think that these words definitely describe God? He is the author of knowledge and of all wisdom. So, as we start out on this journey to the Emerald City, let us totally understand that our sole purpose is to search out and find (wisdom) the wise man. We are pursuing God's complete wisdom and His discernment as we walk in life. We are seeking the one, the only one. In Him all things have been created and exist!

Colossians 1:16, (NIV) "For through Him all things were created: things in heaven and earth, visible and invisible, whether thrones or powers or rulers or authorities; all things have been created through Him and for Him."

James 1:5, (NLT) "If you need wisdom, ask our generous God, and He will give it to you. He will not rebuke you for asking."

This is exactly what the heart of God desires for us on our journey—His wisdom. We need His insight and discernment to see and hear clearly in the middle of all circumstances and to walk hand in hand with knowledge from above. So, we are going to take a moment and shift our mindsets a little, kind of like rearranging a hat that is tilting to the left that needs to be pushed to the right. I can hear your voice now joining mine as we sing the song with Dorothy, *I'm off to see the wise man, full of wisdom and wonder, in this marvelous land!* We are off to seek the true wise man that lives in the land of strength, courage and power.

Never leave home without them

Yes, we must have our rainbow glasses and Red Shoes on for this excursion! As we look ahead, the road is beautiful, and it stretches far beyond everything we can see. The road appears to look long and very winding, up, down and all around. We can't see the Emerald City yet, but we know it is ahead and that it has a great connection to our destiny. What lies beyond calls to us, we *must* go! We have no idea what will transpire, but we shall be brave, let be so! Boldness and true grit seize ahold of us like a strong hand gripping someone's shirt at the neck to get their attention; we step out, one, two, and three … I wonder what will be? We begin to experience the exquisite rolling hills with their lush green grass and the beautifully radiant bright yellow bricks, the sun (*the* Son) illuminates them, they stretch as far as we can see, leading the way. His Glory keeps us carefree.

Habakkuk 3:4, (NAS) "His radiance is like the sunlight; He has rays flashing from His hand, and there is the hiding of His power."

Deuteronomy 31:6 (NIV) "Be strong and courageous. Do not be afraid or terrified because of them, for the Lord your God goes with you; He will never leave you nor forsake you."

Exodus 33:14, (NIV) speaks of the Lord's presence: *"My presence will go with you, and I will give you rest."*

We gather Toto and step out with a song,
Courage and power keep us steady and strong,
Look straight ahead at the beautiful gold,
Our adventure beckons and has yet to be told!

Exhilaration beckons us ahead as we travel. We will be and are full of His weighty presence. He will never leave us or forsake us. He speaks to our spirit and gives us great rest as we keep our eyes on Him the adventure is the best! Our Red Shoes give us the power and the authority to walk the yellow brick road in joy. Toto is snuggled close in our arms and as we look to the Emerald City with hope and eagerness. The Heavenly Father has prepared the way we are in bliss! Beneath us, before us and beside us, our mighty King we can trust!

Psalm 24: 7-8, (ESV) "Lift up your heads, O gates, and be lifted up, O ancient doors, the king of Glory may come in! Who is the King of Glory? The Lord strong and mighty; the Lord is mighty in battle."

Down the yellow brick road,
Swirl the beautiful bricks,
Around and around, up and down,
With all the fun, games and tricks.

We skip and jump, laugh and play,
What a wonderful adventure,
Oh yes, that is what I say,
Jesus is with us every day!

Everything new on every side,
Never knowing what will appear,
So we take the hand of Jesus,
And allow Him to steer.

He does the planning,
He knows right where to go,
I freely rest in Him,
By letting Him run the show.

The evil one may have threatened and
Spewed words of fright,
But the Lord of Glory is with us,
He is ever present in the night.

Just believe! He is mighty in battle,
And fear is not His name,
He looks ahead and has prepared the way,
The enemy He will tame.

John 11:40, (NKJV) "Jesus said to her, did I not say to you that if you believe, you will see the glory of God?"

The name Dorothy means gift of god; we have been given the greatest gift from God, Jesus, through which we have salvation, we have been marked by His blood! We are who we are because of His gift of grace. Let us return and offer ourselves as a living gift to Him and His glory. This name originated from a 4th century martyr name Dorothea.

Ephesians 2:8-9, (ESV) "For by grace you have been saved by grace. And this is not your own doing; it is the gift of God, not a result of works, so that no one will boast.

As Dorothy skips and sings her steps have a spring. She definitely understands she is not in Kansas anymore. This is a new land, so let us believe and see. The old has passed away, all things have become new. The Red Shoes have changed everything. So look to the hills and road ahead, the blood of Jesus has transformed us from one kingdom into another, with anticipation, our hearts stir with a flutter!

Now Dorothy understands that the enemy is lurking about, seeking to devour and destroy, but she keeps her eyes on the prize. In this new land, she never knows what may pop up or occur; so she stays in tune to Glinda's word.

He will see me through, if I only believe,
So I click my heels, one, two three!
My instructions are never take them off,
Or I will pay a very high cost!

I adjust my rainbow glasses, and am reminded of the promises of God, understanding that He is for us and not against us and that all things work together for those that are called according to His purpose.

Romans 8:31, (NIV) "What then shall we say in response to these things? If God is for us, who can be against us?

Romans 8:28, (NLT) "And we know that God causes everything to work together for the good of those who love God and are called according to His purpose for them."

The scripture says in Matthew 11:10, (NIV) "I will send my messenger ahead of you who will prepare your way before you."

Now I understand that this last scripture is talking about John the Baptist, but we need to recognize that the name John also means gift from God, so I believe that God orders our steps if we remain in Him, and as long as we keep our rainbow glasses secure we will see properly. Seeing and being His glory (staying in His weighty presense) will illuminate the yellow brick road of life. What an adventure! We may not always know what is ahead, but the messenger that goes before us is preparing the way. That is truly a gift from God.

2 Corinthians 5:17, (NIV) "Therefore, if anyone is in Christ, the new creation has come. The old has gone, the new is here."

This Glory road started in Munchkin land; this is the land of small beginnings, but nevertheless it is full of such great power. We find that Jesus, the creator and savior of the world, began His journey on earth in a stable in a manger. Now, in our way of thinking, that is a very small beginning, but oh, the glory that came down on the one worthy to wear a crown. No matter how small things look in the natural world, whether it be a manger, a baby or

Munchkins, the power and the destiny that lies within us is the true measure of things. You will only be able to see the promises, the power and the opportunities that will arise for great destiny through your rainbow glasses. You must see what God sees!

No matter where you are in life, looking through the glasses will cause you always to rejoice, for He has much in store for you. Look for the adventure of a lifetime in every encounter with the Father of Lights, as he shines the way.

Philippians 4:11 and 4:4-8

Zechariah 4:10, (NIV) "Do not despise these small beginnings, for the Lord rejoices to see the work begin, to see the plum line in Zerubbabel's hand."

Psalm 37:23-24, (NIV) "The steps of a good man are ordered by the Lord and He delights in his way. Though he falls, he shall not be utterly cast down for the lord upholds him with his hand."

We have all been presented and challenged with small beginnings. Do not despise your time in Munchkin land, just stand. Rejoice and worship God for what He has done, and where we are going. Stay on target as we continue in this kingdom of courage, strength, and power. Remain in a state of wonderment with who Jesus is, celebrate in this place of small beginnings.

Scriptures on glory
Exodus 15:11
Haggai 2:9
Hebrews 1:3
Isaiah 60:1 and 6:1
John 1:14
Psalm 3:3; 19:1; 24:7-8

2 Corinthians 3:18 and 5:14

Zechariah 2:5

Scriptures on wisdom

Colossians 4:5-6

1 Corinthians 3:18

James 1:5; 3:17; 3:31; 3:13

Matthew 7:12

Proverbs 2:6; 16:16; 19:9; 15:33

Psalms 90:12

Pray with me

Heavenly Father, I thank you that I have the ability to walk this road of life with great wisdom and discernment if I remain focused on you. I thank you that we can walk hand in hand through all things and that you never leave me or forsake me. I praise you because through you I can make wise decisions. I thank you for being before me, below me, beside me, above me and around me. I thank you that you are my strong tower and I run in to you. I thank you that in this life you can turn all things for good and that I have the privilege to walk with you. Let me never despise small beginnings. Let me always remember how you came to earth as a baby, small and in a place where no one would know or see your royalty. I thank you for the times on this road when things have been rough and rocky, and I have literally felt you pick me up emotionally and physically and carry me through. When I haven't always had the answers, I could rest in you because you do. I thank you that in life I can sing and dance because of your joy. I repent and ask forgiveness for the times I have not believed, and I have agreed with the assignment of darkness. Let me never forget that the journey is the beautiful gift, just one step, one day, one moment at a time. Enjoying your presence is my greatest gift. I seek your face. I seek your ways. I seek your heart; I seek your glory, for this is the greatest experience, the greatest adventure of them all. I praise your name. Amen.

Declaration

I declare that I will live life with the joy of the Lord and things will work together for my good. I declare that I will walk this glory road with the wisdom and peace of God. I declare that I will sing and dance with Jesus and always look up into His eyes. I declare that my God is for me and not against me, and that He orders my steps.

Bibliography
1. *The Wizard of OZ.* 1939.
2. **Fleming, Victor.** *The Wizard of OZ.* MGM, 1939.
3. *https://nameberry.com/search?q=meaning+of+Oz.* [Online]
4. **Nemitz/Facebook, Colors by Carol.** [Online]
5. www.sheknows.com. [Online]
6. http://www.netstate.com/states/intro/ks_intro.htm. [Online]

16

MEET SCARECROW
(The Mind of Christ)

The fork in the road

What? The yellow brick road splits? Are you kidding me? Which way do we go now? Dorothy I hope you know because I sure don't! No one told us that when we started on this path that we would have to make choices. This is just supposed to be simple.

Here I am with Dorothy doing just fine, skipping along, singing our song, and then there is a suddenly! The road splits in different directions. What do you mean there are choices? Just when I thought we had it all together, and it seemed like such a simple direction to follow, quite a dilemma appeared!

Choices are opportunities and we make choices by our belief system and our estimate of where the choice might take us. So here is Dorothy needing to make a decision!

So then we can totally understand why Dorothy stops, looks around and is puzzled for what to do when the yellow road splits and creates a fork. Now totally grasping the idea of the saying, "There's a fork in the road." When I was young, I felt very puzzled just like Dorothy. It also made me a little nervous about which path was the right direction. The question is staring her down, the roads are calling out to her, *choose me, no choose me*, but which one will lead to the Emerald City? See, you don't know either.

I'm in a quandary. She must get to the city; she has an appointment with destiny, an appointment that will alter her life. So yes, I am concerned, that she selects the correct option. I'm right with her on this adventure, and I need her to make the right choice. Even I don't need to experience any more unexpected, hair rising, nerve-shattering traumas. It's like being in a place where you don't know when or where the next terrorizing, startling thing will come from; anyway that is how I felt when I was young!

Which way do we go? Please someone has to know!

I could feel her perplexing dilemma as she looked all around. Which is the right road to take? They all look good, they all look like the right way, so what should she do?

What do we do as we walk on this road of life with Jesus and we come to a place in our journey where there are many choices, understanding that only one leads to the Emerald City or only one leads to the greatest adventure? Many paths in life will lead to many different doors, and those doors will lead to other doors. So the question is, which door?

Doors in our lives can be made in many shapes and colors. Which do we choose? There's nothing like a little drama in our life, right?

1 Corinthians 1:27-28 talks about how God has chosen the foolish things of the world to confound the wise. I do believe that He is showing us that some doors may look good but are not always the best.

Maybe both roads lead to the Emerald City, but maybe one would take much longer. Or maybe one road has a roadblock or maybe one is more dangerous. Hearing the voice of God is always an absolute necessity and our desire when we face a fork. Personally, forks are not my favorite. They can create a standoff in my heart and mind, producing barriers in life and a need for precise decisions. Decisions can at times lead us into a lot of fear. My preference is that everything be very easy and simple. How about you? But I guess that would be boring if we had no choices or challenges. I have often said to the Father, Could you just write me a letter? That way it is very straightforward. Tell me what to do and I will just do it since you see everything. But, God wants relationship not robots; we are His children. He wants to experience life with us. Fathers love to see their children grow up and mature, but they also love to be needed; they are thrilled when their children come to them for help, conversation and direction. So, guess what, expect to face down those forks in the road and don't be surprised when they show up unexpectedly.

What do we hear?

We stop with Dorothy, and we ponder and contemplate the road she faces. What was that? I heard a voice. But wait, I don't see any one around. Hmmm ...

Have you ever heard the voice of God in that way? Just like Dorothy, we are walking along, singing our song, and then boom! God is speaking! But hey, we are in a brand new kingdom, so it's absolutely no surprise that we hear a voice out of nowhere. I will say this, that usually it is exactly, and I do mean exactly at the right moment in time when we need to hear direction the most.

A brand new friend

Dorothy is about to meet a new friend, one of her new traveling companions. He is the first of three that will join her on these travels. Suddenly, she hears the voice again. Dorothy is a bit confused and very baffled; she turns, but all she can see is a scarecrow.

Now that's impossible! In Kansas, scarecrows do not talk, but yep; it is the only thing she can see. I am sure she is thinking, no way, because that is what I am thinking. But she gives way to chance and looks him straight in the eye. There it is again! Sure enough, he talks! I was shocked!

Through my young eyes, this is like the most amazing fun thing ever. I can't believe it, what an unbelievable surprise that would be. He is alive! Right then and there, once again, Dorothy and I were totally convinced that this was a land of miracles and change. Nothing would ever be the same. Maybe this really was somewhere over a rainbow, where maybe dreams do come true. Yes, just maybe those were her thoughts; I know they were mine.

Rainbow glasses

WOW! Don't you just love it when God speaks to us in the most unexpected and unusual ways, like when God spoke through a burning bush to Moses. I think this might have been a real burning bush moment for Dorothy because let's face it, straw stuffed scarecrows perched up on a post do not talk, just like a burning bush does not talk. Then, to top it off, the fire never consumed the bush. You certainly can't miss the miraculous sign that God was speaking. I'm just saying, be aware. Be very aware because God will speak in the most unusual ways and at the most peculiar times. Keep your eyes and ears open to the brand new because we have the most amazing Red Shoes!

With the rainbow glasses I see so differently. I love how much color and zest the glasses bring to life. What an astounding sight! Without them things can appear so gloomy. As I clean the lens, this is a place with some outrageous wonderful new friends.

A brand new mind

You may not believe, but just roll with me here. I see Scarecrow as the mind of Christ in this new territory of power, strength and courage. I see him as a new way of thinking, new hearing and new seeing. At this point in the trip, Dorothy doesn't even seem surprised at all with this recent development because she chooses to let him join her on this fantastic journey. She releases him down from his pole. Dorothy could have chosen fear, remember she had never seen a talking scarecrow before, but this was a new land, this was a new world, this was a new day! She knew she was somewhere definitely somewhere far, far away.

I Corinthians 2:16, (NKJV) "…for who hath known the mind of the Lord, that he may instruct him? But we have the mind of Christ."

Romans 12:2, (KJV) "And be not conformed to this world; but be ye transformed by the renewing of your mind, that ye may prove what is that good, acceptable and perfect will of God."

Down Scarecrow falls

He joyously tumbles off his perch where he was stuck for such a long time. A little rattled and a little torn, I was so excited that I giggled with glee just to see him free. I knew he had waited for such a time as this to join a great venture. He smiles and picks himself up, stuffs the loose straw back into his shirt; he is no worse for wear. He leaps to his feet and begins to sing and dance from the music that we hear. Dorothy watches him with amazement and a magnificent grin from ear to ear.

Soon, she can stand it no longer,
She must jump in with his song.
The joy that He brings,
Will turn to right all that was wrong!

Scarecrows only focus is to improve his thinking. He wants a brain! I laugh at this statement because I understand desiring that. I have said many times to the Father I need a new brain. Now I understand that I have one, but I have often desired a new way of thinking in situations that have overwhelmed me. Scarecrow felt that he couldn't think deep enough, or that he wasn't smart enough; I can relate to that too. The major times that I have been frustrated with myself are when my mind and my thoughts have been stuck in anger or despair. When heaviness has overwhelmed me and it kept me locked in a prison of sadness, where I felt there was no escape. I knew this bondage was not what the Holy Spirit or the Father desired for me. But I couldn't seem to find freedom. Even now as I write this, tears fill my eyes from the emotion that wells up because of the many battles from within that I have fought in this arena.

Recently I struggled to fight off severe heaviness that was trying to take me down that nightmarish spiral. There were traumas from the past that the enemy wanted to resurrect by placing an unexpected and emotional explosion from a friend right in my face. The situation immediately threw me back in a flash from the past of repeated emotional abuse. I realized as I sought the Lord, that I was free from the feeling of being rejected and also had no anger towards this person. I was at peace, but what did raise its ugly head was fear. I asked the Lord what I was experiencing. He showed me that even though I had forgiven and was healed and had let the past go, there was a residue of anxiousness of not knowing when things could strike again. The ole what's around the corner routine, what's ready to jump out and beat the crap out of me emotionally? This remaining fine line fracture was very, very deep inside and I was quite surprised when it surfaced with a sudden eruption, that emotionally threw my usually quiet peaceful spirit into a spin of drama. There was no denying it. There it was challenging me, staring me directly in the eye and screaming loud. Now the question was, what was I going to do about it?

I can't say that it was easy as quoting a few scriptures, standing on the word and a poof it was gone. Nope this major assault was a tough one. Fear that has been buried for years and attached to trauma can leak into many areas, and all of these areas were screaming loudly, trying to take me down the road of pain and depression once again. I was in a major wrestling match with this darkness, and I needed the love of the Father to come and heal and rescue me. The enemy of my soul was desperately trying to pin me down and keep me in fear. I began to shed many tears with my head resting on the shoulder of the Lord, working through each memory connected to what I was feeling, and then finally, I began to see the light at the end of the tunnel, as I trusted my savior. No matter the unexpected sounds and words that arose, He had me. No matter what unexpected explosive devise the enemy tries to throw to destroy and stop my destiny, I am His and He is mine. His love is sure throughout all time.

In the past I lived many years in a place of depression and fear, but now through the grace of God, I understand how my thoughts dictate my emotions and my emotions dictate to my body. I have through the power and authority of the Red Shoes declared war on depression and I have won! Oh yes, every once in a while he will rear his head again and try to get me to take the bait, to agree with the rejection and the heavy thoughts that the enemy shoots my way. But, now I rule! I rule what my mind thinks through the power of the blood. I take captive my thoughts when they do not align to the word of God and I shift them.

Sometimes the thoughts have me captured, but when I realize this I begin the good fight, for I live in the realm of power and might! Yes, the battle sometimes is more severe than others, but I declare today and every day that I win, and the enemy of my soul loses! I declare the word of God over myself daily, which is the truth and the truth sets me free. I have new thinking. My brain has been rewired one day at a time to the mind of Christ.

I remember a statement that a great teacher named Peter Wagner once said, "The war has been won, but there are many battles in between." He stated such a great illustration of "When the allies in WWII arrived on D-Day, when their feet touched Europe to free the land, the war was won, but there were many battles yet to fight!"

1 Timothy 6:12, (NIV) "Fight the good fight of faith. Take hold of eternal life to which you were called when you made your good confession in the presence of many witnesses."

Stand up and fight. When you are weak, He is strong. Fight! Fight! Fight! Let Him fight for you.

John 8:32, (NIV) "And you will know the truth and the truth will set you free!"

Isaiah 61:3, (KJV) "To appoint unto them that mourn in Zion, to give unto them beauty for ashes, the oil of joy for morning, the garment of praise for the spirit of heaviness; that they may be called trees of righteousness, the planting of the Lord, that He might be glorified."

A call for help

Help us, Father to renew our minds and follow you. Let us not be afraid, let us allow the mind of Christ to be free, let us seek His thoughts and not our own, and His ways and not our ways. Allow the joy of the Lord to attach itself to our thoughts and invade our body by seeing all things through His promises. What a happy day it is for the Heavenly Father, the day we allow Jesus to come down off of the cross and join our everyday living. Too many times we keep Him on the cross, not letting Him join our day, not letting Him be our companion; I encourage you, let him down. Yes, number one He is our savior, but He died so He could be our friend, so He could walk and talk, and be closer than a brother and be with us each minute of the day. He is always there, so invite Him to be a part. Just like Dorothy did with Scarecrow, he was down and then invited! Come with me to the Emerald City, so, down the road they go, I am so excited!

There was a brand new spark! As Scarecrow (Mind of Christ) joined Dorothy, He brought and an expression of joy and dance, and it was only the start! There was no discussion; the steps literally all fell into place. Their feet united together and away they went at a brand new pace!

As soon as Dorothy aligned her thoughts with joy and peace, and her thinking joined forces with his, they were in sync and the choice flowed like water down a beautiful waterfall, creating a force to be reckoned with.

Scarecrow was a little weak and wobbly, but Dorothy continued to pull him up close and tight, it was just right. Changing your stride or your gait is a new way of walking with Him. Keep putting on the praise, wear it every day and speak it in every way. A new mind will emerge, new thinking will come, never ever give up, stay with the Son.

A few years ago, I broke my left foot; the bone broke in a spiral. To my surprise, I had to have surgery and three pins were inserted to pull it back together. I was not allowed to put any pressure on my foot for quite some time. Thank God for scooters! I was able to go faster than most people in some situations, but there were other circumstances that I was totally unable to even think about doing. There was no hiking, which is funny because I don't hike, but I still could not have even entertained the thought. I had to literally crawl up my stairs. That being said, I was still very restricted. Finally the day came, the pressure boot came off and I was released. I was Sooo ready! I was so excited! Ready to walk on my own. But, to my great surprise, I limped severely, I could not walk fast, and I definitely could not run. It took a lot of practice and therapy to walk again totally free of any kind of hindrances. The interesting part is my chiropractor had to adjust the bones in my foot; he had to adjust my gait. Even though I was healed, the bone was mended, and the screws were holding it secure, I still couldn't walk correctly, and it was throwing my back and my knee out. Everything took time. So, please take time with Jesus and meditate on the word and the truth, and let it adjust your thinking. Let your thinking align your body soul and spirit. Get your gait—don't take the enemies bait!

Stay on the Glory Road,
Focused straight ahead,
You will be surprised,
That the adventure will spread!

There was no confusion,
And there was no delay,
All they knew,
Was that they could not stay.

As they linked their arms and spirits too,
The destiny ahead was amazing and new!

John 15:7, (KJV) "If you abide in me, and my words abide in you, ye shall ask what ye will, and it shall be done unto you."

Apples and trouble everywhere

Happily they go, visiting and enjoying the journey together and then they see an orchard full of fruit. Oh they are so hungry, and they have come such a long way, the apples look too beautiful to resist, just like a juicy red kiss (Smile). I gazed upon these apples, and they looked like the best apples I had ever seen. They were perfect in every way, flawlessly round and a delightful scrumptious red. You just knew that they would be succulent, and Dorothy was ready to be fed. Even though I couldn't bite one myself, I could hear the crisp crunch in my mind and feel the juice hit my taste buds. Imagination is a beautiful thing!

Dorothy with a longing look admires the fruit, then reaches for one. She picks it off of the tree, but as quickly as she plucked the apple, a long, skinny wooden arm with a sharp hand immediately slapped hers and grabbed the apple. Ouch! I jumped and was startled with such surprise, as a child, that was definitely not what I was expecting. Trees aren't alive, and they absolutely do not talk. Oh yeah, I have to remember that we aren't in Kansas anymore. Poor Dorothy, my heart was so sad, hurting for her battered feelings. The tree spoke to her with an intolerant grumpy harsh voice. He rebuked her severely for picking his fruit and made her feel extremely bad. He was a nasty brute, accusing her of doing something wrong just as they walked along.

She was hungry and there it was right before her eyes; it seemed that it was prepared especially for her on this journey. But, wait a minute now, that didn't turn out like she had thought it would. Hmm ... Dorothy must remember that she is not in the land of old, but in the new kingdom where everything is changed. All things are alive in the strangest way, so there has to be brand new strategies for today. New methods of thinking, is all I have to say!

Rainbow glasses out and on

Isn't this just like the enemy, we see something good that God has prepared for us on this great journey and just when we have it in our grasp, the Evil One slaps our hands and knocks it away! Oh, but wait, there is a regrouping; God has something to say.

The Scarecrow has lived in this land,
He thinks differently, He understands.

Dorothy had jumped into the situation without thinking; she forgot to stop look and listen; new land, new rules. Scarecrow pulls Dorothy aside and says to her, watch this; I will show you how to get apples. He knew the way to get apples from these grumpy and overbearing selfish trees. Dorothy is protected and then he begins to talk to the trees and call them out for who they really are, and as soon as that happened, everything shifted. The ill-tempered trees begin to throw their apples at Dorothy, and she didn't have to do the work of picking them. The tables were turned, and when it looked like all was lost and that there was no hope to receive the blessing that was prepared for her, Scarecrow set them up and the enemy now just gave it all away. There was an abundance of blessings coming from above, the apples came down just like rain, pouring His amazing overwhelming love!

Now, Dorothy could have made the choice to run, hide or not to listen to Scarecrow. She could have decided that there was no way that anything could change. This enemy was very unexpected, looked huge and overshadowed Dorothy, and the look on their faces were mean, ferocious and threatening. The trees were rooted and grounded in who they were; they probably had done this to many others that had passed by, but this was a new day. Look, believe, and then receive. She made the choice to listen, she stayed, what an escapade. What an experience, what a time to be alive!

Psalm 6:30-31, (NIV) "Men do not despise a thief, if he steals to satisfy his soul when he is hungry, but if he be found, he shall restore sevenfold, he shall give all the substance of his house."

The word sevenfold carries the number seven; it represents full, complete and perfect victory. Yes, the scripture tells us that Satan comes to steal, kill and destroy, but understand that when the enemy steals from us, restoration shall be made if we fight. Follow the master plan from the Father and the Holy Spirit, and the enemy will have to repay completely.

Deuteronomy 6:11, (NLT) "The houses will be richly stocked with goods you did not produce. You will draw water from cisterns you did not produce, and you will eat from vineyards and olive trees you did not plant. When you have eaten your fill in this land."

Through the rainbow, I see God's wonderful ability and desire to supply for us and make it an absolute wonderful encounter at the same time. We can see that when the enemy wants to rob us of a great blessing, God always has a plan to turn it around and instead of sadness; He resurrects hope, laughter and joy. I can just hear the Father say, "I just love it when my plan comes together!"

Looking through these glasses, I also noticed that when Dorothy only looked at the apple, the enemy didn't care. But, when she decided to receive the blessing, the cranky crusty ole tree grabbed it away. The enemy of our soul does not care if you look at the promises of God as long as you do not step into them to receive. That's when the enemy raises his gnarly hand and slaps us down. In fact, he would rather torment us with a belief system that the promises are for everyone else but not for us. I say to you that the mind of Christ has the ability to outwit the enemy and it is time to rise up in the power of the Red Shoes and take authority. It is time that the breaker goes before you and paves the way to abundance physically, emotionally and spiritually. It is time; it is time!

Micah 2:13,(NIV) "The one who breaks open the way will go up before them; they will break through the gate and go out. Their King will pass through before them, the Lord at their head."

Be aware. Be very aware. Have you noticed that I say this a lot? It's just that I want to make sure that you are paying close attention and be on the alert because the wicked one is always lurking behind some tree (Smile) somewhere watching. Her Evilness was watching Dorothy and her companion, waiting patiently for just the right moment to shower more words of tormenting fear over her, to disrupt the journey and steal those powerful Red Shoes. Through this, we must understand that the enemy of our soul will never ever give up he always has a plan!

Dorothy and Scarecrow keep their eyes on the prize, the apples at hand. They are picking up provision as their laughter rings out, enjoying the moment. Joy is the key to moving ahead. One miracle brings another. Just as Dorothy was receiving her blessings that (literally) rained upon her, I want us to recall that this blessing brought her to her knees. As Dorothy was crawling on the ground, picking up the overflow of supply, something caught her eye. If you recollect, it was the choice of not running but listening that brought the marvel of provision that led her to her knees. It was only then, when she was on her knees that the next companion was revealed and it is on our knees that revelation comes, and miracles happen, oh what a joy, so don't be nappin!

Dorothy looks up. Oh me, oh my! What do I see?

Scriptures to meditate
1 Corinthians 2:14-16
1 Peter 1:13
John 2:6
Philippians 2:5-11 and 4:8

Pray with me
Wow, God! How awesome you are! I thank you, Father, that by the gift of your son, we receive the Red Shoes and we have free access to your wisdom and encouragement. We are your children. It is our inheritance to walk in freedom and discernment. I thank you that Jesus is not stuck on the cross but ascended to heaven and sent the Holy Spirit that we might have the ability to walk, dance and live on this road of life with great expectations of blessings from above. I thank you that this journey with you is one expedition after another. Father, I think of an expedition as exploration with great purpose. I truly seek to have more of the mind of Christ. Renew my thoughts Jesus!

I desire to think and speak as you do, and to hear you. Help me not to react to quickly to situations around me but to stay in peace and receive your strategies for living life to the fullest. When the enemy slaps my hands as I reach for your blessings, give me the wisdom and the strength to stand and fight and to never ever give up. Help me to rest in you, which is my greatest weapon of all. Let me always remember that my lifeline is on my knees. Amen.

Declaration

I declare that I will stand, and I will fight! I declare that WE will win! I declare that I am in You and You are in me. Again I say that when You are for me, no one can be against me! I declare that I have the mind of Christ, for I am yours.

17

MEET TIN MAN
(HEART OF THE FATHER)

Dorothy looks up,
And what did she see?
A man made of tin,
Can you believe?

She knocks and listens,
He makes a resounding sound,
He echoes with emptiness,
He is freedom bound.

He desires a beautiful heart,
To be filled with great love,
That he might share with others,
He is as sweet as a dove.

M y oh my, what does my little eye spy? Did you ever play that game as a child or maybe you played that game with your children or grandchildren? Well, here we are, on our knees with Dorothy, just crawling along, picking up apples that have been supplied in such an amazing way and there is a suddenly!

Dorothy is laughing her way all around the ground, giddy with delight of the blessings within sight, and what to her wondering eyes did she see? It's a foot! It's not just any ordinary foot; it's a tin foot! Knock knock! She looks up and there he is, a man made of tin. The echo of the knock is bouncing and reverberating all through his body. Who has ever heard of such a thing? Don't you just love this land? I know I do. It's so full of surprises on every hand.

Such it is with God! When we surrender our lives to Jesus and decide that we will follow Him and live in His Kingdom instead of the kingdom of this world, goodness gracious, how life and our perspectives will change. What a thrill, what an adventure! When Jesus invited the disciples to follow Him, they had no idea what lay ahead. Mass feedings of thousands from two loaves and three fish, healings, water turning into wine and the list goes on. The Kingdom of God is an electrifying, supernatural place of promise, full of strength and courage as we are personally invited to live there every minute of every day; He is stretching forth His hand. Rise up, come forth and step into this land.

Dorothy is explosive with radiant joy!! She stands up and looks him over, indicating that she has come to expect the unexpected. She turns and looks for her friend; she is quick to make sure that this time Scarecrow is by her side, and a part of her experience! Dorothy is learning to not jump ahead like before. With anticipation, she awaits the revelation of who this funny looking silver man might be. I was so excited, how thrilling, a real live Tin Man! He's making a sound; can you hear it? He's trying to talk, it's very muddled, and they barely make it out. He's saying, "oil can!"

Scarecrow and Dorothy jump into action and away they go. They grab the oil, where do we start? He mumbled, "mouth."

It was so exhilarating for this little girl to watch as Tin Man came alive! This new friend is about to become a major part of this great journey to the Emerald City. I could hardly wait to see what would happen next as my little heart was beating furiously with anticipation.

Scarecrow and Dorothy oil Tin Man's mouth, whew! He then lets out a huge sigh of relief. Awe… my goodness that feels so good. Here they go, spreading the oil from head to toe. Every joint begins to let loose as he is set free from the abuse. Tin Man is ecstatic to lower the ax that had become such a heavy burden, when his life was so uncertain. He had held it up for such a very long time waiting for *his* miracle. Hoping and praying someone would travel by and set him free, he was ecstatic with glee! First came the apples, and then came the knees.

One door leads to another, remember? On our knees looking up is always the place to be, so glance up, reach up and receive the promises that the Father has meant for you and me. Seek and see what amazing discoveries are ahead.

Matthew 7:7-8, (NIV) "Ask and it will be given unto you; seek and you will find; knock and the door will be opened to you. For everyone that asks shall receive; the one who seeks will find; and for the one who knocks, the door will be opened."

Tin Man shared his dismal story with his brand new friends. Explaining how he was caught out in the storm and how the rain quickly changed everything. Dorothy definitely understands about storms! Again, we can all relate to being overwhelmed with the storms of life. Let us come under the shadow of the Almighty, let His wings be a shelter, or we will become rusty, and hardened just like Tin Man. Debilitated and paralyzed by our pain, trauma will rule our hearts and crush our joy for life!

Psalm 91:4, (NLT) "He will cover you with His feathers. He will shelter you with His wings. His faithful promises are your armor and protection."

The oil begins to soothe and loosen his joints. He is so stiff, and he squeaks but it doesn't matter. The rejoicing begins, for freedom always brings a celebration. Total freedom is in sight for Tin Man as he slowly begins to move, then walk and then dance. The oil is continually applied wherever it is needed, and then his song flows into the air. All he wants is a heart. He is a little off balance as he tips and sways, swaggers, and unsteady as he staggers, but whoa … is he going down? Nope!

He triumphantly recovers his balance so strong,
He continues on with his dance and song,
This is a happy day,
Surely nothing will go wrong!

Such a joy this brought to my little heart when I watched him dance; it was like he had built-in tap shoes, clickity click, click. He weaved to the right and weaved to the left as the words of his song rang out. His desire was to be tender, gentle and very sentimental, if … he only had a heart. (2)

188

This is exactly what and who the Heavenly Father is. He is tender, gentle and very sentimental towards His children. This is why with my rainbow glasses I see Tin Man as the Heart of the Father.

His desire is for us to learn of Him, interact with Him, know His heart and then *be* His heart on earth. Freedom is such an amazing experience in Christ. As the oil of the Lord is applied, we begin to loosen up with the ability to dance and sing and learn of His love, it is our destiny. The pain of the past that can hold us captive, and unable to move shall be destroyed, free at last!

The first place the oil was released on Tin Man was his mouth. Isn't that where it all starts—with our words and with the agreements that we make? When he begins to release his sound, it was full and overflowing with gratefulness. He was so thankful for the healing balm that was flowing through him, enjoying the freedom that he could feel and see. He was free from the ax that had been so agonizingly heavy for so long. The ax that had been meant for good had turned into a great weight, but now he was free. Free from being incapacitated and unable to move forward, free to dance and to sing, free to share his heart. Freedom is here it is time to start. Freedom! Freedom! Freedom! Tin Man made a wonderful choice; he did not dwell on the storm or the pain of the past. He chose to move on, he took a stance, and it was time to dance!

Remembering once again how the scripture reminds us that there is life and death in our words, speak life, declare His goodness and bless the Lord!

Psalm 103: 1-2, (KJV) "Bless the Lord, Oh my soul and all that is with in me, bless his holy name! Bless the Lord, Oh my soul and forget not all of His benefits."

I was so sad, thinking how Tin Man had been immobilized, confined in time by a storm that had passed by. So sorrowful that he was unable to move or to even cry out for help, that he was all alone day after day, night after night, not knowing when or if anyone would ever see him or stop. My heart was aching over the hopelessness he must have felt. Isn't that how it is in our own lives, sometimes keeping hope alive is the greatest battle. But God! *Fighting to cope, for the healing of our heart, Jesus is our only hope!*

Psalm 3:2-4, (NIV) "Many are saying of me, "God will not deliver him." But you, Lord, are a shield around me, my glory, the one who lifts my head high. I call out to the Lord, and He answers me from His Holy Mountain."

Dorothy and Scarecrow now invite Tin Man to come along. Surely the wise man we are traveling to see at the Emerald City can also help you too. Come with us! We're positive he will be able to assist you with a heart; we have heard so many good things about this great man! Little did Dorothy realize that what this was really all about was the help and companionship that they would bring to her.

Glasses on

Understanding the heart of the Father and His love towards us as Abba (an intimate term for Father) is the most important concept for us to encounter and believe. It determines our relationship with God, others and ourselves. It is through this journey called life (the yellow brick road) that we experience the mind of Christ and the heart of the Father. God the Father so desires for us to be healed just like Tin Man and to experience and know that He is good and that He is good all the time.

Romans 8:15, (NASB) "For ye have not received the spirit of bondage again to fear; but ye have received the spirit of adoption, whereby we cry Abba, Father."

Jeremiah 29:11, (NIV) "I know the plans I have for you, declares the Lord, plans to prosper you and not to harm you, plans to give you hope and a future."

Mark 10:18, (NASB) "And Jesus said to him, "Why do you call me good? No one is good except God alone.""

Psalm 119:68, (NASB) "You are good and do good; Teach me your statutes."

Be aware

The evil one stays out of sight, sneaking around corners, watching and waiting for the perfect opportunity to strike at Dorothy once again. As soon as the enemy sees that there will be yet another helper that will join Dorothy's little troupe, she suddenly makes an appearance and takes advantage of the moment to frighten them once more with a brazen show of unnerving harassment. The enemy is on a mission to create fear in Dorothy's friends so they will choose not to assist her or go along. Maybe they will leave Dorothy to face the enemy all on her own. They are definitely feeling tormented, as Her Evilness stands above and glares at them from up high. She pulls out all the stops and begins to throw balls of flaming fire. Oh my! It seemed like my heart skipped a beat. I sucked in my breath and held it until the danger was past. Please don't hurt Scarecrow, I cried! As quickly as the evil one went into action, Tin Man stepped in and extinguished the fiery threat. His heart is to protect! He jumps on the flames and destroys the danger;

one fell swoop and He is a world changer. Hooray the enemy will not win today!

She may be ugly, she may be rough, she may even sound extremely tough, and she may think she is going to win, but not today! The enemy's plan backfired; instead of fear turning them around, it gave them purpose. They stood straight and tall with a strong resolve. It wasn't about them now at all! Now it was about sweet Dorothy. They will see her to the Emerald City, very quickly! Stay together, it will be much better.

Through the rainbow glasses I can see the promises of God and how when two or three are gathered together in the name of the Lord, there I am with them (Matthew 18:20).

Romans 8:31, (NIV) "What then, shall we say in response to these things? If God is for us, who can be against us?"

With God's perspective from above, I can see that when He is for us, nothing can be against us! What amazing companions we have—The Mind of Christ and the Heart of the Father that lead and direct our steps. Jesus, our High priest, and the word of God are always right beside us. There is no other adventure that is greater than discovering who we are and our destiny in Him through the power of the Red Shoes!

Scriptures to meditate

Isaiah 40:31 and 41:10

Joshua 1:9

Psalm 31:24

Proverbs 18:10

2 Corinthians 1:3-4

Pray with me

Heavenly Father, I thank you for giving me hope in seasons and times of great storms. Thank you for always knowing exactly where I am and being my help in times of need. I thank you for being my sheltering wing. I thank you for always being with me and giving me strength until the storm passes by. I thank you for the oil of joy and grace that you continually pour upon me, so that I might have the ability to dance, sing and rejoice. Father let me always be grateful to you for all my blessings. Help me always to look forward and move forward in love and with love. Help me not to dwell on the pain of the past but always to dance in the freedom that you have provided for my soul yesterday, today and in the future. Give me taps for my shoes so that the sound of my dance may ring out the abundance of your praise. Father, I repent for the times that I have grumbled and complained. May my heart always be in tune with yours, Amen.

Declaration

I declare that I am a daughter of the King. I declare that I will keep my eyes on You Lord. I declare that You are at my right hand and I will not be shaken. I declare that shouts of joy will resound in my tent and that I will dance, dance, dance with the joy of the Lord!

Bibliography
1. *The Wizard of OZ.* 1939.
2. **Fleming, Victor.** *The Wizard of OZ.* MGM, 1939.
3. *https://nameberry.com/search?q=meaning+of+Oz.* [Online]
4. **Nemitz/Facebook, Colors by Carol.** [Online]
5. www.sheknows.com. [Online]
6. http://www.netstate.com/states/intro/ks_intro.htm. [Online]

18

FACING OUR FEARS
(LION APPEARS)

ere we go! Arm and arm with joy, laughter and our song, the mind of Christ, and the heart of God. Around every corner there is a new face-to-face experience on this crusade, surrounded by the Glory of God!

I love it; my nerves are at rest, after that situation with the fire balls of destruction were quenched! Every time Her Evilness threatens Dorothy she gathers her companion's close. They link arm in arm and start to dance down the road. It's like the three musketeers that are sent to protect the queen. Everywhere she goes, they go. They were meant to be by her side through thick and thin, good days and bad; through dark and light, they are the queen's great protectors.

Dorothy has this deep feeling that her new companions seem familiar, and that they may have met before. I believe that is what we sense when we meet Jesus for the first time. He created us and has known us from before the foundations of the world, so when we give ourselves over to a relationship with Him, we have actually come home. Home always feels just right and is very familiar and comfortable. Home is where you always want to be. It's the place where you can flop down in your big comfy chair and totally be yourself. No pretenses or facades. You can just relax, kick up your feet, it's so sweet.

Psalm 139:13, (NIV) "For you created my innermost being; you knit me together in my mother's womb."

Speaking of dark and light that is exactly where Dorothy is headed now, into a very dark and tormenting forest. The forest is full of sights and sounds that could cause your imagination to run quite wild, and that is absolutely and precisely what begins to happen to the travelers and to me. I shared in a previous chapter about my Lion of Judah painting. God created the darkness but the enemy uses it to bring torment and fear, the enemy wants to bring us to tears! But our Father in heaven is right there with us. Through Him is the light that brings revelation when we are unable to see. The enemy of our soul desires to keep us captured and aligned with the agreement that terror is the one in control.

Dorothy holds Toto, and with Tin Man and Scarecrow by her side, they start down the path of this very dark, ominous mysterious place. They pull together all the courage they have and begin to step into the forest with very large strides, singing louder and louder as their steps become faster and faster. They must get through this place of overwhelming blackness quickly, because it is rallying and resurrecting so much panic that their spines feel prickly and their stomachs sickly!

If ever there were a time in our lives that we need to take our thoughts captive, it would be in this tormenting forest. This is the place where everything around us seems to be closing in, and the crushing sound that the enemy sends our way desires to keep us trapped in fear. We must go to the word of God immediately and begin to declare his truth even louder. Declare it out in the atmosphere! It is the light that breaks forth the day and shows the way! It is the sound that reverberates, releasing waves of frequency to open spheres of promise for each step that we take. I love the song that says we should raise a Hallelujah in the presence of our enemy. Keep focused on Jesus the Word and the Sword of the spirit. Like a machete it will thrash through the smothering overgrown pressing darkness, and burst forth His mighty Glory! *This is my story!*

Isaiah 43:19, (NIV) "See, I am doing a new thing. Now it springs up; do you not perceive it? I am making a way in the wilderness and streams in the wasteland."

Proverbs 4:23, (NIV) "Above all else, guard your heart, for everything you do flows from it."

Proverbs 4:23, (NLT) "Guard your heart above all else, for it determines the course of your life."

I have listed two different versions of this scripture because I enjoy how each one shares the warning a little bit differently in how we need to guard our hearts. We have to understand that guarding our thoughts is how we guard our hearts. It is the alignment to the word of God that keeps us safe. Many people that I have talked with and prayed with and mentored have expressed they are guarding their hearts by not having relationships with others. There may be a time in our lives that God does say to walk away from a relationship, because it is a new season and the relationship is unhealthy, but usually that is not the case. Most people have put a fence up to keep people out because of not wanting to be hurt; the motivation of our hearts that cause this type of reaction is fear. I remember a great teacher named Graham Cooke once made a statement that he had been stabbed in the back so many times that he was a sieve. In other words there were those he was in relationship with that had hurt him, but then he said, "Why do I get back up and do it again? Because Jesus heals!" We must forgive. He shared as he wept in pain before the Lord, only to discover a wet spot on his shoulder afterwards from where the Father had wept with him. So, let's make sure we understand what it means to guard our hearts. It is the word of God that keeps us safe, secure and in this place of alignment with Him. He guards our heart and keeps us safe from fears or whatever other spirits that may desire to destroy us. This alignment and relationship to the word will keep a steady flow of life to our inward man, keeping our motives pure. Then our destiny is sure!

One of our most thrilling experiences of all can be to face down an enemy. Because, it is usually in this place that we have the greatest revelation of who we are. It will be in this dark forest that Dorothy and her companions meet Lion. Dorothy could have remained with her friends on the edge not venturing in where threats of evil lurked and probably could have had a very good time, but she would have never reached her full potential or come to know her great strengths and the power she carried. They immediately said, let's go, we will not tarry!

Arm in arm we are linked,
The power within is on the brink,
Look straight ahead to see what comes,
The lion appears, do not succumb!

Fear will always want to rule,
But we will not faint we will not stop,
Let's dance together in this place,
For afraid, we are not, we are not!

I was afraid for Dorothy! As a child, I covered my eyes. I was frightened for what might come out of the darkness and what might be in and behind the trees. I couldn't see what was ahead. Their voices rang out over and over again singing about the lions, tigers and bears. They sang of things that could harm them and eat them. The song and sound of the music set me up and placed my emotions in a whirlwind of panic. My imagination was running wild, I knew something was about to happen, but I didn't know what! Building and building the intensity up! It was not a good feeling, but I had to trust.

Grrr ... Abruptly, there was a mighty deep prolonged ferocious roar! What could be around the corner? This roar came crashing, thrashing and trouncing through the woods like an unexpected hurricane.

Suddenly, out came Lion, he came with a mighty savage full deep bellow! He barged in on them, and they all instantly scattered and hid. The roar resonated as if it was on a loudspeaker. My heart literally skipped a beat as I watched him pounce from his perch. He jumped down from his high place and began to petrify them with his words. He bellowed over and over, right in their face. There was a battle between Scarecrow and Tin Man of who should jump to the rescue as they lay on the ground trembling in fear!

"You go get him! No, you go get him!" We can all relate to our flesh being weak when our spirit is willing (Matthew 26:41).

Dorothy was hiding behind a tree remaining at a very safe distance away with her mind and body rigid with fear! Suddenly, Lion went after Toto and in Dorothy's book that was just not okay. Her protection mode for Toto ran deep and he was the reason for this whole adventure in the first place. Something rose up within her, she stepped out of hiding and her demeanor shifted from meager to mighty. Power and authority came alive! She stepped up to the plate and then took a literal swing as she slapped Lion right on his nose. It was then that the truth was revealed. Intimidation had lied. Dorothy stepped out from behind the tree where fear had bullied and ruled, that was its mission. Keep her in hiding keep her writhing. The instant she broke free and took control, again the atmosphere changed, and the situation shifted. With her mighty Red Shoes she had stepped up, took her place and altered the case!

Dorothy grabbed Toto, her greatest possession; she held him close and rewrote her destiny in that one moment, and a page was turned! Lion began to cry, and the whole truth of the situation was now revealed. Fear had been defeated and a sound mind won. It was not until the arrival of the new companion that Dorothy showed such amazing courage. Never yet on this journey had she arisen to such heights of strength. Dorothy came alive with an enormous action of bravery and fearlessness. As the song goes, we were all born to be a lion and not a mouse. We were born to always rise and shine, to step up and step out for every occasion and each circumstance that calls for true grit.

Whew, that was a close one! Well, anyway, at least that's how I felt when I was little girl. This was a narrow escape, but it disclosed another partner that was to be added to the team's exploits ahead. Fear almost ruled the day and almost shut down the great hooray!

Rainbow glasses

They came face to face with courage because of this terrifying experience. Anytime we have a fear rise up with in us, we need to take the opportunity and face it down because it has come knocking. The challenge is being presented to rise, shine and walk in the power of the Red Shoes, the power of Jesus blood! We must come from behind the tree where we are hiding and build a system of faith that will stand on the Rock of Ages. It is with this new view that we now can see that Lion has arrived with courage, power and strength. With my glasses on, he represents the Holy Spirit. (Ephesians 3:16-29)

Acts 1:8, (KJV) "And you shall receive Power when the Holy Spirit has come upon you...

In chapter 4 of the Book of Acts, the scripture describes the encounter of when the Holy Spirit came in like a *roaring* wind that shifted the early church into a group of people that turned the world upside down. On that day, Peter stood before thousands and preached, even though not that many days prior he had actually run and hid just like Dorothy did. Everything shifted when the Holy Spirit came. Courage and power arrived on the earth like never before. And it now lived within man, this amazing power from on high, Halleluiah, fear is about to die!

Joel 2:28, (NIV) "And afterward, I will pour out my Spirit on all my people. Your sons and daughters will prophesy, your old men will dream dreams, your young men will see visions."

Judges 3:10, (NIV) "The Spirit of the Lord came on him, so that he became Israel's judge and went to war."

Luke 24:49, (NIV) "I am going to send you what my Father has promised; but stay in the city until you have been clothed with power from on high."

Now unified, Dorothy, Scarecrow and Tin Man immediately invite Lion to come along. Come with us, we're positive the wise man at the Emerald City can help you too. If you are looking for courage, please come with us, he will make you new!

So, here we go, Father, Son and Holy Spirit. All for one and one for all. This journey is all about the relationship of Dorothy and her precious companions that will see her through it all, come what may, together she will never stray!

They must be getting close to the end of the yellow brick road that leads them to their promise of provision, a new heart, a new mind and courage to complete this great journey. Dorothy must be close to going home.

They step in time to each other. They jump into the rhythm of the music, to the song that pulls them continually forward with an expectation of the Emerald City! Their steps are visual; they are a cadence of unity and agreement with movement. The expression of happiness and joy gives them strength for what is ahead. Let's pick up our feet and quickly march to the rhythm of worship and get through the dark forests that come into our lives. Release a song, dance and praise His name. Let us move! Move! Move! Allow revelation in the darkness to unfold. Let courage arise within us through the power of the Holy Spirit and our beautiful Red Shoes.

We have turned the corner and wow, what we can see? Can this really be?

Scriptures to meditate

Deuteronomy 31:6-8

Ephesians 6:10

1 Chronicles 28:20

Joshua 1:9-11

Psalm 56:3-4

Pray with me

Heavenly Father, I thank you that no matter how dark the circumstances are around me and how scary the sounds, I can depend on you to light the way. I thank you that no matter the darkness, you are in the midst of it. I thank you that you never leave me or forsake me and that you are the one that puts the spring in my step! I praise you and keep your song in my heart. With the rhythm of your heartbeat, we will sing and dance together and walk through the black forest moments in life until we come to the other side. I am amazed at your faithfulness. Thank you for revealing that good things are in the darkness; we just have to see them through your promises. I look to you for you are the light. You are the author and the finisher of my faith. In Jesus name. Amen.

Declaration

I declare that I am an amazing child of God. I declare that I have the courage and the faith to break through into the light. Father, I declare that you are the light and you are opening the way.

Bibliography
1. *The Wizard of OZ.* 1939.
2. **Fleming, Victor.** *The Wizard of OZ.* MGM, 1939.
3. *https://nameberry.com/search?q=meaning+of+Oz.* [Online]
4. **Nemitz/Facebook, Colors by Carol.** [Online]
5. www.sheknows.com. [Online]
6. http://www.netstate.com/states/intro/ks_intro.htm. [Online]

19

POISON
(NOTHING WILL HARM US)

Dorothy, Scarecrow, Tin Man and Lion turn the corner and there it is! The Emerald City! An intense exhilaration is rushing through their veins; it is revitalizing them with a brand new energy and bringing a fresh breath of life. Oh what a marvelous sight.

Who would have guessed that just on the other side of this dark, scary, frightening, sound-infested forest was the beautiful, bright illuminating promise? It is always the darkest before the dawn!

The place of great promise,
It was just around the corner,
Who would have guessed?
Onward they escorted her!

The atmosphere is ecstatic,
Full of hope and expectation,
As they take off on a run,
They knew it meant their salvation!

But then I remember that the ole enemy is watching, and that Her Evilness sees every step forward that is being made. She is watching closely all of the progress, all of the joy, all of the dancing and the special relationship between the four of them. The enemy does not sleep or rest, for she is continually devising a plot that will put a halt to Dorothy's plans. The Wise Man is just ahead; what will she pull out of her hat now to discourage or bring dread? She continues to try and prevent Dorothy from reaching her appointment with destiny, all because of her intense jealousy!

The enemy will never ever give up, so as soon as you wrap your brain around that and move on, the better. Let your eye always remain on the reward ahead just as Dorothy's are. Straight ahead she sees the Emerald City in all of its glory. The city is exquisite! It rises above the horizon as it radiates and sparkles in the beautiful baby blue sky. The sight of this stunning city is calling them forth with an overwhelming invitation to come, come where there is hope, peace, wisdom and truth. Here live the answers to all of your needs.

As Dorothy and her friends look ahead and see that their glorious destination is just within reach, a smile and an eruption of jubilation flow from the top of their heads to the bottom of their feet. This is for real! Perseverance has been her friend. All she had to do was follow the yellow brick road one step at a time, just one foot in front of the other, and now she has arrived. She, Scarecrow, Tin man and Lion have faced so much opposition where discouragement could have taken root, but they refused. They looked straight ahead, kept their eye on the prize and now they have arrived. They can actually see it, My Oh My!

Rainbow glasses

This reminds me of the story of Noah and the Ark. He heard the voice of God and stayed loyal to his cause even though he couldn't see the rain at the moment—he believed. The pressure was insurmountable against him; he had no friends or any believers to help him, only mockers. But, because of his faithfulness, he saved his family, saved his legacy and changed the destiny of the world. Because he listened and obeyed, we have the rainbow today!

Galatians 6:9, (KJV) "… and let us not be weary in well doing: for in due season we will reap, if we faint not."

Poison

The enemy plots one last desperate ploy to maneuver, destroy and stop this expedition before they arrive at the Emerald City. The city is within their sights. With sinister thoughts she continues to contemplate… What can I do? — Asks the evil one—to turn this around to my favor? Poison, yes, I will use poison!

The enemy begins to mix a concoction of several ingredients to place in the atmosphere to overcome Dorothy and her friends.

As I watched her when I was a child, I thought, *now what?* Haven't you done enough? Can't you just leave her alone? The enemy is relentless. She is constantly scheming, constantly calculating a crafty unexpected way to take Dorothy out. My heart desired for her to be safe and secure. I was so eager for her to arrive at the Emerald City; surely things would be different there. Be safe was my little prayer.

Isaiah 54:17, (NKJV) "No weapon formed against you shall prosper, and every tongue, which rises against you in judgment, you shall condemn. This is the heritage of the servants of the Lord, and their righteousness is from me, says the Lord."

They are so excited, emotions are soaring high and they feel as if they could fly. Scarecrow running is leading the way, come on, come on, he shouts! (2) Hurry! They are running, but suddenly, uh-oh! Something is amiss! I can see a change in the atmosphere as they reach the middle of the poppy field. Dorothy and Lion's steps begin to slow, they are becoming sluggish and tired, and they begin to feel sleepy. Dorothy states if I can just get a little rest, so she lies down with Toto by her side and they quickly fall asleep. Lion begins to wilt and fade. His body begins to sag and droop and then boom! He is down and out! What is that all about?

Now wait a minute; what just happened?

I am crying out—get up Dorothy get up! Her strength and courage have withered; she does not recognize that this is a plot from the enemy. The mind (Scarecrow) and heart (Tin Man) are strong, but they are unable to move Dorothy and Lion. They recognize that this ploy of evilness comes from the hand of evil; this spell of weariness has come from her. They begin to cry out, Help! Help! They look up; their eyes are towards the sky.

As a child I am feeling the desperation, I continue to cry out, "Get up, Dorothy! Get up!" No, This cannot be happening! You are almost there, and you have come so far. If I wasn't yelling it out in the airwaves, it was definitely loud enough in my spirit and my emotions that it felt like I was shouting quite clear!

Get those glasses out!

Matthew 26:41, (NIV) "Watch and pray so that you will not fall into temptation. The spirit is willing, but the flesh is weak."

Attractive to the eye and soothing to the smell, (2) the enemy says, oh how subtle the poison is that the enemy prepares for us. Notice that the poison is aimed at the soul's sphere. This is the realm where the enemy lures our emotions. The poppies were so beautiful that Dorothy did not even consider that there might be danger about. She did not stop, look or listen to detect any evil that might be present. When we continue on the yellow brick road and we're able to view our promise and it's within our sight, let us always be wise. There is always a balancing act between watching, waiting and proceeding.

The vibrant beauty of the poppies distracted Dorothy. Not everything that is enticing to us with magnificent loveliness is in our best interest. This is where the enemy of our soul regularly tries to distract us to keep us from achieving our full and complete destiny in Christ. He will lay a trap that is so subtle and sometimes very beautiful, just like the poppies. Most animal traps are always camouflaged or in disguise, way beneath the grass or in the brush, unable to be easily seen. Sadly the animals are taken unaware. The Evil One wants to snatch us unaware and keep us from the Emerald City!

Dorothy was heading to the City craving wisdom in how to get back home. She needs answers, and the answers are so close! Something crept in unaware and set a trap. Drowsy and weary her eyelids became heavier and heavier and they slowly closed. Dorothy's body began to slump; she fell into a deep sleep with her ever- faithful Toto by her side. They both fall to the ground; She and Toto do not make a sound.

Let's recall this scripture about growing weary. No matter what the cause, be aware be very aware.

Galatians 6:9, (KJV) "And let us not be weary in well doing: for in due season, we will reap, if we faint not."

Isn't this just exactly what is happening to Dorothy as she runs towards the goal? Just as she is in the middle of what seems like the most beautiful surroundings, there is danger everywhere. She is surrounded! It all looked so good, but weary and exhausted, her eyes turn down. It is an assignment of destruction from the evil one, Oh my, it looks like all is lost. My heart is beating fast, hoping for a miracle, no matter the cost!

This is so common in our lives when we are just about to arrive at the objective we have been reaching for in Christ, the enemy sends a spirit of weariness that causes us to slow down, look away and feel there is no use. He then tempts us to give up. He creates a diversion and hopes that we will take the bait. His obsession is to drain us of all our strength. The Evil One desires to put us to sleep with thoughts of, I will never arrive, just stop praying, seeking or trying. Then, he uses a visual reminder that we cannot see any change in our situation, so again he baits us to grow weary and give up. If we are not careful, we look down, unable to see, and slump to the ground. Our joy has been sapped which is our strength, and agreements have been made as our eyes divert down not up. Then, he convinces us to take off our rainbow glasses to blur our vision, we cannot see the promises, and we cannot see the way! Please listen to what I have to say. We must always look up high, for rainbows are in the sky!

1 Corinthians 10:13, (NLT) "The temptations in your life are no different from what others experience. God is faithful. He will not allow the temptation to be more then you can stand. When you are tempted, He will show you a way out so that you can endure."

This is where we find ourselves, needing wisdom for a way of escape. Jesus is always our escape!

He has a strategy. Just as our opponent contemplates on how to ambush us with his plans again and again, never fear, the Father sees it all so clear; please do not shed a tear. He knows the way out. All we have to *do is call, do not sit and pout!*

He is never taken by surprise or alarmed with what the Evil One has up his sleeve. Just as Scarecrow and Tin Man did in the story, all we need to do is cry out for help! Recognize the lies that the enemy wants us to feel and believe, remember he is trying to lull us to sleep.

Proverbs 13:12, (NIV) "Hope deferred makes the heart sick; but a longing fulfilled is a tree of life!"

Looking through the beautiful colors of the rainbow, we can now see that help is on the way. We cry out, angels are then dispatched, so look for them today. They are on the way, and all we need to do is pray!

Those that encamp around us are rallied. Our spirit never sleeps, it is always aware, so let the Spirit rise up and call out! Don't be caught in the snare.

In this illustration right now we can see that the mind of Christ and the heart of God are strong, but courage has faded. Lion and Dorothy are on the ground, their traveling legs have buckled beneath them with heaviness, and they are down.

Will there be times when we are overwhelmed? The scripture says yes, but there is a way of escape. It is through the peace that passes all understanding that flows from the throne of God. It is the trust in His faithfulness that gets us through when the mountain looks bigger than your faith. It is Jesus.

Psalm 46:1-3 says that God is our refuge and strength, an ever-lasting help in trouble. His comfort and joy will pick us back up and send us back down the road. Never believe the lie that you are alone or the only one. Remember the word in first Corinthians as stated above. The temptations (poisons) in our lives that the enemy has concocted are no different than any other that mankind has been tempted with. In other words, the enemy has no new ideas; he uses the same ones over and over. They may be packaged a little different on the outside, but inside they are the same. Press through. Call for Jesus as Peter did for He is there. Look up; be aware (Matthew 14:22-33).

Isaiah 40:29-31, (NIV) "He gives strength to the weary and increases the power of the weak. Even youths grow tired and weary, and young men stumble and fall, but those who hope in the Lord will renew their strength. They will soar on wings like eagles, they will run and not grow weary, they will walk and not be faint.

The enemy in this story is watching as Dorothy and her friend have fallen and collapsed. They are asleep and not moving forward. Her Evilness is quite euphoric she loves what she sees!

Scriptures to Meditate
Ephesians 6:10
Nehemiah 8:10
Proverbs 18:10
Psalm 119:28
2 Corinthians 12:9-10

Pray with me

Father, I thank you that you are my ever-present help when I am in trouble. I thank you that you are not far from me, and that when I call in a time of crisis you come quickly. I thank you that you are my strength. I thank you that you are my shield when the enemy comes to spread his poisonous lies. I thank you that through the Holy Spirit I can recognize them and destroy them by the power of your word. I thank you, Father, that through the power of the blood of Jesus (my Red Shoes) that I can rise again when I have weakened and stumbled. Help me, Father, to always be aware of what the enemy may be up to and give me strategies through your word to deflect the traps and snares he lays for me. Always help me to look up. Give me super-natural resilience just as your breath gave life to Adam. Yes, from death to life. Thank you for vitality from above, for the power and the strength to rise up and speak to the mountains that have come against me. Through you we can do all things! Amen.

Declaration

I declare that I am a child of the most High God. I declare that You are my refuge. I declare that You are my strong tower and I am safe in You. I declare that I will soar with the eagles from on high, and I will see what you see, and that your grace is sufficient for me.

Bibliography

1. *The Wizard of OZ*. 1939.

2. **Fleming, Victor.** *The Wizard of OZ*. MGM, 1939.

3. *https://nameberry.com/search?q=meaning+of+Oz*. [Online]

4. **Nemitz/Facebook, Colors by Carol.** [Online]

5. www.sheknows.com. [Online]

6. http://www.netstate.com/states/intro/ks_intro.htm. [Online]

20

LET IT SNOW, LET IT SNOW, LET IT SNOW

Help! Desperate cries go forth from Scarecrow and Tin Man. The situation at hand appears very dismal. Their eyes are focused totally upon Dorothy, Lion and Toto who have all fallen asleep and are now down. Knowing that they are unable to carry them and that this is definitely not the time to rest, they quickly discern that it is a scheme of destruction sent straight from the enemy that is such a pest! They turn, look upward, and once again their voices ring out a loud sound of despair as they cry for help.

Psalm 34:4, (TPT) "When I needed the Lord, I looked for Him; I called out to Him, and He heard me and responded. He came and rescued me from everything that made me afraid."

Psalm 35:8, (HCSB) "Let ruin come on him expectantly, and let the net that he hid ensnare him; let him fall into it---to his ruin."

THE ENEMY IS GOING DOWN!

Tears begin to stream down the Tin Man's face. Scarecrow then gives strict orders that it is no time to cry because it will cause him to rust! (2) His tears of sorrow would just create an additional set of problems. In other words, there is a time for tears and then there is a time for action. This was a time for action!

I can understand because I remember when I have set up residence in the house of woe where my tears have ruled and flowed. The enemy of our soul has designs for us to remain bound by grief and pain. He pushes us down with the spirit of heaviness, creating hopelessness where we do not reach up and receive healing from the Father. When I went through a full year of several deaths that were close to me in 2015, I looked up the word tears and how God created us to cry because they serve a very healthy purpose. But, with that being said, we are not meant to live in the land of tears. Tears can also take us by the hand and lead us down the road to depression if we allow them. By Special Delivery Heartache and grief can over take our emotions with great authority if we continuously feed them with sorrow and sadness instead of expectation and life. If we are not careful, spirits of darkness that desire to destroy, will then rule us and take us down, down, down into the dungeon of despondency and despair, not able to care. Sadly, the tears that God meant for a good healthy release to our bodies will become a burden and an assignment of heaviness from the enemy.

We are created by God to love and to receive love, so when we find ourselves weary just like Dorothy right now, call for help and look to the word. We must declare life, and be assured!

Rainbow glasses on

Philippians 4:8, (NIV) "Finally, brothers and sisters, whatever is true, whatever is noble, whatever is admirable—if anything is excellent or praiseworthy—think about these things."

Shift your thoughts!

Philippians 3:1, (NIV) "Further my brothers and sisters, rejoice in the Lord! It is no trouble for me to write the same things to you again, and it is a safeguard for you."

Think on the good things of God. Rejoice I say, rejoice! Refresh your mind and heart with what is excellent and praiseworthy. The enemy desires for us to rerun many scenarios through our mind like a record that is scratched and skips over and over again! Saying the same thing continually, thinking of the same painful memories again and again. His mission is to cement these memories in our brain, desiring for us to relive them always keeping these fresh and new. His joy would be for us to remain in trauma. It has been scientifically proven that our emotions regulate what you experience as reality. As Dr. Carolyn Leaf wrote in "Who Shut Off My Brain," you won't believe something unless you feel it is true. So, we must continually speak the truth of the word over our memories of pain, our mind, body and spirit. Speak hope and peace, and *not* the lies of the enemy that are full of rejection and death. When we have shifted our belief system into alignment with the power of the Red Shoes, (His blood), we will hold our heads high, we will stand tall, live in joy, and as Scarecrow did, look to the sky!

Look up!

Then suddenly there is a miracle from up above, an amazing miracle that comes through the Fathers astounding love. It begins

217

to snow. As he looks up Scarecrow begins to experience a wonder, a gift falling softly and quietly. He states that maybe it will help. Little did he know the sensational and remarkable power of this incredible snow.

This is also one of my most favorite parts of the story, as Glinda is revealed once again. She is watching over the travelers and she is bringing holiness and goodness as a source of protection over Dorothy and her journey. As the snow begins to fall, the atmosphere changes in response to the cries for help. All we could see before was the enemy; we didn't even know Glinda was there, but actually, her presence was everywhere!

I love the snow, and I think it's very interesting that as I am writing this particular chapter that it's actually snowing outside. I live in the Pacific Northwest, and while I see some snow it's not very often. Mostly, I see it at a distance on the majestic mountaintops. Oh, but tonight it has arrived, it is here, and God the Father brought it right to my door. I can actually reach out and touch it. I have opened the door, and as I look outside there is such beauty, I am enjoying the visit. It definitely has its own presence and you can feel it. It is like a whisper that you can't quite grab ahold of that brings a quiet, soothing calm and is soft and gentle to the touch—just like God when we need Him in desperate and hopeless situations, just like Dorothy. I can sense the peace, the hush that it brings. It seems to muffle the busy sounds of life. The beauty that it carries is incomparable to anything else. I can't explain it, but my spirit rises within me, it's a call to worship, a desire to lift up the majesty of my Heavenly Father the mighty creator. I could sit and look at the snow for hours; its presence touches me so deeply.

God looks down and sends a messenger with a gift that changes everything, He desire to make us whole.

Can you remember when you have heard snow called a blanket? Blankets are used for comfort, warmth and a shelter from the cold. Isn't this what happens when our sins are forgiven? The Father places His blanket of righteousness around us to protect us from the harshness of the world and Satan's designs on our lives. His righteousness is a shield about us; it produces faith that preserves us from the darts of the enemy that are meant to destroy.

Psalms 3:3, (NLT) "But you, O LORD, are a shield around me, my glory, and the lifter of my head."

Ephesians 6:16, (NIV) "In addition to all this, take up the shield of faith, with which you can extinguish all the flaming arrows of the evil one."

When the snow is untouched by man and man's machines, you can for just a brief moment enjoy a glint of God's amazing heart for the purity and beauty that He so desires for all of mankind.

With our glasses on let's look up snow in the scripture and see what it has to say.

Isaiah 1:18, (NIV) "Come now; let us settle the matter, says the Lord. Though your sins are like scarlet, they shall be white as snow; though they are red as crimson, they shall be like wool."

Acts 3:19, (NIV) "Repent then, and turn to God so that your sins may be blotted out, so that times of refreshing may come from the Lord."

Acts 3:19, (TPT) "So now you need to rethink everything and turn to God so your sins will be forgiven and a new day can dawn, days of refreshing times flowing from the lord."

We have two beautiful scriptures here that are describing snow, and the brilliant white of snow. Snow represents our sins after forgiveness from the Father that brings refreshment from the Lord.

Can't you just see it? That is exactly what Dorothy is experiencing as they cry out for help. The Guardian that is watching over her begins to release the snow, a shower of mercy and blessing. It is bringing deliverance from the poison that the enemy had plotted for destruction. The snow is clearing the air and bringing refreshment to Dorothy's spirit. She begins to awaken and then to arise. She can see clearly now, the snow is returning her strength and bringing the new. The scripture tells us that God's mercies are new every morning.

Lamentations 3:22-23, (KJV) "The steadfast love of the Lord never ceases, His mercies never come to an end; they are new every morning; great is your faithfulness."

This is such a beautiful picture of the mercies of God and His refreshing in times of great need when all seems lost and there is no hope. He sends help, a gift—Jesus—the greatest gift of all from the throne of Grace that lifts us up to a new place so that we can and are able to carry on. The words to an old song written by Thomas Chisholm in 1866 still ring true today as they bring the word of God alive, the word which will stand for eternity.

Great is thy faithfulness!
Great is thy faithfulness!
Morning by morning new mercies I see.
All I have needed thy hand hath provided,
Great is thy faithfulness, Lord, unto me!

Dorothy is up; her strength is renewed, on the way once again His provision is true. Looking up, she regains her focus and sees the Emerald City, grabs the oilcan and uses it on Tin Man. With my rainbow glasses, I see this as a fresh anointing and grace for the remaining road ahead!

Psalm 93: 10, (TPT) *"Your anointing has made me strong and mighty. You've empowered my life for triumph by pouring fresh oil over me.*

Oh drat! The enemy begins to spit and spew a venomous anger, seeing that someone is always protecting and helping Dorothy. She throws out ferocious words into the atmosphere, "Shoes or no shoes, I'm still great enough to conquer her and woe to anyone that tries to stop me!" (2) I am sure this is why Glinda wanted to make sure that Dorothy definitely understood she must never take off the Red Shoes.

It brings a thought to mind,
Always be covered by His blood,
Rain or shine,
Be surrounded by His love!

The Evil One grabs her broom and out the window her flight begins, the plot for another rendezvous is full steam ahead! Her scheme is to meet Dorothy right where she is at, so it's straight ahead, no holds barred, not holding back! Even as a child, I could see that she is quite impressed with her abilities of evil right from the start, on a mission with revenge in her heart.

I was wondering what plan of action is in her playbook now? What does the next chapter hold for Dorothy? Being young this dark wickedness on a rampage made me cringe!

Dorothy, Toto, Scarecrow, Tin Man, and Lion do not worry or fret. Their eyes are focused directly ahead—it is the Emerald City in its entire lustrous splendor; there is no time to entertain any fear, not today not here, not ever! Up they jump, refusing to linger in the past where the enemy caused them to stumble or to fall. They are looking relentlessly ahead at the beauty, radiance and glory of it all!

They link arms again,
As a sound comes from heaven,
The song from above,
Is filled with His great love;

Let us skip to the rhythm,
And the beauty of His grace,
Let the sound of freedom,
Bring us close to His face.

At last, once again they are off to the City of Emeralds as it is called in the original story. I believe that is a great description of the wealth of this beautiful city.

Scriptures to meditate
Hebrews 4:16
Matthew 7:7
Psalm 107:28-30; 121:2; 143:1-11
Psalm 121:2

Pray with me

Father God, I thank you for your righteousness and for my salvation and that my sins are as white as snow. I thank you again that when I cry out, you hear me. I thank you that your loving kindness, your goodness and your holiness is always around me and pursues me. I thank you for the peace that comes from above that wraps around me like a blanket. I am thankful that I can feel your warmth consoling me when my heart is hurting from the pain that comes my way in this world. Father, I ask you to help me never to feel ashamed when I stumble or fall and help me always to feel the freedom to call upon your name when I need help. Help me to keep my eyes on your righteousness and who you are. Help me to always look up and see the rainbow! I praise you for your power and redemption! Amen.

Declaration

I declare that I am your child. I declare that the peace of God rules my heart. I declare that my mind will stay in perfect peace as I keep my mind steadfast upon You! I declare that I am covered by your righteousness and it is your righteous right arm that holds me up!

Bibliography
1. *The Wizard of OZ.* 1939.
2. **Fleming, Victor.** *The Wizard of OZ.* MGM, 1939.
3. *https://nameberry.com/search?q=meaning+of+Oz.* [Online]
4. **Nemitz/Facebook, Colors by Carol.** [Online]
5. www.sheknows.com. [Online]
6. http://www.netstate.com/states/intro/ks_intro.htm. [Online]

27

WE HAVE ARRIVED
(The City of Emeralds)

Just look ahead
Such a beautiful city
I shout with joy
I am over the top giddy!

ere we are, looking up at this glamorous Emerald Green City. It sparkles and shines and is so inviting; it takes my breath away! You just have to know that there is something absolutely amazing inside. My heart is racing just a bit as my expectation begins to anticipate what is through those spectacular and remarkably stunning doors. I can hardly wait to experience what has been prepared and is waiting for our grand entrance.

We have walked, skipped and danced with Dorothy through many dangerous and crazy encounters to arrive at this city. Oh how the anticipation rippled through me. My expectancy to have those doors open and Dorothy step inside was over the top. The memory of this scene is still vivid, and to this day as I recall those amazing emerald green doors, that same excitement is revived!

I so desired to behold what had been prepared for Dorothy and her friends. This had been a long trip, so let's put on our rainbow glasses and get ready for the show. Okay, here we go! Brace yourself for some amazing, dazzling and astonishing moments that will change your life forever. What is ahead? What suspense! What do you think will appear before our very eyes? What is behind those stunning green doors?

I Corinthians 2:9-10, (NKJV) "Eye hath not seen, nor ear heard, nor have entered into the heart of man the things which God has prepared for those who love Him. But, God has revealed them to us through His Spirit. For the Spirit searches all things, yes, the deep things of God."

The scripture teaches us that if we seek Him and seek the deep things of God, He will reveal to us through His Spirit astonishing, lovely, and absolutely beyond our imagination revelations. Let's go behind the doors called search and desire, for the great unveiling of His character and nature. The scripture says the eye hath not see, nor our ear heard, or has it entered the heart of man what the Father has prepared for those that love Him. So, when we arrive at our own personal Emerald City and we are seeking the pouring out of profound wisdom and a deeper encounter to be unveiled, open the doors of our heart to Him with an overwhelming burning enthusiasm, and wait. Take time and wait for what He has prepared. It will be worth it all. Let's go, we are ready. Do not stall!

Ephesians 1:17, (KJV) "… that the God of our Lord Jesus Christ, the Father of Glory, may give you a spirit of wisdom and revelation in the knowledge of him."

Ephesians 3:19, (KJV) "…and to know the love of Christ which surpasses knowledge, that you may be filled up to all the fullness of God."

What has God prepared for us? What has He prepared for me? I know that as we walk through life with the Father, Jesus and Holy Spirit right by our side, that the Emerald City is such a great visual of what is in store for us. It is not until we step through the new doors to this city that we can actually see and participate in what is available. It took continual persistence to arrive and determination to push through the tough times for the new doors to be accessible. Now, here we are! Open! Promises, revelation and destiny are on the other side.

"No," I cry out!

Her Evilness is quite bold as she erupts, grabs her broom and announces that she is going to the Emerald City! Feeling and thinking that there still must be time, that there still might be a chance to stop this little girl and her friends. She acts quickly to create something that will work to crash this party. She flies off in a flurry to once again intercept Dorothy's objective. She simply must have those shoes!

Off she flies as fast as she can,
For She is on a mission,
The enemy has great intent,
But it will not come to completion!

She is in the atmosphere;
Her darkness is coming near,
Her plan is to strike with fear,
Yep, the same old tricks she is almost here!

If the enemy's design is to derail us from what the Father has in store, then never be surprised or dismayed. I have always shared with people that life can feel like a rollercoaster ride; it goes up and down and all around. We can either hang on for dear life, grip the bar in front of us with an intense panic or we can raise our hands in the air with praise! Let's worship and rest. Place your life in the Father's hands and shriek with joy as He takes you on the ride of a lifetime, for He is right by our side laughing or crying, sharing every minute with us.

Step up to the ride past the fence,
The ticket has been bought,
Yep, sometimes it will be incredibly intense!

You can hear the powerful words that they are singing as Dorothy, Scarecrow, Tin Man and Lion skip up to the entrance. The words are so encouraging! They have come out of the dark, out of that terrifying forest, out of the night and into the light!

I could feel the suspense in the air. Can you believe it after everything we've been through, we've made it! We are here! We're at the Emerald City! I felt so much emotion as a child; it brought laughter to my little spirit. I was giddy with anticipation for what was ahead, and great relief brushed over me from the top of my head to the bottom of my feet, as I danced with joy, this is oh so sweet!

There are just no words that can describe this city. It glistens in the sun and the light illuminates its beauty. There are flowers everywhere and it sits on a hill. Ooh, what an amazing view, it doesn't seem real. The entrance door is enormous. I felt that it must mean that there are great and elaborate blessings on the other side. Not every day mundane experiences of life, but rollercoaster ride experiences. These are the doors of promise and expectation. These are the doors that night after night they have dreamed of arriving and knocking on! These are the doors that they have dreamed of over and over again that would someday open to them the very innermost desires of their hearts. Yes, it is definitely a time to skip, dance and sing!

Dorothy rings the doorbell. Out pops the doorman, what a joy to see. He is just like you and me, except all he wore was green! I laughed the first time I saw him, and I still laugh today when he pops out of his little round window and scolds them for ringing the doorbell. He tells them that it doesn't work, that they need to knock and then he slams the door in their face. How funny is that, especially when it did work.

Wow! Now wasn't that quite the greeting? Well, personally I thought that it was quite rude, but Dorothy just listened and obeyed; she did not get flustered, she remained in peace. After all, she was on a mission to be allowed entrance into this beautiful, breathtaking city that she believes holds the answers to her prayers.

Galatians 6:9 shares with us to not grow weary in doing well, to stay steadfast and believe, to keep knocking, and to trust and know that the door will open.

Knock, knock, knock!

Out pops the doorman again, curly mustache and all.

They state their request, "We would like to see the wizard."

His reaction was astoundingly over reactive with a great emphatic, absolute no way, no!

No one sees the wise man! No way! No how! (2) He turns to shut the window once again.

Please, stop, wait, we must see him, and they stated their case to the doorman who has the authority to give entrance or not.

My heart was breaking as I watched this scene. "What do you mean she can't see the wizard?" I knew that she must see the Wiseman because he had all the answers for Dorothy and she must get home.

Dorothy began to share the story of how far she had come and what she had gone through to get to where they were. Her companions spoke up and stated that Glinda (goodness and holy) of the North had sent her. The doorman wanted proof. "She has the powerful Red Shoes," they stated very emphatically! Dorothy shows off her beautiful Red Shoes, as they gleamed and sparkled in the light of the sun (Son).

Oh my, what a difference that made to the man in charge of the door. "That changed everything! You should have stated that from the very beginning," he said and suddenly there is breakthrough. "Come on in!"

Wow! What a difference the shoes made. They gave Dorothy entrance to a city that otherwise would have been shut to her. The power of the Red Shoes opened these magnificent doors. Here they were after this long journey, looking at a closed door. They had even pleaded their case, but in the end, it was the shoes that opened the way. When everything looked hopeless, there was a suddenly again. Dorothy had it right in her possession all of the time. She held the key to the entrance of this magnificent amazing city. As of yet, Dorothy still has no comprehension of her powerful Red Shoes and the authority that she possesses because of them. She sees them, wears them and even admires their beauty but with no real understanding.

With my rainbow glasses I can see that the Red Shoes changed and turned everything around. The blood of Jesus opens many doors of destiny for us that transform the world around us. The doorman then began to laugh and smile and celebrate Dorothy's arrival. The double door, representing a double blessing, is so tall and so wide it begins to swing open slowly and gracefully. Once opened completely it reveals the abundant festivities inside where the Wiseman lives. Look what has been prepared for their arrival! Look what this city contains! Yeah! No more hindrances, no more games!

It felt like I had waited for so long to see Dorothy and her friends reach the Emerald City, and because the journey did have so many ups and downs, laughs and tears, I was a little shocked that the door could have possibly been shut to her once they finally did arrive. Thank God for those Red Shoes!

What promises are now becoming clear?

2 Corinthians 1:20: The promises of God are always yes and amen!

2 Peter 1:4, (NIV) "And because of His glory and excellence, he has given us great and precious promises. These are the promises that enable you to share his divine nature and escape the world's corruption caused by human desire."

Exodus 14:14, (NIV) "The Lord will fight for you; you only need to be still."

Each of us has our own Emerald city as our stories are being written in this book of life. And, yes sometimes the enemy has shut the doors to our promises, but if we could only understand the power of our Red Shoes. The blood of Jesus opens doors where there seems to be no way, and suddenly, there can be a break-through, and the breakthrough is for today!

It removes the enemy's schemes,
To stop our destiny,
Launching us forward into the amazing.

These sensational Red Shoes open doors,
That would otherwise be shut and locked,
They are the key,
You cannot be stopped!

Philippians 3:14, (NIV) "I press on toward the goal to win the prize for which God has called me heavenward in Christ Jesus."

Isaiah 43:19, (NIV) "See, I am doing a new thing! Now it springs up; do you not perceive it? I am making a new way in the wilderness and streams in the wasteland."

Jeremiah 29:11-14, (NIV) "For I know the plans I have for you, declares the Lord, plans to prosper you and not to harm you, plans to give you hope and a future. Then you will call on me and come pray to me, I will be found, and I will listen to you. You will seek me and find me when you seek me with all of your heart. I will be found by you, declares the Lord, and bring you back from captivity."

The Father has a plan for our lives, and it is to prosper us and not to harm us. Jesus paid the ultimate price that we might walk the yellow brick road in freedom, joy and hope. He will reveal and open our eyes to see the way ahead and to be able to see the Emerald City. To seek and to receive wisdom, discernment and courage is our promise. The Father has prepared the best for our future. He has prepared a beautiful table in the presence of our enemy. (Psalm 23: 5)

We understand by Dorothy's example that she pursued her future by continuing to knock on a door even when she was unable to open it. At times it looked as if Dorothy might get discouraged, but there was always someone that cared, someone that was watching over her and her friends. There was a greater design and plan for her life, and the outcome was inevitable because of the power of those Red Shoes.

This is where we make sure that we keep our rainbow glasses on so we can see and believe that God has a plan. This plan wrapped in adventure has been prepared and created with great detail just for Him and us. Look up, keep knocking and expect God to open doors by the power of Jesus blood, then the laughter will roll in like a flood!

Doors that were only,
Created just for you,
Remain and stay true,
He has promises that are new!

Tomorrow may be the day,
Tomorrow may be the time,
He is faithful, Seek His face,
He has an amazing design!

Emerald

Let us take a look at the color emerald through the rainbow glasses and see what God has to say about it and what it represents.

Emerald green (Rev. 4:3 NIV) is described around the throne of God. (4) Emerald is the background color of the flag of Judah who was one of the four main standard bearers for the tribes of Israel. Dark green includes the attributes of green and black, a fruitful intimacy that tramples our enemies under our feet like ashes. Yes, I do believe and know that we have been invited to the throne room because of those powerful shoes that represent the sacrifice of His son, Jesus. His blood has opened the path, and the scripture says to come to the throne boldly.

Hebrews 4:16, (NIV) "Let us then approach God's throne of grace with confidence, so that we may receive mercy and find grace in our time of need."

Green in of itself is the combination of blue and yellow. Blue represents peace and yellow represents his Glory and Grace. One view of the color green is that it stands for fruitful intimacy with Jesus. Pastures are green where the shepherd leads His sheep. Finances or money to fund God's wishes and desires are colored green. Green is what happens when God's (yellow) Grace mixes with (blue) peace. This information about the color green came from "A Collection of Prophetic Meanings of Color" by Carol Nemitz.

I personally see the color green as restful because it is the most prominent color in nature. To me, nature without the touch of man is peaceful and brings us into alignment to what I believe heaven is like. It is not loud, but yet there is a gorgeous sound. The trees dance with the movement of the wind, and the exquisite sound of the Holy Spirit. He whispers in our ears wonderful, graceful words of tranquility. He is a God that brings us into rest, body, soul, and spirit. Be still and know.

Open

Open, open, open, the doors swing wide, the sound of the city begins, music and singing are all about, we step inside and what to our wondering eyes do we see? It's a horse and carriage pulling up just for you and me. What fun there is inside, such a joyful, jubilee! Smiles are everywhere. It is such a delightful welcome after so many frustrating negative experiences with the wicked one. Singing and laughter seem to be the way of life in this dwelling place. Surely nothing can threaten them now that they have entered the city of grace. They laugh the day away in the very ole land of Oz. (2) This will be a time of refreshing and pampering. They are stuffed and oiled, shinned and buffed, combed and curled, preparing and refreshing the team for the assignment that is just ahead. Music, song and dance are continually around them; how happy their hearts must be. The city is surpassing all of their expectations; I know that as a child it sure surpassed mine. This was definitely sublime.

There is such an atmosphere of fun because everything is green, everything except the horse that pulled the carriage that Dorothy and her friends rode in; he was like a walking flashing neon rainbow sign. As the horse continued to change into beautiful colors, with my glasses I see this fabulous horse as one that represents the never-ending adventure of what God has in store for us all. I choose to see the rainbow horse as the Father's phenomenal promises that want to take us on an extraordinary ride through life. Allow the Father to spread His beautiful blessings over you, and always remember that for there to be a rainbow, there must also be some rain. But the sun is always present to show the way and shine through, just for me and you.

Matthew 5:45, (NIV) helps us to understand that "He causes His sun to rise on the evil and the good and sends rain on the righteous and the unrighteous."

No matter who we are or where we live,
There will always be rain and sun.
Be expectant for the promises of God,
And for the rainbow that will come!

Color color everywhere! I think that is why I love Disney Land so much because it is alive with vibrant color that is everywhere. I live very close to a famous farming area called the Skagit Valley in Washington State. It is famous for growing tulips. Their bulbs are shipped all over the world. Once a year, people come from everywhere to see the fields when these flowers are in bloom. The colors are beyond any word you can describe. The rows and rows of color that are so bright and beautiful, they are bringing forth life. To me it radiates the heart of the Heavenly Father for color brings joy and creates movement. Now we can undoubtedly understand why the

Emerald City is radiating with such an uplifting energizing vitality as we step through the doors. It is full of praise.

In the Bible, the tribe of Judah is the one that leads in worship. If you remember the color emerald is on their flag, and the color emerald is around the Throne of God. Worshipping at the Throne of God should always be our greatest desire; it should always be our focus. Live in a place of praise!

Psalm 22:3, (KJV) "But Thou art holy, O thou that inhabits the praises of Israel."

2 Chronicles 20:21-22 speaks about Jehoshaphat appointing men to sing to the Lord of His splendor and holiness and to give thanks that His love endures forever. As they began to sing and praise the Lord, God ambushed and destroyed the enemy!

This is where Our Father God resides; He lives in the midst of our Praise. It is our worship and praise that keeps our hearts in tune to heaven. I have heard people testify that when they have seen glimpses of heaven that the colors are so vibrant that they cannot describe them and that the flowers dance. I can believe it because no matter how magnificent our experience is here on earth with nature and His creation, I know that heaven has not been damaged by sin and that the very essence and presence of God is its life and light. Nothing of our earthly imagination can even touch what heaven is like; so to me dancing flowers seem very probable and quite normal. Just like this new land Dorothy is in, with its magnificent beauty and sound, she could have never imagined it if she had not experienced it!

Dorothy and her companions were all polished up, rested and happy and having such a grand ole time. This is indeed the land of strength power and courage.

EEEKKK! SURRENDER!

Are you kidding me? Here we go again! Right in the middle of the most beautiful blue sky, in the middle of the most restful pampering fun time, the enemy has shown up.

The enemy shows up

SURRENDER DOROTHY is written with the black fumes of her flying broom high in the sky. It is written so everyone can see, so no one can miss the intensions of the Evil One. The enemy is ejecting ugliness and demanding that the people in the Emerald City give Dorothy over to her! The enemy seems to feel like she has the power and authority to demand this. There is a moment where overwhelming fear grips all of the people in the whole city, but the guard comes forth with a powerful word and brings peace; he calms the crowd. Well, that didn't go very far. Her Evilness traveled a long way to make more threats, which diminished into thin air and were shut down very quickly. Oh well, that was an anticlimactic affair!

Isn't that just like the enemy of our soul though? When we are having a really good time, he seems to show up out of the blue to try and ruin everything. He arrives to steal our peace and as the old saying goes, to ruffle our feathers. Then, as Jesus steps forth and speaks words of reassurance, "Be not afraid," He calms the storm. We have mentioned before, that He shares with us in the word to be anxious for nothing, that His peace will guard our hearts and minds, and that He has overcome the world and so can we. So, when the enemy flies in with accusations screaming that we must surrender the places of our lives where we have gained peace and joy, and he is spouting ugly, black smoke and putting on a good show, remember it is only smoke. Allow the Father to speak to your heart, let Him wrap you in His feathers, let Him shut down the fear that will want to grip you and take control. The enemy bows to us; we do not bow to him, by the almighty power and authority of the Red Shoes. The enemy has no more authority to abuse.

Scriptures to meditate
Ephesians 2:13
Hebrews 9:14 and 13:12
Matthew 26:28
Revelation 12:11

Pray with me
Father, I am so grateful for the blood of Jesus! Thank you for the lamb that was slain. Lord, I thank you that the blood of Jesus opens many doors that would otherwise be closed to me. Father, I am thankful that once we choose to enter into your presence, we are blessed beyond anything we could ever possibly imagine. Thank you, Father, for opening doors of destiny to my legacy. I thank you that you are concerned not only for me in the now but for eternity. I thank you that your promise is that the generation of the upright will be blessed. Thank you for the place of wisdom that, as we abide in you, will be our inheritance. Forgive me, Father, for the times that I have not stayed in a place of worship or have been timid to come to your throne when your son paid the ultimate price, so that I could come boldly. I praise you and worship you now for all things. Amen.

Declaration

I declare that doors will open for me by the mighty hand of God. I declare that when I abide in Christ and I speak to my mountains, mountains will move. I declare that the power of the living God lives in me and I change the atmosphere wherever I walk!

Bibliography

1. *The Wizard of OZ.* 1939.

2. **Fleming, Victor.** *The Wizard of OZ.* MGM, 1939.

3. *https://nameberry.com/search?q=meaning+of+Oz.* [Online]

4. **Nemitz/Facebook, Colors by Carol.** [Online]

5. www.sheknows.com. [Online]

6. http://www.netstate.com/states/intro/ks_intro.htm. [Online]

22

GREAT MERCY

Time to see the wise man

We are positive that he will have the answers and will know what to do. His reputation of knowledge goes before him and speaks so highly of his wisdom. All four comrades step up and ask to be presented and brought into his presence. The guard immediately marches off to announce their request.

If I were king

Their hearts leaped with joy! We've done it! We've made it! They begin to dance and sing. Elated, their steps have a special zing. This sends their emotions into an expression of euphoric delight, oh, what a marvelous sight! Knowing soon they will see the man that will show them the way, they are celebrating for this is the day!

In their rejoicing, they crown Lion, roll out a royal carpet and then place a regal robe upon his shoulders. The words break forth that He is the king! So much excitement in the air, they continue to sing!

That is exactly who he was created to be. Full of courage and strength; he was born to rule. Lion declares the truth of who he is. He has struggled in the past with anxieties and fears and to be all he was meant to be, but, from deep down inside comes the sound of a roar as his heart begins to soar—I am king of the forest! He declares who he is! He is meant to reign in the darkness, and for others to step aside when he steps up. His friends are celebrating and declaring what will be. This impressive beast of courage has not yet prevailed, but he will, he will! There will soon be a time that he will not cower, shiver, shake or hold his tail.

In Romans 4:17, the scripture speaks about believing and bringing into existence what you cannot yet see. In order to believe the promises of God, we must agree and speak them. If we do not, we will stay in a place of pain, disappointment and discouragement. The Heavenly Father told Abraham, "I have made you the father of many nations." This came true because Abraham trusted the voice of God. He couldn't see it in the natural, but by faith, he packed his bags, left home, stepped out and believed.

Call it out! Always speak the truth about exactly who Jesus says you are. If we hide and keep the lies of the enemy in darkness, we empower him to keep us bound by his sound! Our voice and our sound is then silenced. The door of torment remains open, and we will continue to feel that we are not a lion but a mouse. The Father has created within us marvelous plans that are direct from heaven above. We may not see them yet, but we must believe because of

His great love. There is a very old saying, "Cut a Rug," meaning dance dance dance, dance on the head of the enemy and disintegrate his schemes! Raise a mighty note of who we are that will shatter the boundaries and the lock that keeps us restrained, for you are a daughter or son of the King. We were created to be just like Lion that walked with Dorothy on this great journey. Raise your voice, shout out a sonic boom of life-giving words powered by the Red Shoes, and the chains of active lies will be broken. Let your words resonate and thunder. Be a human trumpet that cuts through the air, awakens and shifts everything within your body, soul and spirit. Let God run to you and place His royal robe upon your shoulders and His ring upon your hand. With our rainbow glasses let us see ourselves through the colors of God. You are a Lion; you are not a mouse!

Hope through the rainbow glasses

As I write this now, I just received a message from a friend sharing that a young man we have known has taken his life. Dear God, I weep, help us to know you and to encounter you as the living water and hope. The enemy has silenced this young man's voice and his sound. God had a plan, He had a purpose, He had a dream and He had an answer for whatever this young man needed or faced. My heart grieves for the unfulfilled promises and the amazing life that was cut too short. God had a table spread; it was prepared just for him, but he did not see through the rainbow. His view was dark with the enemy's lies. My heart is gripped with a heartache for the loss of a precious life and how the ripple effect of the pain he succumbed to will now go out. Jesus is the healer, He is our refuge, He is our peace, and He overcame the world in a

243

time of great oppression from the Roman government. Jesus tells us that He overcame the world and so can we. He came and gave His life that we might have life more abundant. (John 10:10)

Every morning stand tall, put on your crown and regal robe, speak who you are, take the hand of the Father and be a light to those around. Encourage and inspire. You have the answer; you have the power of the Red Shoes, the blood of Jesus that overcomes, always always, always remember that we are daughters and we are sons! Speak up and speak out, rigorously give a shout!

Revelation 12:11, (NIV) "They triumphed over him by the blood of the lamb and by the word of their testimony ..."

We can make a difference

I encourage you right now to stop and dance! Stand up and act! Release a sound of worship and praise into the atmosphere. Shift the very air around you and in you to the vibrancy and the frequency of the colors Of God! Be a rainbow. Be His presence.

Many around you need to see your rainbow. I believe that as Gods colors illuminate through us, we will change hearts and lives and give hope. Believe! Step out like Abraham did, pack every emotional bag you have, every pain and every trauma, every disappointment, every hope and every dream, and give it to Jesus, give it all. Walk with Him and radiate His colors. Believe and change the world!

You are denied

This cannot be happening! The guard comes back and tells Dorothy and her friends that there is no entrance—you are unable see the wise man. Immediately, as quickly as there was a high with singing and rejoicing, there was a drastic falling down a dark hole emotional low. What a letdown. The words ring out, *YOU CANNOT ENTER!* Don't tell me that words are not powerful!

Dorothy's immediate reaction is a deep heartsick cry of pain coming up from her inner most being. She melts to the ground. She cries out and names all of her regrets. If only I had not run away, I would be with my family. Her heart yearns intensely to be back home. She is not thinking about the reasons why she ran away in the first place right now. Somehow, in this moment, the reasons don't even seem very important—they don't even come to her mind. What will she do now? Her friends gather around her with comfort and a sheltering love, the companions make a statement that they will get her in to see the wise man somehow. Their love and caring for her is precious. They have been through a lot together and this little hiccup in their plans is not going to deter them from helping Dorothy. There will be a way; that's all I have to say!

Promises

Philippians 2:13, (NIV) "… for it is God who works in you to will and to act in order to fulfill His good purpose."

Romans 8:28, (NIV) "And we know all things work together for good to them that love God, to them who are the called according to His purpose."

Pull out the glasses

Let us stop for just a moment and reach into the memory banks of our mind and recall the life-changing story of a man named Peter. He ran away also and denied His close friend Jesus when

245

Jesus needed him the most and was at a place in His life where He needed his friends more than ever. He was alone, He was in danger, and He was in pain. But Peter was afraid and ran, not to Jesus but away from Him. Even though he loved him dearly, Peter did not have the strength or courage in an extreme situation to stand strong. Not once but three times he denied knowing Him. We can all relate to the times in our lives when we have run away instead of standing. Dorothy is sitting right in the middle of extreme regret; she is lamenting the choice of leaving instead of facing the day. If you recall in the scripture, Peter then went outside and wept bitterly for turning away. (John 18:13-27)

In our own lives we find that it is not unusual when we have not had enough courage or strength to face a situation. Regret, whether it be then or later has always come back to torment and haunt us. So Dorothy's meltdown is quite believable.

The guard looks on with empathy as Dorothy's tears begin flow, then his own heart is moved with mercy. Tears of compassion begin to drop to the ground. It is mercy that will open this next door for Dorothy.

God collects our tears in a bottle (Psalm 56:8). He sees every tear and has feelings of concern for everyone; whether it is from joy or pain. Dorothy is in a very fragile emotional state. She is very aware that if something does not change, her dream of going home may never become a reality. As lovely and as fun as this new land is, she is missing her family, if only they were here with her. Dorothy has been learning from this unprecedented escapade that nothing can take the place of home. Home is where her heart is. It has taken this awesome journey down this yellow brick road with these awesome extraordinary friends to bring her to a place of revelation, finally comprehending what is really important in life. She is seeing everything through a new pair of glasses. Hmm ... I wonder what glasses those are?

Her tears have been seen, a heart is turning, and they are now activating Mercy.

Once again we want to remember this scripture in Lamentations.

Lamentations 3:22-23, (ESV) "The steadfast love of the Lord never ceases; His mercies never come to an end; they are new every morning. Great is Thy Faithfulness."

Psalm 56:8, (NKJV) "You number my wanderings; put my tears into your bottle; Are they not in your book?"

Psalm 57:1-3, (KJV) "Be merciful unto me, O God, be merciful unto me: For my soul trusteth in thee; Yea in the shadow of thy wings will I make my refuge, until the calamities are overpass. I will cry unto God Most High, unto God who performeth all things for me. He shall send from heaven and save me from the reproach of him that would swallow me up. God shall send forth His mercy and His truth."

What a masterpiece this is, a painted picture with perfect strokes for our minds eye to see, showing off the mercy of God and just how much our tears move Him. Move Him to open doors when it seems that nothing else will. Our journey in life is full of many different experiences and situations, but just as the scripture reminds us, His love never ceases, and His mercy and faithfulness is new every morning. So no matter what comes our way, no matter our reactions or unwise decisions, God's love and mercy can overcome it all. It will get us through, it will cross us over to the other side, and He will make things brand new! He is absolutely everything we need. The Father's compassion and love for his children run deeper and wider than the ocean, and Higher than any mountain. Dorothy looks up; she receives mercy and the doors open.

History says that the words to the hymn "The Love of God" were written on a wall in an insane asylum. The words proclaim the amazing mercy, grace and love of God.

"Could we with ink the ocean fill and were the skies of parchment made; Were every stalk on earth a quill, and every man a scribe by trade. To write the love of God above would drain the ocean dry, nor could the scroll contain the whole though stretched from sky to sky."

Dorothy was just handed the beautifully wrapped gift of mercy through love.

Peter receives mercy

Now, let us go back to Peter, the friend of Jesus that left him when He needed him the most. After His death and resurrection, Jesus sought out Peter. I love that! Jesus went looking for him. Jesus extended him great mercy, grace, love and words of encouragement. Jesus did not bring up the past but thrust him into his destiny of being one of the most amazing men in scripture. This man that denied Christ because of overpowering fear was martyred for his faith. History tells us that Peter asked to be crucified upside down because he did not feel worthy to be crucified as Christ. Wow! All because Jesus knew that Peter's past did not define him or his future. The Savior viewed Peter through rainbow glasses, through the promises and the things yet to be fulfilled. Jesus saw the man he would become. Do we always make the right choice? No. But mercy and grace make the difference all because of the blood of Jesus, praise God for the Red Shoes! I bow my knee and lower my head in reverence.

Enter

The Guard weeps for Dorothy. He sees her heart and her plight and opens the way. Mercy has prevailed and his face has a grin. Up they jump with such gratitude and forward they step into the great Hall of Fame. Again, a suddenly has shifted the mood; nothing will be the same!

Whoa! This is nothing like I imagined as they step into the long corridor looming ahead. Creepy is the word that enters my mind as the lengthy hall stretches forth. My emotions did a bit of a shudder and my teeth did a bit of a clatter, but they are not turning back for it doesn't matter! Linking arm in arm, they are in this together, it is an unshakable power of unity facing whatever is ahead. Forward and march. Arm in arm, hand in hand; nothing is going to break up this little band, together they will stand!

They dreamed of this day and when it would come, but I'm sure this is not what they envisioned. What a peculiar package has arrived, this dark shadowy passageway that is the entrance to the so-called impressive man of wisdom. Well, let's just see what is ahead and what shall come next; there are absolutely no regrets!

So let us link arms.
With the Father, Son and Holy Ghost,
Let's go; let's face it together!
What fun we will have, it is the most!

They have arrived. They are in the room of this great wise man. Well, that's what they have been told anyway, that he was a great man and that he had the answers for them. I want to share this thought though. This does not look like anything that I anticipated when I was a little girl. His voice begins to boom and bellow! It reverberates loudly! Explosive fire is raging! Lion is shivering and shaking; he is losing his grip with courage as it begins to slip. I understand because I am right there with him! He is pulling and pushing, he wants to turn and tare back down the corridor, definitely pointing AWAY, but his true and faithful friends refuse to let him go! With their hands clinched tight, they hang for dear life!

You want us to do what?

After this long journey and all we have been through, you are asking us to go seek out and find the evil one? I am sure if we just wait a little bit, she will find us. We've spent all this time trying to stay out of her way. This surely cannot be!

This is the requirement: you must bring back her broom. Wow! You've got to be kidding! That would mean facing our fears to the highest degree possible and meeting her on her turf. Dread wells up within them like a balloon being stretched to the max before it suddenly pops. That would mean looking her straight in the face, eyeball to eyeball. Oh My Gosh! I was shivering in my own boots along with the clan. I couldn't believe what I was hearing either. It seemed way beyond anything that should be asked, I didn't know if I would have been up for the task!

Now without question, they do absolutely understand that it will be impossible to get the broom from the Evil One without destroying her. To me this is beginning to sound like the showdown at Okay Corral back in the old West. So, right now is a decisive and defining moment in their lives for sure, what do you think their answer will be?

This mission, this assignment is going to change their fate forever. It will realign their thoughts and establish a new view of themselves and how they look at evil. It is too late to back out now; they are going all the way! Somehow they will complete this task, they shall be victorious I pray!

Right now I can hear the music running through my thoughts to an old television show called Mission Impossible that seems quite appropriate, and the words, "If you should choose to accept this mission…"

Here we go, we press on, we press forward, and we pick up the glove and accept the challenge. We embrace The Great Assignment, a mission that seems impossible!

Scriptures to meditate
Ephesians 2:4-5
1 Peter 1:3
Hebrews 4:16
Psalm 145:9 and 86:5
Titus 3:5

Pray with me
Father, I thank you for your precious mercy that you bestow on me each day. Lord, I praise you for your compassion and grace. May praise always be on my lips! Father, you abound in love and I thank you that it continually flows. You cover me as I feel your abundant and deep affection towards me. Abba, I am so grateful

that you never give up on me. Thank you for constantly pursuing my love towards you. Lord, I thank you that you see my tears and your heart is for me. May I always bless your name and give you my highest praise for your continued mercy in my life. Amen

Declaration

I declare that I am a mighty child of God. I declare that I will stand and be strong by the grace of my Father. I declare that I will praise your name forever. I declare that my heavenly Father believes in me and I will not walk in fear and brokenness, but in the power of His might.

23

THE AMAZING ASSIGNMENT

One, Two, Three,
Here we go,
Can you see?

It is dark,
And it is scary,
I see the shadows,
Let us be wary.

It is the unknown.
So let's grab arms,
We can do this,
Do not be alarmed!

Walk straight ahead,
With weapons in hand,
Do not be distracted,
Together we stand!

Victory is ours,
The enemy will go down,
We will reach our goal,
We will release our sound,
Until the enemy is bound!

Y ou can definitely see that I am passionate about the sound that God has created with in us. God's power was carried on the wings of sound as He created the universe and all living things. We are His children and are made in His image (Genesis 1:27). The Father desires for us to speak up and speak out. The scripture instructs us to speak to the mountain and to believe, and then it will be removed. Right now, the major mountain that Dorothy and her friends face is fear. Uneasiness is racing through their veins as they move towards the castle. Tormenting fear again raises its ugly head; it seems to be the common thread. It weaves itself in and out and shows up repeatedly. Fear seems to be the glue that keeps Dorothy bound, and I see that this bond must be broken. What gives it the right to ooze and squeeze through the cracks and torment her life?

Just like Dorothy, when we think fear has been totally been conquered, it shows up in the most unexpected place. It may not be huge, but its tentacles have slipped through the smallest crevice, wrapped themselves around our feet, pulled, tripped us up, and slammed us face first down to the ground.

The words that spring forth now will make the difference in how this endeavor plays out. Do we speak to the mountain or do we run and hide? What will Dorothy's choice be?

Mark 11:23, (NIV) "Truly I say to you, whosoever says to this mountain, be taken up and cast into the sea, and does not doubt in his heart, but believes that what he says is going to happen, it will be granted him."

Jeremiah 32:27, (KJV) "I am the Lord, the God of all mankind. Is anything too hard for me?"

Ephesians 4:29, (ESV) "Let no corrupting talk come out of your mouths, but only such as is good for building up, as fits the occasion, that it may give grace to those that hear."

Psalm 119: 105, (ESV) "Your word is a lamp unto my feet and a light unto my path."

PRAYER: Father, let my words be your words because your word lights the way and clears the path. Your word moving on the wings of my sound, united with my faith, by the power of the Holy Spirit will move any mountain. Speak through me!

Let's go!

We are on our way! The challenge is accepted; Dorothy, Scarecrow, Tin man, and Lion head for the open road with darkness all around, as they shiver from tortuous thoughts that abound. But they continue to march forward I know they will succeed! I love their weapons of warfare. The big net and the bug sprayer are over the top. I am not quite sure what they intend to catch with that net, but I do know that it will be crazy awesome. After all, it's not like they're going after a giant butterfly. The bug sprayer is ginormous! It looks like we sure could choke and gag the enemy with that! Let's spray a little Holy Spirit in his face and watch him run for his life. Then, they have a gun and a huge wrench that they're packing, I'm not quite sure what the thinking is behind the wrench either but I'm sure it was a good thought. As we recall, it turns out that these tools were very ineffective for what was needed to take down the evil depraved powers that lay ahead.

Rainbow glasses

Taking out the enemy and destroying his plans is such an interesting experience. It involves, the power of God and I will say that again, the power of God. It will take strength in God, perseverance, focus, and weapons that you cannot see. In fact, the scripture tells us that we don't fight against flesh and blood but actually we wrestle against principalities, against powers, against the rulers of darkness of this world, and against spiritual wickedness in high places.

Ephesians 6:12, (KJV) "It is in the next verse, number 13 that states to take unto ourselves the whole armor of God. His armor will defeat the enemy, not ours."

1 Samuel 17:45-46, 48, (NIV) "David said to the Philistine, 'You come against me with sword and spear and javelin, but I come against you in the name of the Lord Almighty the God of the armies of Israel, whom you have defied. This day God will deliver you into my hands, and I'll strike you down and cut off your head.'"

As the Philistine moved closer to attack him, David ran quickly toward the battle line to meet him. Goliath had continuously and profusely shouted threats of foreboding intimidation into the atmosphere for 40 days, twice a day, that God's people could not shake off, but there came a time when it was one day too many. David prepared himself and addressed the threats. It was at this juncture that he ran to the battle line under the power of the Almighty God. His throw was confident and sure, the enemy crashed like a fallen tree to the ground, David then cut off his head with the giant's sword and the defeat was sound!

Zechariah 4:6, (KJV) "Not by might nor by power, but by my Spirit, says the Lord of Hosts."

We can do nothing in our own strength!

There is another event in the scripture that I would like to review concerning the seven sons of Sceva, a High Priest. If you read the account in Acts 19:11-20, the story shares that God was doing amazing miracles through Paul. Numerous people were being healed of sickness; disease and evil spirits came out of many. The times then were no different than today, so the sons of Sceva that were Jewish exorcists wanted to jump on the bandwagon and they decided to invoke the name of Jesus over someone that had evil spirits, saying, "I adjure you in the name of Jesus whom Paul proclaims." But the evil spirit answered them and said, "Jesus I know, and Paul I recognize, but who are you? And then the man in whom the evil spirit was in, leaped on them and mastered all of them, so they fled out of the house naked and wounded. Basically, he beat them up! This teaches us through a very convincing warning that only the power of God reigns over evil. It is the blood of His son and the authority of knowing Him personally that takes away the rights of Satan and all of his helpers. We never come against the master of darkness on our own. These seven men did not know Jesus personally. They had only heard of the great works that Paul was doing through the name of Jesus and decided it was something they would like to try. It sounded good, but I will guarantee the end product was not so enjoyable. Never go out on your own. Jesus, His name and His blood are the only armor that protects and is the only authority. So, I say once again, destroying the plans of the enemy takes the power of God! The authority of the marvelous Red Shoes!

Nope, we can't see any of these things with our natural eye that we actually fight against or fight with, but the enemy would like us to think that we do. He deceives us with the lie that we are fighting against friends, family or our neighbors. He creates chaos by having people look at color or race or what has been said or done. If we would just look up, encounter the Father's heart and perceive what He sees, anger and pain would melt away like ice cream on a hot summer day. We would know the truth, and the truth would set us free. There would be no more war, whether it is in our own hearts, homes, our cities, our churches, and our nation or across the globe. The Prince of Peace would reign; we must see through our spirit man, not through the natural, in order to understand.

Just like Dorothy and her colleagues, let's go after the real culprit! The real enemy! Let's strip the lies that create his disguise.

So then, what is the real assignment?

Number one we step up and then we step out. Dorothy and the troupe are way beyond their comfort zone, but just like David, the challenge has been made so they decide to meet the enemy on their own terms. Number two; we must take back the land that the enemy has stolen. Has he stolen your peace, your family, your health, your joy, or your finances? Where has he come in, made his bed, set up house in your life arrogantly and taken over? Do you remember when we talked about Miss Gulch clear back in the beginning chapters and how she had come to the farm with a paper in her hand, and that paper had given her the right to take Toto? Those are the areas that we need to take care of in our lives. That is the great assignment! Go! Face the enemy and take the broom. Face the things within your heart that give the enemy a right and a landing strip to come and to torment you. Pray and seek God's face, seek His counsel, receive wisdom from the courts of heaven by the authority and power of the Red Shoes, step up, step out and step on the enemy. We can all relate to the voice of the evil one that comes to lie, torment and destroy, but freedom is what Jesus paid for so sound the charge, go after it with a vengeance, do not allow the enemy to stay at large. If we are going to step into the ring for a fight, let's fight and take our freedom, let it be our resolve, Evil shall be vehemently beaten!

This is the great assignment !

Luke 10:19, (NIV) "I have given you authority to trample on snakes and scorpions and to overcome all the power of the enemy; nothing will harm you."

Take your authority over the enemy where he has invaded our lives. Rip up every verbal contract that we knowingly and unknowingly have made with the kingdom of darkness. You ask, and what would that be? Any and all repeated statements that you have made that do not agree with the word of God that have created your belief system. Any and all-negative feelings that are lies that want to crush your spirit. Let the Holy Spirit that leads and guides show you where the enemy has a foothold, and then break them off through the power of the blood of Jesus Christ through prayer.

A small, simple prayer:

Father God, I come to you now and I ask you to show me where I have made agreements and believed lies. I repent and choose to turn to you and your truth. Please open my ears to be able to hear the words of the enemy that I have spoken over myself, others and situations. I come now to the throne of mercy and grace and I repent for speaking and agreeing with the lie of _____. I now break the lie of _____ off of my heart, my mind and life and I choose to come out of agreement with this lie of _____ through the power of the blood of Jesus Christ. I now choose to covenant with you that I will speak the truth of the word of God concerning this untruth that has operated in my life.

Then, begin to rejoice, be thankful and praise God! Worship His mighty name!

Repent for each untruth that the Father brings to your mind and begin the road back to freedom one prayer at a time. You must now speak over yourself and fill yourself with the truth of the word of God concerning each individual lie. At this point, you are beginning to dissolve the emotional chains that have kept you bound for many years, months or days. Even if the bondage has been only for a few moments, it is too long! Break the chain now until only freedom remains!

If you can visualize someone that has had chains on them for a long time, when they are taken off there is usually a place on the skin where there is an open sore. The chains are gone but there is a painful reminder of what once was. This can be the same emotionally. This is why we continue to bathe ourselves in the healing balm of the word of God and forgive over an area where the chains once rubbed. Eventually, there is no more pain, and through the continual emersion in the spirit with the word, only a forgotten scar remains and a whole heart we will regain.

Psalm 139: 23, (KJV) "Search me, O God, and know my heart; Try me and know my anxious thoughts."

He will shine His light on the evil that is hidden. He desires to eradicate guilt, shame, and all of your fears. Exterminate the tormentors wherever they may lurk. Wear those Red Shoes proud; allow the power of the blood to conquer the kingdom of darkness and bring victory to you, your family and legacy. Let your shoes change history. As for my house, we will serve the Lord!

Joshua 24:15, (NIV) "But if you refuse to serve the LORD, then choose today whom you will serve. Would you prefer to serve the gods your ancestors served beyond the Euphrates? Or will it be the gods of the Amorites in whose land you now live? But as for me and my family, we will serve the Lord."

Micah 4:5, (KJV) "Though all the people walk each in the name of his god, as for us, we will walk in the name of the Lord our God forever and ever."

Today we are making decisions. Being free and staying free takes action. If you notice with Joshua, it is a choice to stand, and with Micah, they choose to walk. I encourage you this day to take a stand, stake a flag in the ground, and fight for your freedom! Be free! Choose this day who you will serve. Look up and listen to the Father's voice. It's a choice!

Another dark, scary forest

Dorothy and her crew look to each other for help, encouragement, strength and might. When one wants to turn and run, another will grab on and hold tight, they all continue to stay away from fright! The forest is dark, and it is scary, and yes, it has a lot of unnerving sounds. The sign does say, "If I were you, I would turn around." But, they must continue on, keeping their eyes on the prize, they have chosen not to leave town.

Philippians 3:13, (NIV) "Brothers and sisters, I do not consider myself yet to have taken hold of it. But one thing I do: Forgetting what is behind and straining toward what is ahead."

Now look, Her Evilness is not just sitting around twiddling her thumbs you know, or just waiting for them to come and take her broom, the scepter of her authority. Like an eagle up high, she is watching and waiting, very aware. Evil ponders, then steps up to the plate in the dark, and she hits the ball out of the park! In an instant, a demanding command screeches forth from her lips to her flying squadron of tormentors. "Bring me that girl and her powerful Red Shoes!" The monkey's wings begin to flap in the wind, in obedience they are off. With the enemy's focus on the shoes, she underestimates the power, strength and courage that reside with Dorothy's traveling friends. This will eventually lead to her demise. But, in the meantime, I was quite distressed watching the sky become gloomy with a shadowy movement from the monkeys on assignment. Please God, I prayed, please protect Dorothy and her friends. Place your arms around them; let your shield of love ascend.

Trouble is on the way

Look up to the sky! Oh no! Horror is about to arrive, and it's looking for a place to land. The taunting oppressive monkeys dive in for the kill with great skill, they are thrilled. They begin to harass and wreak havoc on the three companions. Dorothy and the crew respond in fear. They turn, run and scatter as they release screams of terror! My question is this, I wonder what would have happened if they had come together and united as one? Maybe they could have formed a mighty shield of protection? Now it's just a thought, but unfortunately, the dangerous, chaotic panic prevailed, and their immediate plans were derailed! The flying monkeys (tormentors) chase Dorothy down, swoop her up in their arms, grab Toto and they are in flight once again.

Strict orders have been given; do not harm Dorothy and especially do not let any harm come to those Red Shoes, for isn't that what this is all about, those beautiful, amazing extraordinarily powerful Red Shoes!

Dorothy screams, hollers, and kicks, trying to wiggle herself loose as she is carried through the air, but to no avail, the tormentors will complete the mission. She is delivered like a FedEx package right to the door. Mercy mixed with grace and peace will now be her only companion.

The wickedness that lives within this castle believes that there can be no escape. I'm watching evil revel in the power surge that is produced from the enemy's warped ego. With this, her confidence hits an ultimate high. She now reflects on her past triumphant schemes that have won many great victories, but I will state this emphatically that this battle will not be any ordinary everyday battle! This turf war is about to shift the powers that be, for this is no ordinary prisoner, and these are no ordinary shoes!

As a child, I could feel my heart beating as fast as the music was playing. There seemed no way out of this difficulty, what was going to happen now? Before it had been about closed doors, but this situation was different, this was about having been snatched up and placed behind enormous walls. Dorothy was an actual prisoner now. The castle in the distance seemed so black and ominous, strong and authoritative. When you're little, it's one of those cover your head with a blanket moments and let me know when it is over! My young mind just knew this was such an evil kingdom. Most heavy thick darkness does seem overpowering, but isn't that exactly what the enemy of our soul wants us think? He bluffs his way in with his shadowy lies until the light becomes dimmer and dimmer then the gloom covers and controls our every thought. We then believe a lie and accept that he is larger and more powerful than the one true God, the God that framed the universe and holds it all together.

Hebrews 11:3, (KJV) "Through faith we understand that the worlds were framed by the word of God, so that things which are seen were not made of things which do appear."

We even forget that God created the enemy himself. God gave a choice to Satan when he lived in heaven, whom will you serve? Sadly, he puffed himself up, thought himself greater and chose poorly. Let us choose wisely.

Tears well up in my eyes. How could Dorothy ever escape from this fortress that I was viewing? I watched as the castle became larger and larger. It became more and more menacing the closer we approached. I went by what my eyes could see and that is exactly what I believed: she will never ever be free!

Scriptures to meditate
Ephesians 6:11-18
1 Corinthians 15:57
1 John 4:4
1 Peter 5:8-9
James 4:7
Romans 8:37

Pray with me

Lord God, I thank you that you have equipped me with the ability to fight the enemy on my terms because you have given me weapons to combat the forces of evil. Help me to not be caught unaware of his tactics. Help me to be alert to his sly ways. Help me to be prepared like David and run toward my enemy with the power of your might and face him without fear. Lord, I desire to know you as the mighty God of Israel and the Lord of Hosts. I desire to know you like I have never known you before. Let me see what you see, help me not to fight battles that are not mine to fight. Help me to see and call the enemy's bluff when he rails lies of fear against me. Give me courage to walk through the darkness when it comes, knowing that you are there and will always be there. Reveal the deceit that I have believed that plunders my strength, so I might repent and walk free. Amen.

Declaration

I declare that I am a child of the King. I declare that I have the authority through the power of Jesus Christ and His blood to tread over all of the power of the enemy. I declare that the Lord will cause my enemies who rise up against me to be defeated before me. I declare that I will not walk in fear for the Lord God fights for me.

24

THE MIGHTY FORTRESS

Oh My Gosh! Look at poor Scarecrow!

Now we might be thinking as we look at Scarecrow, that this could very well be the end. He is upside down, sideways, shredded and torn. Is it possible that the time has come when finally this adventure will take a left turn off the edge of the earth with no hope of return? Maybe this is it, a down for the last count moment? Isn't that what it looks like with his body scattered everywhere? This brought tears to my eyes once again. He was scattered and my heart was shattered. Haven't you ever felt like things could never be the same? Even Dorothy was gone now. She has been carried off and imprisoned by an evil diabolical essence of black heartedness. What's going to happen next?

But, just when we think hope has been extinguished like a flame of a match with a gallon of water, we are going to put on our rainbow glasses and take a look at this situation in a colorful way. We are going back to the filing cabinet of our memory banks and pull out the file that states that Scarecrow represents the mind of Christ.

Yep, Scarecrow is on the ground. He is torn apart, tossed and disheveled, and yes, as you can see the stuffing has been kicked out of him! His body is dismantled, and he cannot move without help, wow! But, remember there is always hope! That actually sounds very familiar to me because there are times in my life, when I have felt exactly like that. How about you? I've been scattered from the emotional stuffing being kicked out of me by a sucker punch right to the gut by life that I didn't see coming. It takes the breath right out of you and pins you to the ground, not knowing which way is up or down. In times like these when my world was spinning all around, I was a mess and definitely not at my best, but there is always hope, and His amazing name is Jesus, with Him we are able to cope!

The heart of the Father and Holy Spirit (Tin Man and Lion) were always there for me to direct my path, comfort and help, just like Humpty Dumpty; they put me back together again. Lovingly, the Father has always been ready, willing and able to pick up the broken and cracked pieces when I have fallen off the wall in life, just like Tin Man and Lion are now helping Scarecrow for he was unable to do it alone.

They shook their heads and rolled their eyes as they viewed the mess. Come on, move it, Scarecrow shouted! We are not going to be stressed! His companions wasted no time; they jump and scramble into action. The battle is on, the line has been drawn;

they will rescue Dorothy. Whatever it takes, what a turn of events, they won't be late!

Psalm 34:18, (GNTD) "The Lord is near to those who are discouraged; He saves those who have lost all hope."

Psalm 147:3, (GNTD) "He heals the brokenhearted and bandages their wounds."

1 John 4:10, (GNTD) "That is what love is: it is not that we have loved God, but that He loved us and sent His son to be the means by which our sins are forgiven."

When you feel your emotions are being tossed in the air like a salad and it feels impossible that you will ever be straight or strong again, remember that hope lives and again I say, His name is Jesus! When I looked up at poor Scarecrow, seeing him scattered and every which way but loose, my thought was, how in the world is he ever going be able to help Dorothy in that kind of condition? I could feel the tears welling up in my eyes. Can you tell I have a gift of mercy? You talk about trauma, but to my amazement, before I knew it, he was stuffed, fluffed and tightly tucked, totally back together again. Sharp as a pointy pencil and determined to face the immense evil that has captured the one he loves. Wow! He is now ready to write a bright new ending to the next chapter on this adventurous road.

Scarecrow seems to be the leader of the pack, as he gives the commands! We absolutely cannot go anywhere without him, and that is exactly what it is like for us, the mind of Christ must lead the way, our thoughts must be steadfast and unmovable, totally and completely established in the word of God.

Psalm 18:2: "The Lord is my rock and my foundation …"

I have such good memories with my dad when I was young. Often I refer to my dad as my rock; he was the one that always pointed me to Jesus, the ultimate rock. He would continually tell me, "Debbie, the word of God is your only truth and if it is not in the word, you don't believe it or follow after it."

Fortunately, those words have been the foundation for my whole life, and his legacy continues to this day, as I have shared those words with my children and grandchildren.

The wise and foolish builder

Matthew 7:24-27, (NIV) "Therefore, everyone who hears those words of mine and puts them into practice is like a wise man who built his house on the rock."

These scriptures describe two men, one wise and one foolish. The foolish man built his house on the sand, but the wise man built his house on a rock. When the storm came, and the winds blew and the rain fell, the sand shifted, and the foolish man's house fell apart and was destroyed. The wise man's house that was built on the rock stood firm, once again teaching us that our lives, emotions, and experiences, must be built on the rock. We must have a firm foundation so when the storms of life come, and they will come, we will then be able to stand, stay strong, go forward and live life with a capital L! It doesn't mean that we don't experience emotions; it means that we can withstand the storm and come out on top, sturdy on the rock, *The Rock Of Ages*.

Psalms 18:1-19, (NIV) "I will love you, Oh Lord, My Strength. The Lord is my rock, my fortress and my deliverer; my God, my strength, in whom I will trust; My shield and the horn of my salvation, my stronghold."

I call upon the Lord who is worthy to be praised so shall I be saved from my enemies.

Please go to the scripture and continue to read this passage that David wrote on the day that God delivered him from his enemies and the hand of King Saul.

Just then, Dorothy's friends find themselves perplexed. Which way do we go? They hear a sound! It is a marvelous sound—it is the sound of Toto. Remember, Toto means priest and Jesus is our high priest, Jesus always meets us right where we are at. Toto has come to shine and lead the way.

Psalm 119:105 (KJV) "Thy Word is a lamp unto my feet and a light unto my path."

Let us take a quick look and see what was going on in the house of evil where Dorothy has been dragged, for this miracle of Toto to suddenly appear.

The stronghold

Dorothy is experiencing great overwhelming fears from the scare tactics that have been concocted by the enemy and directed at her and Toto's lives. The Evil One directs her minions to take away Dorothy's little dog and drown him. Poor Dorothy is absolutely beside herself, but evil is pleased. She feels quite empowered knowing that she has captured and entangled Dorothy in an emotional stronghold, believing that she is trapped and can do absolutely nothing about it, believing that she is defenseless, and that her death is quickly approaching!

Dorothy feels that her helpers are far far away. She has lost any and all hope of any freedom or protection with being trapped in the castle, this fortress of great strength and sadly she *still* has no hint of the power that lies within her Red Shoes.

Dorothy's emotions are ravaged by this nightmare. They swing completely out of control. They gain the best of her and the thought of losing Toto is too much. She buckles under the pressure! With heartbreaking tears and anguish, Dorothy relinquishes to the threats of evil.

Take the shoes! You can have them, please, just let my dog live!

The enemy cackles with glee, she is thrilled. Reaching for the shoes though she suddenly receives an extreme reality check. To her great surprise the authority attached to the shoes reaches out with a severe, harsh and electrifying instant warning! The shoes let her know who is boss; they strike her hands, and instantly there is the smell of smoke and a substantial singe! Evil is stopped, quickly and abruptly. Authority is established, no access! Her Wickedness begins to rant and rave as she realizes that her gnarly wretched hands have no power to take what is not hers, not on this day, not in this hour, not *EVER*!

Yes, and Amen! I began to dance and sing as a child. This is glorious. The wicked ole Evil One loses this battle, and she is put in her place. I was so happy when it was revealed she had no power to take the shoes.

It's the blood of Jesus applied to our lives that stops the enemy in his tracks. He has no right to take our salvation and no power to do so. When we walk as a son or daughter, we continue to live under the protection of His blood. At times, our choices may put us in jeopardy, financially, emotionally or physically, but nothing can take our salvation or separate us from the love of God.

In Romans 8:31-39, Paul speaks of many situations in life but none of them can separate us from God's love. He continues to work things for our good, for those that love Him and are called according to his purpose. Yes, we are all called.

Remember in the previous chapter when we talked about the blood and it was placed upon the doorposts to protect the children of Israel. If you remember, death passed over them all. We want to always remember that the blood of Jesus that represents the Red Shoes in this story sanctified us. Sanctification is the act or process of acquiring sanctity, of being made or becoming holy. To sanctify is to literally "set apart for a particular use in a special purpose or work and to make holy or sacred." (Wikipedia)

The blood of Jesus has set us aside and nothing, and I do mean nothing, can cross that line and take away what God has purchased. Now, I also want you to understand that we have the right to choose, we do have the choice to walk away, just as King Saul did in the Old Testament. He chose to disobey and walk out from under God's protection, but it was his choice. I am a believer that Dorothy could have sat down, chose to remove the Red Shoes and given them away, but the Evil One had no right to take them! Always remember that one of God's greatest gifts to us is our free will, our power of choice.

The enemy jumps back as she cried out in pain! When she looked at Dorothy, fear gripped my heart. I observed the piercing evil in her eyes, I could see and feel the hate, oh boy, now she was really angry; she was in quite a state!

Then the enemy recollects; I can only have those shoes if you are dead! My heart fluttered from a shot of terror fueled by adrenalin when she stated, "But how to do it? (2) This must be done

273

delicately!" (2) Gosh, how much she hated Dorothy! How much those shoes meant to this sinister villain. They had made Dorothy her greatest adversary.

Dorothy was in tears, but then there was a suddenly, just when everything was so intense and focused on the enemy, Toto took a chance and he jumped. Whoo hoo! He is free! Off he ran as fast as his little legs would carry him down the stairs with the threat of death intensely chasing close behind. Her Evilness shouted out with fury that he must be caught before he leaves the castle! (2) Toto comes to the edge of the enormous steel ramp as it is pulling up. If it closes, he will be sealed in forever. He looks down and without a thought, leaps to the ground. He is splitting this joint! Dorothy is thrilled, her heart sighs with relief as she watches with tears in her eyes that her precious companion has leaped to safety.

With tears in my own eyes I was right there with her hoping and praying for the miracle, and then it happened, he was free! I wept as my heart rejoiced with hers, I was hoping for the best. Whoo hoo everything had changed, and it only took a moment. What had looked totally despairing and absolutely beyond repair, once again suddenly shifted liked greased lightening! With a total turnaround of events, expectation and anticipation was alive once again, where disheartenment had once been.

Toto is now off; he must find the others for he knows the way back to the stronghold where Dorothy is being held. Miracles do happen! Things that look impossible can shift, like I have declared before there is always hope.

Dorothy was totally in the dark concerning the adventure that is about to transpire. She is enclosed and sealed behind large overwhelming walls that made it impossible for her to see. These walls have stolen any image of deliverance or any prediction of freedom. She is in a place of just being grateful that those she loves are now safe and liberated. She has no more fight, wilted and discouraged within, she will now just sit and wait for the bitter end. But, little does she know that there is a plan, it is revving up into high gear and has already began.

The mighty fortress

What is a fortress? What is a stronghold?

According to the Google dictionary, a fortress is a heavily pro-tected and impenetrable building. It is a fort, castle, citadel, and stronghold. Fortis means strong in Latin and fortress means strong place in French. These are military terms. This is where we get the word fortress, and this is where we find Dorothy, totally enclosed.

What is a stronghold? A stronghold is a place that has been for-tified so as to protect it against attack or a place where a particular cause or belief is strongly defended or upheld.

I want us to take a quick look at Dorothy's circumstances and where she is, so let's make sure we stop, put on our rainbow glasses and take a look at this part of the adventure through the colors of God.

My first question is, "Have you ever felt trapped like Dorothy by a situation which is totally out of control or there is no control?" Have you ever wanted to change a destructive habit or pattern in your life that you were in bondage to? Have you ever wanted to change how you have reacted in certain situations, but because of hurt and pain, shame, anger or fear you were locked up inside of yourself with no ability to be free? You are able to see that the door to freedom is right in front of you. You can also see that you have access to the door, but yet you are bound, imprisoned by your circumstances, emotions, pain or fear. Sometimes, even if you have the key to the door, the feelings of hopelessness, or intimidation have stolen your ability to even try and use it. These questions I have just asked you describe a stronghold. The enemy of our soul is seeking to devour our ability to even fight. God wants us to be free; He gave His son so that we could be.

I feel this is exactly where I find Dorothy; in her case, she is trapped with access to a door that could set her free, but she has no key.

She sits in tears,
Wishing to be free,
Calling for help,
How can this be?

There must be a way,
Someone has to come,
Pushed to the limit,
She feels lost and undone.

Without a miracle,
All will be lost,
For the door is shut,
And great is the lock.

Who has the key?
Can anyone hear?
Her cry is desperate,
The end seems near!

Scriptures to meditate

1 Peter 5:6-7
Matthew 11:28-29
Philippians 4:19
2 Corinthians 5:7 and 12:9

Pray with me

Father, I thank you that no matter what situations I find myself in emotionally, you have a way of escape, you have a path to freedom. Thank you, Father, that no matter the stronghold that seems to have me bound, You have the key to the great doors. Father, I thank you that your word is always alive through Holy Spirit and working on my behalf; all I have to do is use it. Father, I thank you that Jesus always meets me right where I am at and that you sent your son to bring peace to the world that we all might be saved. I thank you that when I feel torn and tossed that You are my hope, that You are my rock. I thank you that you are steadfast and unmovable, and that in you I am secure. Father God, I repent for the times that I have wanted to go my own way and have not chosen your way, which is righteousness and truth. Keep my mind and heart stayed on you and looking up. I place my life in your hands even when walls seem to be all around me, I will still trust you. Amen.

Declaration

I declare again that I am a child of God! I declare that You have a key for every situation. I declare that if I hope in the Lord that I will renew my strength. I declare that I will soar like an eagle and that I will run, and I will not be weary. I declare that I will walk, and I will not faint! (Isaiah 40:31)

Bibliography

1. *The Wizard of OZ.* 1939.
2. **Fleming, Victor.** *The Wizard of OZ.* MGM, 1939.
3. *https://nameberry.com/search?q=meaning+of+Oz.* [Online]
4. **Nemitz/Facebook, Colors by Carol.** [Online]
5. www.sheknows.com. [Online]
6. http://www.netstate.com/states/intro/ks_intro.htm. [Online]

25

HELP IS ON THE WAY!

The Wicked One is totally out of control with her terrible raging anger towards Dorothy! Nasty threats are being spewed with a violent wild rampage; the enemy is in total disbelief that Toto just escaped. Realizing that she has now lost the leverage she needed with Dorothy to release the Red Shoes, you can almost see smoke come from her ears. Her penetrating gaze stares Dorothy down as she picks up an hourglass and turns it over, leaving a tormenting thought of agony behind, knowing Dorothy will watch the falling sand, anxiously foreseeing that the end is near. The last threat pierces the air like lightening, "This is all the time you have left, and then those Red Shoes will be mine!" (2)

Motivation

The immense drive inside of the Evil One to have those shoes is eating her alive; it motivates her every thought. Every moment is consumed with a desire for their enormous power, it rules who she is. This spirit combined with hate feeds and springs up every action that is coming forth to conquer and dominate Dorothy.

If we could possibly grasp the understanding that this is exactly the picture of whom Satan, the enemy of our soul really is. We need to catch a glimpse, really receive and believe the dire need that burns within him to destroy our lives and ultimately take us out. This picture of wickedness that has Dorothy captured with intimidation and has threatened to kill her is a great visual of the spiritual reality we face.

Dorothy is sinking in despair, but help is on the way, be aware!

As Dorothy weeps, as a child, my heart was breaking with her and for her. Tears also streamed down my face as I associated with her pain. Fear was ruling her (and me). What was going to happen? How could she possibly be set free?

Dorothy is calling out to the one she loves, the one she left back home so many days ago. She actually thought she was on the right path and making the right choice when she left home, but now with hindsight, she realizes that home is where she should be, and where there is true safety. How she must have imagined things so differently when she walked out the door with Toto close by her side and her bags clutched in her hand. I believe as these memories flood her mind in the moment, of the little farm in Kansas, she must seem many light years away as she fights this opponent!

You and I both know we can't turn back time and life isn't always fair, and we don't always make the right choice, but even so, God is in the midst reaching out to help. He is a redeemer! He is a good Father. His heart is to walk us through and to shut the door to created chaos and leave it behind. The answer? Call on His name! Listen for His voice, take His hand that is graciously extended and let Him provide you with peace. There is a place that His love overflows, step in, don't walk it alone, for he is Shalom!

Psalm 23: 4-5, (KJV) "Yea, though I walk through the valley of death I will fear no evil; for thou art with me; thy rod and thy staff they comfort me. You prepare a table before me in the presence of my enemies."

Dorothy cries out for help! "Aunt Em, I am so afraid." Help me! "I am locked up in the evil castle! Help me!" (2)

Ultimate intimidation

Suddenly, the enemy appears in the hourglass and mimics Dorothy and her cries for help. She ridicules and mocks the intense desire and expression to be rescued and the cries of her broken heart. Miss Evilness feels nothing for Dorothy as she watches her plead for someone to come to her aid. She actually enjoys watching her suffer Dorothy is dismayed!

It is the same with us, and the enemy of our soul. He plots and schemes to bring us into a place of imprisonment (a stronghold) through our experiences in life. He continually baits us to hang onto the pain of rejection, traumas and fear. He loves to watch us as we continue to roll around emotionally over and over in past circumstances like a swine that wallows in the mud for refreshment on a hot day, not knowing that there is something much better just outside the fence. His plan is to keep us stuck in the pigpen, away from fresh water, never to escape our feelings of despair. His scheme is for us to remain in heartache, suffering, torment and fear for the duration of our days. Satan loves it when we make emotional choices just like Dorothy did. She overreacted in a panic, leaving behind those that loved her and kept her safe. The enemy will go to absolutely any extreme to keep us from turning back towards home; his mission is to seek and to devour, and to strip us of all our power!

1 Peter 5:8 (NIV) "Be alert and of sober mind. Your enemy the devil prowls around like a roaring lion looking for someone to devour."

Help is on the way

As we can see, Dorothy with four walls around her is in need of another miracle. This great story is full of them so let's take a look in on her friends and see what miraculous wonders they have up their sleeves and are about to perform.

Her companions' extreme love for Dorothy is what drives them on; no matter the cost, they are committed. Despite the hazardous dangers that may lurk ahead, they are declaring every threat shall be shred. Exhilaration floods there hearts as they hear the sound of Toto and realize that he has come to save the day he shall prepare the way! The rough terrain as they advance and scale the mountain height is no match for their determination in order to see Dorothy free.

Free from her pain and fears,
Free from the threat of death!
Continuing to move forward,
They can hardly catch their breath!

Toto directs them on the path,
The stronghold is just ahead,
Do not veer to the right or left,
They absolutely have no dread!

There is no return,
Forward they must go
There is no looking back,
They are ready to defeat the nasty foe!

I'm laughing as I watch Tin Man; he is hanging onto Lion's tail as they climb higher and higher to reach the fortress. My thought was I sure hope this doesn't fail. It certainly does look a little shaky and very precarious as they maneuver this mighty mountain. When you're young the darkness that surrounded them on the mountain felt ugly and oppressive like a weighty suffocation. I even questioned how they could possibly see. The rocks looked so sharp, jagged and dangerous, I just had to continue to believe.

They continued up, up, and away,
Thinking of a better day,
Knowing freedom was at hand,
For Dorothy they will take a stand!

Thinking only of Dorothy, her friends knew that this posse was her only hope of survival. Scarecrow, Tin Man, and Lion would not be intimidated with the invading force of evil, for it was nothing in comparison to the victory that they envisioned ahead. I sat on the edge of my seat, anxiously watching as they continued to climb the hazardous, very wicked mountain full of its menacing clefts and crevices. Nothing will turn them around as these great and faithful friends, these trained battle buddies and comrades-in-arms, march forward to see that she is never harmed!

There they are,
Up they pop,
They can see,
Things are about to get hot!

They look down below,
It's the big, dark stronghold,
They have traveled far to see,
They are about to be bold!

Seen by the enemy's spies!
They are jumped from behind,
Oh boy, what a tussle,
These guys are one of a kind!

One, two, three, as the enemy tries to take out those arriving, Rescuers,
they are down for the count, Tin Man, Lion and Scarecrow finish the
fight, Oh what a night!

They are always at the top of their game,
The enemy they shall tame!

They are up and on their way,
In disguise and staying on task,
An undercover covert operation,
They are going in to harass!

Off they go,
The door is open,
It's the Great Escape,
The Evil power is about to be broken!

Open her eyes

Oh, if Dorothy could only see, blinded by the walls she does not realize what is about to be. Her heart is broken and in despair, if she only knew how much they cared. They have crossed the mountain named impossible; her friends are coming, they are unstoppable! The walls will come down, for love conquers all, so let the adventure begin, the enemy shall fall! Help is on the way!

Rainbow glasses

I recall two stories in the Bible that I feel we can look through the lens of the rainbow glasses into this circumstance. One tells of not being able to see in the middle of an enormously dangerous state of affairs, and the other is right in the middle of a very sinking and desperate time. In both cases, Jesus reached out and saved the day! So let's quickly go to the scripture and refresh our memory.

Matthew 14:22-33, (NIV) Remember the words, "take courage" that Jesus spoke? The disciples were in the boat crossing the water because Jesus had sent them ahead. Then later, as He came walking out to them they thought it was a ghost. I can definitely understand why. They were calmed by His voice calling out to them, "Take courage! It is I, don't be afraid."

Remember what Peter did next? He said, "If it is you Lord tell me to come to you." Jesus said, "Come." Now we can all recall that Peter got out of the boat and began to walk on the water to the Lord. He did really great until he looked at the waves and he took his eyes off Jesus! The scripture says that he saw the wind and he was afraid; it is then that he began to sink.

Just like in this story of Dorothy, she is only looking at the walls (waves), and because of this, she is sitting in a mess of despondency and unbelief. The beautiful story of Peter is that he cried out, Lord, save me! Immediately Jesus reached out his hand and caught him. Jesus said, "Why did you doubt?" Like Dorothy, even though she cannot see, I want her to know they are coming to set her free!

2 Kings 6:17, (NIV) In this scripture, the servant of Elijah was very afraid. The enemy came and when the servant saw the men he was blinded by fear and didn't know what they were going to do. But Elisha could see in the spirit realm because of his great trust in God. He prayed to God that his servant's eyes would be opened and that he could see the truth. God then opened his eyes and as he looked, he saw the hills full of horses and chariots of fire all around. One of the reasons I believe this story was recorded, was so that hundreds of years later we can still understand that when we are in a tight place, whether it be emotional, physical, or spiritual, we can put on our rainbow glasses and be reminded that we must ask God to open our eyes to be able to see the real truth. There are more for us then against us! In situations when we feel like Dorothy and we are surrounded by a great fortress of fear, just like Elijah's servant, let God show us

the mighty horses and chariots of fire that surround us. We must keep our rainbow glasses near.

Scriptures to meditate

Hebrews 12:1-3

Isaiah 41:10

Joshua 1:9

Mark 10:27

2 Chronicles 17:17

2 Timothy 1:7

Pray with me on fear and intimidation

This prayer was sent to me from a dear friend named Phillip Martin, when I was going through a very intimidating time from the enemy in my life. I now share it with you.

Intimidation returns because it has won in a previous season, or we have received it by default through iniquity. It has attached to you by an agreement. (Remember throughout the book, we have talked about our agreements) So again, I ask the question, what are your agreements?

1) Recognize that God has not given you a spirit of fear and intimidation.
2) Intimidation is fear in a dress. It stops you and causes you to believe less then what God has said about you concerning what you are called to, anointed for, and appointed to do.
3) We need to take authority over it in the name of Jesus, then bind and cast it off.

4) We need to command the spirit of intimidation to stop its assignment.

Father God, in the name of Jesus, I repent for coming into alignment with the spirit of intimidation. Show me Father where the agreements are that I might break them by the blood of Jesus. I now declare and decree every place that intimidation has held me back or stopped me that I will launch forward in boldness. Every assignment that the enemy has played against me with intimidation will now be removed and all will be restored. I recognize that this spirit is also assigned to the spirit of thievery that steals from me my rightful inheritance and rightful ability to process what God is telling me to do. It limits my blessings. So now with the authority of Jesus and His blood, I release the Kingdom of God to take its place and declare that every evil work will be turned to good. Fill every area of my heart that has been cleansed and healed of the spirit of intimidation, fill it with your love. Seal it by the power of the Holy Spirit. In the mighty name Jesus, Amen!

Declaration

I now declare that I am a child of the living God! I declare again that I have not been given a spirit of fear, but that I have been given love, power, and a sound mind. I declare that all things are possible through God. I declare that I will not live under the oppression of the spirit of intimidation by the power of Jesus Christ.

Let this scripture ring out

Psalm 93:1, (NIV) "The Lord reigns, He is clothed with majesty; The Lord has clothed and girded himself with strength; Indeed the world is firmly established, it will not be moved."

Bibliography

1. *The Wizard of OZ.* 1939.

2. **Fleming, Victor.** *The Wizard of OZ.* MGM, 1939.

3. *https://nameberry.com/search?q=meaning+of+Oz.* [Online]

4. **Nemitz/Facebook, Colors by Carol.** [Online]

5. www.sheknows.com. [Online]

6. http://www.netstate.com/states/intro/ks_intro.htm. [Online]

26

WALLS COME TUMBLING DOWN
(THE STRONGHOLD)

an you feel the power surge in the atmosphere? It's a combination of expectancy and the unknown filling the air with breathtaking and electrifying excitement! It is time for a stronghold to hit the ground, it's time for it to come tumbling down.

They are in

In this story of Dorothy and the journey with the powerful Red Shoes, help has arrived, and the mighty rescue is about to commence. This is war! This is a matter of life and death! Of all the challenges that this team of travelers has faced together, this will be the greatest confrontation, the most dangerous assignment of them all. This challenge will be a face-to-face showdown like never before. The broom must be captured at all cost, and there cannot be a loss!

Ready, set, go

The rescuers look around, Toto leads the way; Dorothy's destiny is about to be met, let's shout out a mighty Hooray! Swiftly they turn as Toto scampers up the cold dark stairs (the Word of God always leads the way) as her rescuers follow close behind. When they reach the gigantic door, they knew they had to act quickly for the Evil One was very close by, plotting to return soon to finish what she had started, Dorothy's demise!

When you're little, everything looks extremely large, and this was one of those moments. I knew that this plan had to work!

The mission to rescue Dorothy is well on its way. Scarecrow (the mind of Christ), Tin Man (Heart of the Father), Lion (Holy Spirit), and Toto (Our High Priest and the word of God) have come together as one and have entered the stronghold that keeps Dorothy incarcerated! It is a time of immense despair, but some big walls are about to come down and that meant freedom was near!

As a child, I recall singing a song that stated, "And the walls, came tumbling down!" The song even had these great actions to it— you would engage your whole body demonstrating that the massive walls that surrounded the city of Jericho were falling down. Finally at the end you would totally fall down and completely crumple to the ground. It was a perfect demonstration of the total and complete collapse of the walls at the battle of Jericho, which is recorded in scripture. In obedience, the children of God marched and then shouted as instructed, and then God demolished the protective wall around the city. The children of God could now go in and possess the land, it was a promise fulfilled to them and to their descendants. What a mighty God we serve, just take His hand! (Joshua 6:1-21)

Just like in the story of Jericho, at times, all of us have to face the music. The children of Israel wandered for 40 years in a very desolate place, they were either going to have to cross over and take what was promised to them or stay in a place of continual round and round the gerbil wheel of wandering for more generations to come. It was time to choose. Someone had to step up, take the leap of faith, believe God and take down some giants! God allowed the past to die off, and the new generation decided it was time, so they trained for war and took a stand. Only those that had stood by faith in the past, crossed into the Promised Land!

In our lives, we need to take a good look at the walls that are holding us back from moving forward and just like the walls of Jericho that kept God's children from receiving their inheritance, we must make a choice, train for war and look to God for deliverance. The walls inside the castle definitely have Dorothy stuck, stuck physically and emotionally from moving forward and receiving her promise. Walls that have become prisons must come down and giants must be destroyed, they are battles that we cannot avoid!

We have talked before about 1 Samuel Chapter 17 where it tells the story of David, God's giant killer. David knew who and where his help came from. He stood in the gap for his people and took out the enemy that held the army of the Lord at a stand off through fear. The giant was the mighty wall. He prevented God's people from going forward. David shifted his destiny and the destiny of his nation through standing alone and believing. Pick up your weapon, as David did, no matter how small you feel, and through the strength and power of God, be a giant killer! Let the Holy Spirit arise, and release your faith, throw the stone, God will take the giant down right between the eyes. David must have looked amazing as he rushed towards Goliath and then took off his head with the giant's own sword. Just like Jericho, this mighty wall came tumbling down! God did the work, but the stone had to be thrown!

Toto leads the way and signals to Dorothy's rescuers to follow him. The word of God is the only weapon that Jesus used to defeat the enemy and it is the only weapon that will take him out today. It is the stone placed in the sling, when hurled through the air with faith it will destroy the plans of evil and take him down. Jesus is our only example. He taught us to use the living word of God when tempted by Satan, and there are no substitutes; it is the only way he will be taken!

In Matthew 4:1-11, Jesus is tested in the wilderness. Every hook the enemy threw out to Jesus, hoping He would take the bait, was destroyed by the word of God.

The ax of deliverance

Deliverance is an action word. It is the act of being rescued or set free. With hearts full of courage and strength, up the stairs they go as fast as they can run, they are on the move! It is very interesting to me that even though they left the Emerald City with a lot of different weapons, the only weapon that they have with them now is the ax. So, let's take a look and see, what is an ax? An ax is an instrument that can strike, especially violently and destructively to take down massive barriers, and in this case a mammoth locked door. The ax blade is made of steel that is sharpened to demolish whatever it impacts; it is built to make a difference! The name of the ax in this story is called deliverance and truth.

Let's look back and remember where the ax came from; it has been a part of this adventure and traveled with them virtually since the beginning. It first showed up when Scarecrow and Dorothy found Tin Man rusted and still as a statue by the side of the road. If you remember, Tin Man had held the ax up for such a long time; he was weary and yearned to be released. Let's rejoice that when the oil was applied, it set Tin Man free. The ax had turned into such a heavy burden, but that burden has now become a weapon of deliverance through the beautiful colors of God's amazing grace. Let His oil heal the pain of the past just like Tin Man as we release our hearts to Him. Let it go!

We see that Tin Man, Scarecrow and Lion are now at the door using this magnificent *ax* to break it down. The pain and heaviness healed from the past is now powerful with authority. It is in this same way that God will use our former healed traumas to break down the walls and the doors that hold us in bondage today. They can also be the instruments that will be used to set others free. What was meant for evil and harm, the Father will now use for good!

John 8:32, (NIV) "And you will know the truth, and the truth will set you free."

Hebrews 4:12, (NIV) "For the word of God is alive and active. Sharper than any double-edged sword, it penetrates even to the dividing soul and spirit, joints and marrow; it judges the thoughts and attitudes of the heart."

Still locked in this fortress, Dorothy looks at the hourglass in shear panic; she sees that time is running out! The sand is disappearing. Wait, wait I cried out as a child, surely we have a little more time! I could barely deal with the anxiousness that was overwhelming me. When you are young, yes, you know that it is just a story, but it doesn't matter, you are still drawn in. As the emotion raced through my body and my mind, I am living it with her, one breath at a time.

Genesis 50:20, (NIV) "You intended to harm me, but God intended it for good, to accomplish what is now being done, the saving of many lives.

WHAM! WHAM! WHAM! CHOP, CHOP, CHOP! Over and over again the rescue crew is smashing in the door with their trusty weapon. The ax will do the job, if they just do not give up; a major wall is about to come tumbling down, soon freedom will abound!

Now, depending on the wall or door that is your stronghold and how long it's been standing, there might need to be many mighty blows for it to be destroyed, just like Dorothy. Maybe there are areas in your heart that you have held offense, you will need to forgive. You can recognize these places when they come to the surface for they will be covered and bound in pain or anger.

Maybe your wall is fear, self-hatred, jealousy, or rejection, there is also bitterness, hopelessness and unbelief that are major hindrances, and I am only mentioning a few of the walls that can keep us from being free and unable to move. *Chop, chop, chop!* Let the ax of truth create the greatest potential that God the Father desires for us to be, chopping away to set us free! Always remember that we were designed to be shakers and movers, made to shift destinies and nations just like David. Don't choose to remain behind closed locked doors. You are made to be giant killer! Just like David, face the enemy, prepare the stones, step out in faith, and release! Let God do the rest He is the best!

Psalm 2:8, (NLT) "Only ask, and I will give you the nations as your inheritance, the whole earth as your possession."

It takes many blows to break a stronghold down to the place that it has absolutely no more power or effect over us, for the walls are built by the power of many lies. You don't build a wall overnight. We can see visually in this story that every time the team strikes the door, it is becoming weaker and weaker; it is being demolished and dismantled one assault at a time, keep the stones coming, and then there will be a suddenly! The tremendous wall that imprisoned Dorothy came absolutely and completely crashing to the floor, Dorothy could now soar!

Declare with me that this is the day! This is the day that the Lord has made, and it is on this day that wherever we are being held captive by the enemy, that those walls are coming down! Take the challenge, pick up the mighty ax and start chopping! Let the Lord dismantle the things within us that keep us bound; over and over we must attack to destroy the lies with the word of God and continue to declare the truth. I have said it before, but I must say it again. Yes, and then the lock will be broken, and the door will be opened!

Swing that ax with all of your strength, great strength given by God, and He will do the rest, you just need to do your best. Over and over, swing the ax of forgiveness and release the pain to Jesus, then allow the oil of His love and grace to wash over you until you are completely free. Over and over swing the ax, a declaration of truth, declaring healing over your body, mind, soul and spirit, until the health of Heaven reigns. All I can say is this, that whatever the ax is that the Father, is asking you to pick up, pick it up and through the power of the Red Shoes swing, swing, swing!

Philippians 4:13, (KJV) "I can do all things through Christ that strengthens me."

Break down the door,
Escape and soar!
Arise and fly above the prison cell,
Break away from fears' great spell!

She is heard

Psalm 34:17, (NLT) "The Lord hears His people when they call to Him for help. He rescues them from all their troubles."

Psalm 34:17, (NIV) "The righteous cry out, and the Lord hears them; He delivers them from all their trouble.

Dorothy's friends heard her frantic cries. The hourglass was almost empty. The enemy's timeline has now come to an end; the threat, the line that was drawn in the sand will now be crossed. That last swing of the mighty ax and the lock was broken. The door swung wide open!

Hurry! This situation is still dire, they tare swiftly down the stairs together leaving the old prison that held Dorothy in such terror. She is loose, she is free, or is she? Quickly, there is no time to lose!

They are racing together towards the main door to make a great escape! But wait, stop! Haven't they forgotten something? Oh My Gosh, I am thinking. Noooo … don't forget the broom!

The only thought that seems to be on their minds now is to run, run hard and run fast but wait, they MUST have that broom! They need to stop and face the enemy straight on, all together united as one. Dorothy was shaken and unable to stand strong when she faced the evil alone, but now the situation has changed, and in the flurry of the moment, they have lost track of their original assignment.

Get that broom! Hey, let's rise up together and shout out, get that broom! If they do not confront the enemy now, when will they? Go back! Don't run away! We can see that they have come so far and now is definitely not the time to fail the mission; now is the time for completion!

They run towards freedom, knowing the door is just ahead, complete freedom seems so close, but where is the Evil One? They continue to swiftly scurry towards the door thinking if they can just make it out, there will be no more problems, no more troubles, but that really isn't the total truth is it? The real truth is that they need to stop, stand their ground and fight! They are so close; they reach the door and what happens, it slams shut. It slams shut with a mighty, thundering boom just as they arrive. Oh what a fright! They need to get that broom!

In my own mind, I am thinking maybe this might be a good thing; it will cause them to turn and to do battle from the inside and take down the giant from within! They are stopped in their tracks; they hear the shrill screech of the enemy's voice behind them. Her hideous words harass them once again with ultimatums that would cause anyone to shrink and shrivel into a puddle of desperation and fear. She puts on a show of having great power to impress. She explodes into a tantrum, which includes dispensing hideous and sharp piercing intimidating darts of torment. Those darts feel like penetrating fire searing their emotions. She is warning them to be afraid, be very afraid!

We are trapped like rats, says Lion, (2) for they are cornered by the very nucleus of evil. She instructs her hideous army to stand in front of Dorothy and her friends, pointing their long weapons of destruction, threatening their lives with harm; their backs are against a locked steel door! What to do? What to do? It looks very impossible and like there will be no escape, but then, just as quickly as the enemy arrived to torment and finish her despicable act, there is another suddenly!

Scarecrow starts to think. He sees a way that will disrupt her plans! He swiftly follows the lead; he takes the ax and boom! The power is released, like lightening he strikes the rope, it is severed in two, the heavy wooden light that hung above them fell, it entraps the tormentors below with its weight. Fire caused the threat to be neutralized; here's their chance, they speedily bolt and dash away. There must be a way out of this major fortress, there must be!

Some freedom has come,
From the walls that be,
But they find themselves,
In a place they cannot see.

The stronghold continues,
To surround their every move,
So round and round they go,
Which way, if they only knew!

Chased and chased,
What do we do?
Look straight ahead,
Oh my, what a scary view!

Darkness is everywhere,
What is the plan?
How can we be free forever?
Freedom would be grand!

The walls will come tumbling down!
Arise and take back your land!
Let's put on our rainbow glasses,
We must stop and take a final stand.

Scriptures on hope
1 Corinthians 15:54-58
1 Samuel 17 (the story of David and Goliath)
Jeremiah 29:11
Luke 18:35-43
Mark 4:30-34
Psalm 3:2-6

Pray with me
Heavenly Father, I thank you that you are always pursuing me in
my times of darkness when doors in life seem closed and locked.
Particularly when I feel there are no answers and the hourglass of
time seems to be running out. Thank you, Father that you always
have a way of escape from the imprisonment and torment of the
enemy. I thank you that your love is destroying the doors that want
to keep me from running free. You are my hope! You are the answer!
You are the key that unlocks my heart to believe! I praise you for
bringing the walls down in my life that have kept me trapped. Help
me to always speak the truth of the word of God. Restore my faith in

you that I might believe no matter how dark the surroundings may look. I thank you that you always come to my rescue and demolish the door and bring the walls tumbling down. Amen.

Declaration

I am a child of the king. I am mighty through the power of the Holy Spirit! I am a giant killer. The weapons that I fight with are not of this world; on the contrary, they have divine power to demolish strongholds! (2 Corinthians 10:4, NIV)

Bibliography

1. *The Wizard of OZ*. 1939.
2. **Fleming, Victor.** *The Wizard of OZ*. MGM, 1939.
3. *https://nameberry.com/search?q=meaning+of+Oz*. [Online]
4. **Nemitz/Facebook, Colors by Carol.** [Online]
5. www.sheknows.com. [Online]
6. http://www.netstate.com/states/intro/ks_intro.htm. [Online]

27

IT'S A MELTDOWN DAY

Have you ever had one of those days, where the moment you are awake and have opened your eyes, you instantly can feel an outrageous energy in the air, knowing a shift was about to happen? I mean a major life-changing shift! The kind of day where you can perceive it in the atmosphere way down deep in your gut. The kind of day where you keep looking over your shoulder and feeling goose bumps run up and down your spine, because you know, you just know that your world is about to take a sharp right or left turn and go down a different path then you have ever traveled before.

When you have a day with those feelings, it can usher in great fear, but instead of fear I want you to look at this day as the day that the Lord has made, and He has good plans for you. We are on an adventure that only can happen through Jesus and it's going to be the adventure of a lifetime! It is the day that this fateful foe is going down, down, down. It's going to be a great show!

This is where we find Dorothy, living this day out in the story. Today is the day! It's kind of like when you are little and you have waited for Christmas morning to be able to open up your gifts and you haven't a clue what is behind the wrapping paper, but with a great sweeping expectation, you have waited and waited, and the day has finally arrived. Little does she know that Her Great Wickedness is about to be destroyed and obliterated in a most unusual way, and yes, it is absolutely going to happen today!

As Dorothy runs to escape her thoughts are definitely not about the Evil One at all, her focus is only get out! Get out! Oh my, she is so surprised, she is trapped! But this evil trap will set her up for victory! This particular circumstance will dictate absolutely no more running.

Dorothy will now be forced to face her ultimate and highest level of fear head on, her arch nemesis! Things are on the move, the lever has been pulled the tracks switched and it is clear there is a change in the air. She will be astonished at the profound courage about to arise and be discovered deep within her. Dorothy will go from running in terror to amazing fearlessness.

Scarecrow takes Dorothy by the hand as he leads the way and the others follow. Dorothy hangs onto Toto with everything she has, making sure he doesn't slip from her grasp. The enemy allocates her assailants into two separate groups relishing in her plan to surround Dorothy and her friends, stopping their way of escape. They are trapped! Closed in on both sides, they face absolute evil and hate in every eye that pierces them. Her Wickedness steps forward with great confidence as her army parts the way and opens up a free and easy access to her prey.

Oh how exciting! My heart was dancing with joy! We can now see the broom and it is within Dorothy's reach. The broom actually is leading the way; the evil one carries it like a scepter of authority, but she has forgotten that it is Dorothy that actually has the powerful Red Shoes. She continues to intimidate and terrorize with words that surge like a waterfall, forceful and unrelenting. My gosh, she is like the never-ending energizing bunny that goes on and on and never shuts up. That would be our adversary, continually trying to be scary. If they will just keep their eyes on the broom, on the prize, and not on her or her tormenting words, an amazing way will be made.

Determined to have Dorothy watch as her friends suffer, she takes the broom, lifts it to a torch, and lights it on fire. Then, she moves closer, step-by-step with wicked tantalizing ultimatums towards Scarecrow. She looks him dead straight in the eye and shoves the fire uncomfortably closer and closer, believing that she has the power to destroy him.

My heart seemed to be bursting with so much stress. Noooo, Noooo I cry out, this must not happen, this has to stop! I just need to rest; this cannot be the end! Scarecrow has always been by Dorothy's side since the fork in the yellow brick road. He has been there through thick and thin, no matter what was ahead during this amazing journey, encouraging and leading throughout all of the challenging times, times of great sadness and the times of great joy. It was with Scarecrow that she had her first major dance in this new Land of Oz, a land full of courage and strength, and it is this precious relationship that the enemy is now intending to completely annihilate. We can see that everything Dorothy loves and holds dear to her heart is in imminent danger once again. I feel we are watching a replay of the earlier experience that Dorothy went through if you recall. In the first round she chose to run when she left home, but on this occasion her back is to a wall and there will be no more running, no more running at all.

2 Corinthians 4:8-10, (NIV) "We are hard pressed on every side, but not crushed; perplexed, but not in despair; persecuted, but not abandoned; struck down but not destroyed."

I have noticed when a situation arises in my life and I am forced to make a decision quickly with no real options, with hindsight I can see that many of those decisions I have made were some of the best. I had to rest and obey, I looked up and He made the way! I will say it again, look up!

My eyes are on Dorothy and my emotions are being seized with fear. I probably held my breath, but obviously I lived through the experience. (Smile)

I'm thinking that something has to be done and it has to be done now! Move! There has always been a way made before; there must be a way now. Scarecrow has his arms around Dorothy in a position of protection, his love for her is beautiful and steadfast, and he is unmovable, even when faced with his own destruction. They all stand by her side in this distressing situation, but, it is at this moment that it will all come down to Dorothy!

Scarecrow is on fire!

In an instant there is an amazing awakening and transformation in Dorothy as she acts and reaches behind.

She grabs the bucket that waits,
It will accommodate,
For it is prepared for this great fate!
Full of water that will refresh,
Out go the flames,
This is the very best!

The water is released. It flies through the air, immersing Scarecrow like a shield, drenching his straw and quenching the fire, I was in awe! WOW! What a scare. Dorothy puts out this dangerous outrageous threat all because of her love in action. There will definitely be no regrets. It was natural for Dorothy to protect her wonderful companion, and in the instant that she stepped up and took charge just like David; she threw the stone and became a giant killer! She shifted her destiny in a moment and the fate of all those around her.

My Oh My!
What do we see?
What do we hear?
The shriek of the enemy,
Going down in fear!

The book of Esther gives the written account concerning a beautiful queen that stood in the gap for her people. The Israelites were scheduled for death because of an evil law that a wicked man named Haman who had gained great power instigated. He manipulated the king in the land of Persia to place his seal upon this law. Esther, through the wisdom and favor of God, rose to the occasion, went to the king, plead her case and the future of her nation was saved. Haman, the enemy was destroyed on the very gallows he had prepared for someone else. I encourage you to read this book as a refresher to what can happen if we step up and stand in the gap for such a time as this. Be a giant killer!

The Wicked one looks at Dorothy in complete disbelief as she loudly shrieks, then begins to shrink and shrivel. As moments pass she begins to disappear; this is going to be a complete meltdown day! Hooray! The water has diffused her power; I like to say that it short-circuited her. How could this possibly happen? How could this little girl destroy so much evil? The enemy seemed to be in such control, it looked as if there would be no way for any kind of escape, but this little girl with the powerful Red Shoes made *the* difference, and everything is coming into perfect shape!

After all of the unrelenting harassment that followed Dorothy days with no end, and all the threats that were right in her face, it was an act of love that destroyed this tormenting monster. Is was the love of the Father that sent His only son, that has destroyed the ultimate evil. We forget how powerful love is. The Evil One melted into oblivion, shrieking all the way, her voice dwindling more and more until it was barely a whisper, and there was nothing she could say! The Wickedness continued to vanish from sight, until all that remained was a vapor of smoke and her oppressing clothes that were lifeless and dead. Her power had been stripped. Dorothy had done it; there was nothing more to dread! This was definitely a Hallelujah moment!

Ephesians 5:26, (NLT) "... to make her holy, cleansing her by the washing of the water through the word ..."

Who could have known?
Who could have guessed?
All it would take was water,
That would bring her death!

Rainbow glasses on
One action of love,
One action on the cross
Changed the world forever,
Jesus paid the cost!

What do we do with water? Water is for washing; it keeps us clean and takes away the dirt and germs that attach to us from a busy day. It is also life. We cannot live without drinking water. It replenishes every organ in our body; we are made up of 60% water. According to a study by H.H. Mitchell that was presented in the Journal of Biological Chemistry 158, the brain and the heart are composed of 73% water, and the lungs are about 83% water. The skin contains 64% water, muscles and kidneys are 79% water and even our bones are watery at 31%. Wow! We need the watering of the word for us to be able to function properly and stay healthy, healthy in our thinking, breathing, and cleansing. Remember every word you speak, that your body is listening to and obeying, so make sure you speak life!

The scripture mentions water in many different ways; Ephesians says that it is the washing of the water through the word that makes us holy. We cannot live without the word. It washes over our souls, empowered by the spirit of God and it literally destroys the darkness. What a great illustration of water destroying evil, when we watch the Wicked One in this story melt away, powerless, being liquidated and evaporated.

John 7:38, (NIV) "He who believes in me, as the scripture said, from his innermost being will flow rivers of living water."

Exodus 17:6, (NIV) "Behold I will stand before you there on the Rock of Horeb; and you will strike the rock, and water will come out of it that the people may drink."

John 4:14, (NIV) "… but whosoever drinks of the water that I will give him shall never thirst; but the water that I will give him will become a well of water springing up to eternal life."

The water of life comes from the word activated by the spirit. Isaiah 44:3 talks about the Father bringing water to a dry and thirsty land and streams on the dry ground. He also says He will pour out His Spirit on our offspring and blessing upon our descendants. Water is essential. It is a life-giving force. Just as in this story Dorothy destroyed the enemy with the water, we destroy the effects of the enemy in our lives by the water of the word activated with Holy Spirit. In the above scripture, it talks about how water came out of the rock to save God's people, He is our Rock and He desires for us miracles in the dry places. He will supply water where you cannot see water. Jesus is the water of life! John 4:10-13, states that He gives us living water.

Scriptures to meditate
Isaiah 58:11; 43:2; 12:3, 43:20
Isaiah 43:2
Isaiah 12:3
John 7:38-39
Nehemiah 9:20

Pray with me

Heavenly Father, I thank you and praise you that you give fresh life when I am in need. You are my refreshment in the desert times of life. You quench my thirst as I seek you. Father God, thank you that you are a miracle-working God and in times when I cannot see where the water of life might be in a situation you have prepared the rock, you are the rock that the water springs forth from. Father, I thank you for the water of the word that dissolves the enemy. Lord, help me to speak forth your truth continually to dissolve the plans of the enemy over my life. Lord, help me to step up and look around at what you have prepared for me to take out the enemy in a time of great pressure. I praise your name forever and ever! Thank you for always providing a way of escape when my back is against the wall. Thank you for the joy of my salvation. Amen.

Declaration

I declare that I am full of the spirit of God, full of His joy and full of His refreshing water. I declare that your living water will flow from me and give life to those around. I declare that I will speak the word and will dissolve the enemy right in his tracks by the power of your name!

28

THE GREAT REVELATION

Dorothy can't believe her eyes!

She is watching the wicked one literally and slowly dissolve and disappear right in front of her. I am reacting the same exact way. How could this be? This is a shock! Such a long journey of ups and downs fears and tears and then suddenly she is gone? No way! And all it took was water? Well, that was definitely a very well-kept secret because it seems that if that would have been common knowledge Dorothy and her friends could have ended this seemingly never ending torment days ago.

"You have killed her!" they stated. Dorothy's immediate and timid response to the evil army was that she didn't mean to do it. She's frightened as they stare at her in disbelief! Yikes! What is going to happen now!

Freedom rings out

Thank you Dorothy you have saved the day! Wickedness is dead! Wow, the atmosphere in the castle changed instantly. Looks of trepidation suddenly turn to relief and smiles with magnificent jubilation. Dorothy's bravery has even freed those around her; they were also chained and bound emotionally by the vile depravity of this villainous Evil One. There are no words to express what I felt when I realized that her army was also being held against their will because of fear. Anxiety, dread, worry, and many other forms of fear are such major opponents. They slink into most every part of the battle for our freedom. So yes, they were elated to hand Dorothy the broom, the symbol, the trophy of her great success and triumphant victory. I was so impressed!

With wonderful delight, and all as one, the mighty warriors head back to the Emerald City, their sentiment is flying as high as a kite! Hope is rising anew; Dorothy can feel and knows that going home is almost true. If there were an apple pie in the window cooling at the farm, she would be able to smell its magnificent aroma, that's how close she senses her return. The troupe of travelers will soon see their hearts desires come alive for the battle has been won; there is no more strife!

They arrive back and enter the Emerald City; they present themselves to the Wiseman and display the broom with pride! It has almost cost them everything, so they are quite ready to receive the reward that I am sure is just in sight. Being faithful, steadfast and loyal to what had been asked of them surely will bring this to an end. Hope and expectation have been revived weariness has been defeated. New life is abounding, but something is amiss, something is about to be revealed that is a strange twist!

They're baaack!

Dorothy lifts the broom up so that it may be seen clearly. The Wiseman speaks to them very abruptly, almost with a hint of anger that they are back. Why have you returned? We have done what you have asked; please keep your promise for we have been through so much and gone way beyond to accomplish the task that was at hand. He spits and fumes and says, "Come back tomorrow!" Dorothy is in tears, "But I want to go home now!" (2) There is now suspicion in the air, something is off, it is very clear! Little Toto, faithful and true begins to sniff out and search for reality. He starts by investigating and inspecting the surrounding area. He discovers a veil that is covering the truth. He snatches the curtain with his teeth and pulls, he continues until the great revelation is told!

The curtain slides open,
And shows what is hidden,
My heart sinks into sadness,
This should be forbidden!

What is this?
What do we see?
This almost brings me,
Down to my knees.

As a child, I was hit hard by this betrayal for I was taught to be honest and true, and that deception was not an option, that to deceive was hurtful and wrong. This Wiseman revealed behind the scenes was just a person trying hard to help, but was actually putting on a sham, he was just a man. He had been proclaimed and announced that he was great by others, he had fallen into the trap of declaring and professing his own excellence, but he was still only just a man.

What will they do now? Their eyes are opened and in disbelief, this changes everything, they are instantly in grief!

Promises

The warriors began to demand the promises that he had made. What are you going to do about your pledge they shouted in anger? We want answers today! The heart, the courage and the wisdom that was promised! We have come so far to receive, what are you going to do now; we believed and have been deceived!

The man was not a bad man; he had just been put on a pedestal by people that looked up to him for things he was unable to do. He had no great powers as they had been told; he should have come forth with honesty, he should have been bold. He wore a façade to please those around him and now consequently, what a mess he was in! And, needless to say, this is quite a difficult and embarrassing day!

Encouragement

The Wiseman reaches deep into his bag of knowledge and begins to encourage and share the wisdom that he does have, and it does change their lives. For even though he is not a God, or a Wiseman with supernatural powers, but words are empowering and as he gives them what he does have, it fuses with their hearts, which results in an explosion of an amazing brand new, off the charts, connections with faith.

Faith changes everything!

With Scarecrow he shares that higher thinking comes from studying, that we can learn from the best and we can then progress into greater accomplishments. We can change the world. He was given a diploma and recognized for his intelligence that he already had been created with; it was just a matter of tapping into the source, the mind of Christ is our course!

2 Timothy 2:15, (KJV) "Study to show thyself approved unto God, a workman that needeth not to be ashamed, rightly dividing the word of truth."

Proverbs 1:7, (KJV) "The fear of the Lord is the beginning of knowledge; but fools despise wisdom and instruction."

Colossians 2:2-3, (NIV) "My goal is that they may be encouraged in heart and united in love, so that they may have the full riches of complete understanding, in order that they may know the mystery of God, namely, Christ, in whom all the treasures of wisdom and knowledge."

Speaking to Lion, the Wiseman shares the understanding that to go around certain situations and not to go in headfirst without good sense and consideration is awe-inspiring wisdom. He exhorts Lion for his extraordinary valor and assures him that he does have great bravery and courage. He was given a medal of recognition and declared a hero, for that is really who he is deep down. He is a Lion and not a mouse! I love that his medal was a cross, for the cross of Jesus where He shed His blood gives us the true ability to walk in courage.

James 1:5a, (KJV) "If any of you lack wisdom you should ask God, who gives generously to all without fault finding, and it will be given to you."

1 Chronicles 28:20, (KJV) "And David said to Solomon his son, Be strong and of good courage, and do it: fear not, nor be dismayed: for the Lord God, even my God, will be with thee; He will not fail thee, nor forsake thee, until thou hast finished all the work for the service of the house of the Lord."

Deuteronomy 31:6, (CEB) "Be strong! Be fearless! Don't be afraid and don't be scared by your enemies because the Lord your God is the one who marches with you. He won't let you down, and He won't abandon you."

The Wiseman then begins to share with Tin Man that he has an amazing character and that he is sentimental. He explains that the sacrifices that he made for Dorothy showed that he operates in true love. Below is the biblical description of true love, and we can see that Tin Man definitely operates in it. He has a heart, but he has to believe. When he held it in his hands, it was tangible; when he heard it, he could truly listen. Allow God to bring your heart alive; I will say again, "Be His Presence."

1 Corinthians 13:4-5, (NIV) "Love is patient. Love is kind. It does not envy, it does not boast, it is not proud. It does not dishonor others, it is not self-seeking, it is not easily angered, it keeps no record of wrongs."

Proverbs 23:26, (NIV) "My son, give me your heart and let your eyes delight in my ways."

Proverbs 51:10, (NIV) "Create in me a pure heart, O God, and renew a steadfast spirit within me."

Matthew 5:8, (NIV) "Blessed are the pure in heart, for they will see God."

Psalm 19:14, (NIV) "May these words of my mouth and this meditation of my heart be pleasing in your sight, Lord, my Rock, and my Redeemer.

The beautiful part about this story is that when the Wiseman (he was full of wisdom after all) began to exhort, encourage and declare over them who they were, immediately there was a transformation by the truth that was forthcoming. It literally set them free! Their identities, always full of potential, were now being resurrected and brought to the light; they had been hidden beneath a tomb of heaviness and unbelief, sealed by the enemy's continual words of rejection and fear. This was a beautiful sight, my heart was exploding with delight!

When the great revelation came that the Wiseman was not who they depended on him to be or thought he was or first appeared, it was quite alarming. I was very disheartened also, but he was able to bring many answers and he was equipped with impressive knowledge that did teach and shift things. It's just that Dorothy and her friends had listened to others and had not experienced who he was for them selves. We've all done that somewhere in our lives through this walk on the yellow brick road. We have put our faith and trust in people along the way and they have disappointed us, but it's okay, it happens. God still uses it for our good, so let's forgive, let go, and move on!

Now wait a minute, you're thinking even Glinda said to go and seek him out! Yes, she did, and the knowledge and experience that was attained on this journey were beyond measure. We have to remember that it's the journey that is the true gift. The participation and the insight that was gained by the relationships during this adventure that Dorothy was exposed to are impossible to replace. She learned how to persevere, how to fight through the dark times, how to recognize and cling to the good. It was the personal encounter that brought authority and wisdom, so Glinda was right in sending her to the Emerald City.

Proverbs 4:6-7, (MSG) "Never walk away from wisdom–she guards your life; love her—she keeps her eye on you."

So, it's okay when things don't turn out as we originally have planned or imagined that they would. The true measure of growth will show up in how we react. Trust in the journey. Believe and receive the gift.

What about Dorothy?
He works in ways we cannot see,
He will make a way for you and me,
Just hang on to your hats and believe!

Scriptures to meditate
John 14:1
Joshua 1:9
Psalm 9:10; 13:5; 20:7; 31:14
2 Samuel 7:28

Pray with me
Father God, I thank you that I can seek your wisdom and I will never be disappointed. Father, you said you would give your wisdom liberally to me; I praise you for that. I can always trust you and I thank you for that. Even if man disappoints me, Father, you will never disappoint me if I trust that you know best. Circumstances may change quickly in my life and not look like I had envisioned,

but I choose to believe and receive your love. Let me know you in a greater way and experience your hope, joy and peace as I learn to trust you more as I overflow with hope by the power of the Holy Spirit. Help me to always keep my eyes on you and you alone! Amen.

Declaration

I declare that, as I believe in the almighty God, my heart will not be troubled. I declare that I am righteous, and I will thrive. I declare that I am safe as I walk in God's wisdom. I am a child of God!

Bibliography

1. *The Wizard of OZ.* 1939.
2. **Fleming, Victor.** *The Wizard of OZ.* MGM, 1939.
3. *https://nameberry.com/search?q=meaning+of+Oz.* [Online]
4. **Nemitz/Facebook, Colors by Carol.** [Online]
5. www.sheknows.com. [Online]
6. http://www.netstate.com/states/intro/ks_intro.htm. [Online]

29

THE POWER OF THE RED SHOES
(GOING HOME)

here is a song that plays during one of the most amazing rides at Disney Land that is called Zip-A-Dee-Doo-Dah, lyrics written by Ray Gilbert and composed by Allie Wrubel. If you have been there, you might recall this tune that plays along with the log ride down an amazing waterfall. Well, that's what I call it, a water-fall, because it is a ride on water, and you fall! My stomach always does a huge flip-flop every time I go over the side and down. No matter how many times I ride it, I cannot keep my eyes open as I am falling. Now I am laughing and screaming, but my eyes are closed.

As we get ready for Dorothy to prepare to go home, I am hearing that song that they sing during this ride, yep, you got it! It's a fun happy song that gives a lift to your step, with a big hoo-ray! It's got to be one of the most delightful lyrics and music ever recorded. It leads you into laughter and smiles and once you hear it or think of it, it is totally stuck in your head. It is a song that will give you a boost along the way. I do believe this is that kind of day that is ahead for Dorothy, a Zip to your step with a big hoo-ray! (Please Google and listen to the song)

After such a long journey to find her way back home, with so much wicked darkness that had to be pushed, shoved, sliced, diced, and removed so this moment could take place, yes, *that* is the song that I hear.

The Wiseman looks at Dorothy and promises that he will take her home, that he knows the way.

She is overwhelmed with emotion,
And tears fill her eyes,
The preparations begin,
And the day finally arrives!

The Wiseman is in the ride,
Dorothy and Toto join by his side,
There is excitement in the air,
She is saying a little prayer.

The Wiseman begins to brag about his abilities … oh dear!

He gathers the joyful city for a time of celebration to say goodbye and make a speech transferring authority and giving honor to Scarecrow and his wisdom, Tin Man for his heart and then finally Lion for his great courage. They will serve and rule you well.

What a royal force to lead the way,
Sing a Hallelujah chorus,
This city will be transformed today,
They have conquered the very dark forest!
He does well to leave them in charge,
The city is happy as can be,
Dorothy is so ready,
Home is where the heart is, you see.

Oh My Gosh, what just happened? Toto jumped and ran, Dorothy jumps out to save him, the rope is loose, and the Wiseman is drifting away! Stop, Stop! Don't leave! I begin to cry as a child; now what's going to happen to Dorothy? The Wiseman can't leave, he just can't, and this was her last chance, but that is exactly what is happening. Dorothy pleads to no avail; he doesn't know how to stop what has already been put into motion. He has no control over the hot air balloon!

Trusting in God and staying in peace as we prepare for things one way and then see them suddenly turn and go another is truly believing that He is the almighty and that He is good.

Joshua 1:9, (NIV) "Have I not commanded you? Be strong and courageous. Do not be afraid, do not be discouraged, for the Lord your God will be with you wherever you go."

Isaiah 55:8-9, (NIV) "For my thoughts are not your thoughts, neither are your ways my ways," declares the Lord. "As the heavens are higher than the earth, so are my ways higher than your ways and my thoughts higher than your thoughts."

Rainbow glasses on as I look around,
What colors are running free?
Promises of safety are clear,
How do we get out of here?

Tears of sorrow begin to stream,
How in the world can this be?
Please stay with us, we love you so,
We beg you again, don't go!

Dorothy's companions,
With her until the very end,
Their love surrounds her,
They are her closest friends.

The color of love is fresh in the air,
When suddenly out of nowhere,
What is it that they see?
A miracle has arrived just believe!

Scarecrow lifts his eyes; he catches a presence coming softly, like a song from heaven that floats to earth like a butterfly. Hearts are prepared; Glinda has arrived through the air.

With my rainbow glasses on as I continue to write, my memories surface from a child, soft wispy memories. They are not memories of fear, but Glinda has awakened tranquility, total peace and joy for I know that this lovely messenger has come to bring Dorothy Gale good news, with Holiness and Goodness we cannot loose!

I don't know how she will save the day, but I know she surely will. I feel deep down in my "knower" that when she appears, life changes when she is near. You can feel the rest and ease that she ushers in as she waves her star-studded scepter; she has always been Dorothy's great protector. A quiet calm flows over the great city, they bow as she gracefully moves, yes, her very appearance radiates pure royalty.

Dorothy begins to petition Glinda for help. Please, can you help? Glinda says you don't need any help; you have always had the power to go home! Dorothy is astonished at hearing this news, she thinks no way! Glenda states, you would not have believed if I told you, you had to learn it for yourself; it took the journey to understand, to believe and to see.

Then, Tin Man inquires of Dorothy what had she learned? She ponders for a moment and then shares her heart. She realizes that what she always looked and longed for was no further than her own home sweet home. Home is where your heart is.

Jeremiah 29:13, (KJV) "And ye shall seek me and find me, when ye shall search me with all of your heart."

Matthew 22:37, (KJV) "Jesus said unto him, Thou shalt love the Lord thy God with all with all thy heart, and with all thy soul, and with all thy mind."

Dorothy's desired rainbow experience, the love and life she desperately longed for, needed and was always searching for, was right in front of her eyes all of the time. This yellow brick road glorious journey has brought her understanding that home is where you're meant to be; *now* it is so easy to see. If you are looking for the pasture that is greener on the other side, look to Jesus, in Him you can abide.

Home is where Jesus is, for Jesus is our Home!

Ephesians 2:6, KJV "He hath raised us up together and made us sit together in heavenly places in Christ Jesus."

John 15:4, (MSG) Live in me. Make your home in me just as I do in you. In the same way that a branch can't bear grapes by itself but only by being joined to the vine, you can't bear fruit unless you are joined with me."

(2) Glinda then shares that Dorothy needed the experience; she needed to walk this road, for it was this amazing adventure on these golden yellow bricks that brought the understanding of the powerful Red Shoes. It was the amazing Glory road that highlighted and enhanced their *SPARKEL*! Dorothy had to believe!

No one can walk our path; no one can take our place on this glory road with Jesus. It was meant for you and me to be able to see, teaching us to believe and to receive; there is no one else that can ever wear our custom fit beautiful Red Shoes!

It's Jesus and me,
Without Him,
I will not be free!

Dorothy turns and expresses love to her friends as she says goodbye. Moved emotionally to tears, she realizes that Scarecrow, Tin Man, and Lion have been with her through thick and thin, through pain and life, but she must go. She hangs on tight to Toto and speaks out that she is ready. Dorothy closes her eyes and taps the heels of her powerful sparkling Red Shoes together *click, click, click*. Her heart looks up, her faith rises; with expectation she knows she is finally ready to go home. My eyes were not dry.

Tears of great relief streamed down my face, as I looked on this beautiful sight as a little girl. Dorothy is resting in Glinda's guidance as she gently begins to repeat the words; there is no place like her beautiful, wonderful home. As quickly as she arrived in this marvelous Land of Oz, the land of strength, power and courage, from a ride on a twirling, whirling wind, she was now back home, a place of peace never again to roam. She was not alone.

Click! Click! Click!
Father, Son and Holy Spirit,
Jesus is our home,
He is the dearest.

Dorothy arrived safely; placed at total rest in her own comfy bed. She looks up into faces that are familiar and kind, full of love and compassion. Her family and precious friends are reaching out, tending to her every care; happy she has returned, shedding a little tear.

Now let's take a little trip down memory lane, if we may. As we recall, these are the very same faces and relationships that fear caused Dorothy to run away from. The friends on this great adventure had always been right beside her; they had been on the farm all of the time, and right in her own back yard, but she was blinded to who they really were by a need to always be looking and searching for that something or someone that was over a rainbow. Praise God, now she can see! Her eyes are finally opened; she is really truly and totally completely free. She will keep her rainbow glasses near, never again to react to fear!

May I encourage you to never ever take off the rainbow glasses. Stay in Jesus, abide in His promises and love, for He is the way, He is the truth, He is life everlasting, He is the beginning and He is the end. JESUS IS OUR HOME. He is right where you are. Live in the realm of Victory, gaze upon the beautiful Day Star!

2 Peter 1:19 KJV

John 14:6, (NIV) "Jesus said, I am the way and the truth and the Life. No one comes to the Father except through me."

Isaiah 32:18, (NIV) "My people will live in peaceful dwelling places, in secure homes and in undisturbed places of rest."

Look up, instead of around,
Contentment in Jesus,
Will never bring a frown,
Praise will always be the sound!

He is our home,
There is nowhere else to go,
A table is always spread,
Take His hand and follow.

He will always lead the way,
To great adventures every day,
Stay refreshed in Him,
Bow your head and pray!

Scriptures on abiding

Colossians 2:6 and 3:1-3

Colossians 3:1-3

Galatians 2:20

John 15:4-9; 1:9, 2:28

Pray with me

Father, I thank you that you promised that if I abide in you and your words abide in me that when I pray, whatever I ask will be done. Father help me to hear your voice and walk in your steps to honor you. Let my will be your will. Let my thoughts be your thoughts. Let me see and hear what you see and hear. Help me not to be blinded to the truth around me. Let this adventure; called life in you be full of your joy and peace. Help me to always remember that you are my home, and I do not need to look any further then You. Remind me daily to keep my rainbow glasses on and look at life through the color of the promises in your word that are given because of your love. Let me continue to see every situation through Your rainbow. Father, I thank and praise you for my powerful RED SHOES, the mighty blood of Jesus. Let me never forget to click my heels together and to believe, by calling on the power of the Father, Son and Holy Spirit, all three. For when I am weak, you are strong! Take me to places in you that are far beyond anything I can imagine, let me experience your rainbow. Amen.

Declaration

I declare that I am a child of the Living God bought by the Blood of Jesus Christ. I decree and declare that I am redeemed and walk in the power and authority of His blood daily by the mighty name of Jesus. I decree that this is my time to rise up and be all I was meant to be. I decree that I will see!

So, put on your Powerful Red Shoes,
Dance to a tune and kick your heels in the air,
Let the sun (Son) Shine so bright,
There is none to compare!

Bibliography

1. *The Wizard of OZ.* 1939.
2. **Fleming, Victor.** *The Wizard of OZ.* MGM, 1939.
3. *https://nameberry.com/search?q=meaning+of+Oz.* [Online]
4. **Nemitz/Facebook, Colors by Carol.** [Online]
5. www.sheknows.com. [Online]
6. http://www.netstate.com/states/intro/ks_intro.htm. [Online]

30

HOME SWEET HOME

I t is often said that home is where the heart is. This statement, I believe, is the complete truth. The Bible tells us that where your treasure is, there will be your heart also (Matthew 6:21, NIV).

My question to you is, where is your heart? Where is your home? The things I have shared through these many pages have hopefully come to you in a fun and memorable way and caused the question within yourself to be raised, where is my heart? Where am I living? Where is my home?

It is said that home is where you are most emotionally attached. Let us be totally and completely fastened (attached) to Jesus!

Remember this whole journey and adventure that was presented each day to Dorothy on the Glory road of life was all about revealing and unraveling the truth within by how she responded. Matthew 15:18 teaches us that what is coming out of our mouth is really what is in our heart. Dorothy had to learn who she was and the power that she carried through her amazing Red Shoes just as we do. This is our greatest revelation.

In the beginning, Dorothy was totally on the right track; she was heading home as fast as she could get there. In the original story, Dorothy was given silver shoes, and in a spiritual context, silver represents redemption (Colors by Carol Nemitz on Facebook).

Dorothy's direction of redemption was the way to go! Even though she made a very sad choice and walked where she should not have walked, she knew where her help came from.

Psalm 121:1-3, (NIV) "I will lift up mine eyes unto the hills, from whence cometh my help. My help comes from the Lord, the maker of Heaven and Earth. He will not let your foot slip. He who watches over you will not slumber. We must know where our help comes from!"

Home sweet home is where the heart is. Her heart knew that she needed to be home, it was a place of safety, but little did Dorothy realize what else lurked inside. Soon fear would twist her thoughts and rule her movements. Her choices would then dictate to her an unexpected pilgrimage through a major door into the marvelous Land of Oz. New revelations would come to the surface and appear from deep down in her soul.

All of us, no matter how the journey looks, must walk this path of having our hearts unlocked and exposed to our truth, our belief system. In Dorothy's case, we found that her choices were motivated by major fear, and because of this, her trip down the yellow brick road was definitely filled with a lot of interesting escapades, but what I loved more than anything is that her deepest desire was still to be free and to reside at home. No matter the fear that continued to arise, she continually pushed ahead through it all, with her loyal companions of faith by her side. Continuing to seek freedom from it all, Her unrelenting perseverance brought her home safely through the squall.

Let us choose to do the same. It is through the gift of intimacy with the Father, that no matter the decisions that we have made, God will stay with us throughout any storm and He will turn it around and use it for our good. Our choices may not be what He has desired for us, but no matter the path we have chosen, He will turn it into an adventure of a lifetime. Stay close, take His hand and trust, follow the *Yellow Brick Road of His Glory, it's Home or Bust!*

Let's reminisce

1) Seek the Wisdom of God in the land of strength, courage and power.
2) Keep your perspective through the colorful rainbow glasses clear and sharp, viewing life through the promises and covenant of God. Let them lead the way.
3) Let this road of life be filled with His glory.
4) Ride the storms of life out in His rest.
5) Celebrate that the cross has taken out the power of evil.
6) Continue to walk and dance on this road with the Mind of Christ, the Heart of the Father, and the Power and Courage of the Holy Spirit.
7) Celebrate and learn the Power of the Red Shoes.
8) Face your fears.
9) Thank and Praise God each day for the amazing assignment and the ability to take down every stronghold in your life

by every word that comes out of your mouth. Each word is equipped by the power that is in the Blood and the authority of the Word of God. The word of our testimony will melt any influence and strip the license to kill, steal and destroy from the enemy. We testify Jesus and only Jesus! Bless His Holy Name!

1 Chronicles 16:11, (NIV) "Look to the Lord and His strength; seek his face always."

Isaiah 41:13-14, (NIV) " For I hold you up with my right hand, I the Lord your God. And I say to you, "Don't be afraid. I am here to help you. I am the Lord, your Redeemer. I am the Holy one of Israel."

Psalm 37:7, (NLT) "Be still in the presence of the Lord and wait patiently for Him to act. Don't worry about evil people who prosper or fret about their wicked schemes."

Psalm 136:23, (NIV) "He remembered us in our weakness. His faithful love endures forever."

Home sweet home

Through the power of the Red Shoes and her great desire to be home, Dorothy clicked her heals together three times and voiced the words within her heart.

In our story, as we look at it through rainbow glasses, it is the power of the blood with our companions, the Father, Son, and Holy Spirit as we speak our desire, that we have the ability to come home to Jesus, no matter the path we have chosen.

Who is Jesus?

He is the Almighty One! Revelation 1:8

He is the Alpha and Omega! Revelation 22:13

He is the Advocate! John 2:1

He is the Author and He Perfects our Faith! Hebrews 12:2

He is our Authority! Matthew 28:18

He is the Bread of Life! John 6:35

He is the Son of God! Matthew 3:17

He is the Bridegroom! Matthew 9:15

He is the Chief Cornerstone! Psalm 118:22

He is our Deliverer! 1 Thessalonian 1:10

He is Faithful and True! Revelation 19:11

He is the Good Shepherd! John 10:11

He is the Great High Priest! Hebrews 4:14

He is the Head of the Church! Ephesians 1:22

He is the Holy Servant! Acts 4:29-30

He is the great I AM! John 8:58

He is Immanuel! Isaiah 7:14

He is the Incredible Gift! 2 Corinthians 9:15

He is the Judge! Acts 10:42

He is the King of Kings! Revelation 17:14

He is the Lamb of God! John 1:29

He is the Light of the World! John 8:12

He is the Lion of the Tribe of Judah! Revelation 5:5

He is Lord of All! Philippians 2:9-11

He is our Mediator! 1 Timothy 2:5

He is the Messiah! John 1:41

He is the Mighty One! Isaiah 60:1

He is the one that sets us Free! John 8:36

He is our Hope! 1Timothy 1:1

He is our Peace! Ephesians 2:14

HE is our Redeemer! Job 19:25

He is the Risen Lord! 1 Corinthians 15:3-4

He is the Rock! 1 Corinthians 10:4

He is the Sacrifice! 1 John 4:10

He is our Savior! Luke 2:11

He is the Son of Man. Luke 19:10

He is the Son of the most High! John 11:25

He is the Resurrection and The Life! John 11:25

He is the Door! John 10:9

He is the Way! John 14:6

He is the Living Word! John 1:1

He is the True Vine! John 15:1

He is the Truth that sets us free! John 8:32

He is the Victorious One! Revelation 3:21

He is the Wonderful Counselor, Mighty God, Everlasting Father, Prince of Peace! Isaiah 9:6

And, of course, there are many more! This list was compiled by Debbie McDaniel and can be found at Crosswalk.com.

The scripture tells us that there is not enough room in the world to hold the books that could be written that tell of everything Jesus did when He walked the earth (John 21:25). Even today, the living books continue to be written in the minds and on the hearts of the generations that have been and are yet to be, full of the stories of Jesus.

I declare today that there is not enough time or ink to write down everything He wants to do for you and with you!

Choose today to say,
There is an amazing way,
This journey is full of life,
Through Jesus there is no strife.

So put on your powerful Red Shoes,
Wear them, what an honor,
Rise up and become,
An amazing son or daughter!

Jesus you are my Peace,
Jesus you are my Home,
May I always stay in You,
You are the Great SHALOM!

SHALOM! Peace, harmony, wholeness, completeness, prosperity, welfare and tranquility to you all. (Wikipedia)

Shalom is the absence of chaos. Living in Him is a lifestyle every moment of every day!

LET THE JOURNEY BE THE JOY.
Go forward in

THE POWER OF THE RED SHOES!

ABOUT THE AUTHOR

B orn and raised in the Pacific Northwest, Debra has been in ministry most of her life. She and her husband Mark pastored for
many years in the state of Washington and Colorado. Currently
they are involved with various ministries in the church they now
call home. Debra is also a teacher, speaker, apostolic prayer coor-
dinator, prophetic painter and certified prayer minister. She is passionate about equipping the Body of Christ to come into her full
expression of what God has intended. As an apostolic prayer coor-
dinator with SPAN (Strategic Prayer Apostolic Network) under
Apostle Rebecca Greenwood she currently spearheads a team of
regional strategic intercessors, and also partners with others traveling the nation and the nations of the earth.

Her art has blessed and influenced many through the years. She
was thrilled to be involved with restoring a mural in a 12th century
chapel in the country of France.

She still resides happily in the state of Washington with her
husband, two children and her grandchildren.